An Orgy of Thieves
Neoliberalism and Its Discontents

Praise for *Orgy of Thieves*

"Ugly is the detritus left behind by the scorched earth policies of the US ruling class, a class that can tolerate sophisticates such as Obama as well as barbarians such as Trump as long as it continues to hoard the bulk of the social wealth. Alexander Cockburn and Jeffrey St. Clair chronicle the assault on the United States by the Wall Street Horde, their chronicle pickled in hatred but written with beauty."

— Vijay Prashad, author
Washington Bullets: A History of the CIA, Coups and Assassinations

"For astute and informed analysis, brilliantly presented, Alex Cockburn was incomparable. These essays with Jeffrey St. Clair are as fresh and timely as the day they were written, and as indispensable for understanding this sad world."

— Noam Chomsky, author
Requiem for the American Dream

"This collection could not be timelier. In the bad times that engulfed the world, Alexander Cockburn had to frequently combine in his writings past and present. He had to combat the state-organized amnesia sweeping the Western world. Become the vanguard and rear-guard rolled into one: at the center of what was going on, but far removed from the accommodationists who began to dominate the liberal media and write glibly against those like Cockburn and St. Clair who 'find themselves at the wrong end of history.' Cockburn was both sentinel and outrider in an age when star columnists and self-important anchor men had eclipsed mere reporters and editors and journalism proper was dying. The job of the 'stars' was to distract the audience from the crimes being perpetrated in full view and, which were later exposed by Wikileaks. Together with a tiny band of brothers and sisters Cockburn held the armies of reaction at bay. He was happy doing so and reading him was always a pleasure."

— Tariq Ali, author
Churchill: His Time, His Crimes

"What a gift to have access to a collection of some of Alexander Cockburn's commentaries in one volume! His brilliant analyses remain fresh and vital as when he wrote them, his insights and warnings relevant today."

— Roxanne Dunbar-Ortiz, author
An Indigenous People's History of the United States

"Cockburn was the greatest writer of a generation, who used rapier wit and the force of history to demolish venal bullies. Everything he wrote, in defense of the underdog, was a feast to be savored. A treat to look forward to."

— Sue Coe, artist
Dead Meat

"Alexander Cockburn was a marvel. A skilled journalist and superb writer, his knowledge was both broad and deep. It was almost unfair to the rest of us that he could write intelligently, wittily, trenchantly, and well about food, classic cars, interior design, art, music, not to mention economics, politics, and history. And he did this while always maintaining the deepest integrity, championing those without and pillorying the rich, who rule us so callously. With respect to the nature of this vicious system and the need to overthrow it, Alex kept his brilliance shining brightly. Oh, that there were more writers like him today. Fortunately, his legacy lives on and will endure for those who cannot stomach hypocrisy, who like Olaf, in ee cummings poem, say steadfastly that 'there is some shit I will not eat.'"

— MICHAEL YATES, author
Work, Work, Work

"A needed project, that can't come too soon, with its acid prose cutting through the machine's wicked fabrications, and preparing us with hoe and spade for the seed time of the future. Good talk and lots of laughter as we pulverize their castles and redoubts right down to their last squalid maggot."

— PETER LINEBAUGH, author
Red Hot Globe Round Burning

"Alex Cockburn was a journalist who broke media criticism barriers at the Voice in the 1970s. pissed off almost everyone at one time or another, had more enemies than there were names in the 1980 Manhattan White Pages, and reveled in it all. In my opinion, he was one of the greats."

— RUSS "MUGGER" SMITH, editor
Splice Today

"During the decades of descent into neoliberalism, many of us endured bolstered by Alexander Cockburn's razor-sharp dissections of the political and social scene. It is a gift to the future to have some of the best of his piercing legacy assembled here, his perceptions still radical as our reality."

— Susan G. Davis, author
Dirty Jokes and Bawdy Songs: the Uncensored Life of Gershon Legman

"In the 19th century, Jeffrey St. Clair would be the publisher of fugitive slaves who had a bounty on their heads. In 2022, he is the publisher of fugitive opinion, which would be censored elsewhere."

— Ishmael Reed, author
Mumbo Jumbo and "The Conductor"

CounterPunch
PO Box 228
Petrolia, CA 95558
www.counterpunch.org

Copyright © 2022 CounterPunch
All Rights Reserved.

First published by *CounterPunch* 2022

ISBN: 978-0-9982292-2-5
Library of Congress Control Number:
2022949221

Typography and design by Tiffany Wardle.
Typeset in Minion Pro, designed by
Robert Slimbach for Adobe Systems Inc.
and Founders Grotesk, designed by Kris
Sowersby for Klim Type Foundry.

An Orgy of Thieves

Neoliberalism and Its Discontents

Alexander Cockburn
Jeffrey St. Clair

For Harrison, Charlotte and Lilly

"...laden with fruit, and stained
With the blood of the grape…"

— William Blake, "To Autumn"

"The ideas of debtor and creditor as to what constitutes a good time never coincide."

— P.G. Wodehouse, *Love Among the Chickens*

"I've always been a religious man, I've always been a religious man
But I met the banker and it felt like sin, he turned my bailout down
The Banker Man, he let into me, let into me, let into me
The Banker Man, he let into me and spread my name around
He thinks I ain't got a lick of sense cause I talk slow and my money's spent"

— Drive-By Truckers, "Sink Hole"

Table of Contents

A Note on the Text	XI
Prelude: Mornings With Cockburn	1
An Orgy of Thieves	7
The Curious Case of Stephen Breyer	14
The Making of Hillary Clinton	17
The NAFTA Saga	32
NAFTA and the Shameful Seven	40
How NAFTA Ate the West	43
The Neoliberal War on the Poor	47
When Democrats Ran the Culture Wars	60
How Goldman Sachs Killed the Peace Dividend	62
The Clintons and the Rich Women	64
Shattered Promises, Toxic Towns	74
A Secret History of the Monarch	77
The Political Economy of Dead Meat	81
From Mitch to Katrina: Nature is Politics	86
Fukushima and the Ring of Eternal Fire	88
Fukushima Mon Amour	94
The Price America Paid for Madeleine Albright	97
Serbia: the Neoliberals' War	104
Venezuela and the Imperial Script	109
Julian Assange: Wanted by the Empire, Dead or Alive	112

The Libyan Enterprise: Hillary's Imperial Massacre	**118**
Camus in the Time of Drones	**123**
The Origins of America's Vicious War on Its Own Kids	**126**
The Bi-Partisan Origins of the War on Drugs	**130**
The Real Purpose of the Drug War	**136**
Options in America: Kill Yourself or Have a Baby	**140**
The Whack 'Em and Stack 'Em Mentality of American Cops	**142**
Hate Versus Death	**145**
The Death Penalty and the American Mind	**148**
Constitutional Entropy	**151**
Agency of Fear	**154**
America Enters a New Time	**157**
The Myth of Microloans	**161**
Creatures of Capital	**164**
The Economics of Contempt	**166**
Making the Rich Happy	**169**
Masters of Perfidy: The Crash of AIG	**173**
The Fall of the House of Stanford	**180**
The Myth of the Knowledge Economy	**190**
Temple of Mammon, Planet of Doom	**194**
The Strategists of Urban Destruction	**197**
An Architecture of Doom and Dread	**200**
The Parable of the Shopping Mall	**204**
The Dollar General Theory of Money and Employment	**207**
Gratis	**212**
Index	**213**

A Note on the Text

THIS PROJECT ORIGINATED in 2010, one of several ideas Alexander Cockburn and I had been tossing around, including A Book of Monsters, which may yet see the light (or at least twilight) of day. "Neoliberalism is too soft of a word for a system that grinds so many people down," Alex wrote me in an email. He wanted to dump the word in the tumbril and cart it off to the guillotine for summary execution. Of course, we'd been writing about "neoliberalism" since we started working together 20 years earlier and were both guilty of overusing that anodyne term. So a book was in order to set matters right. Alex took the first stab at compiling it. After weeks exploring the CounterPunch archives, he sent me a file with 152 essays, divided into 5 sections he labeled: Dogpatch, Jackboot State, Cutthroats, Swindlers, and a Touch of Nature. The whole packaged totaled well over 500,000 words. We both decided this was perhaps a little too much Cockburn and St. Clair for even our most devoted readers to feast upon. Then his health began to deteriorate and he turned his attention to finishing the book that would become *A Colossal Wreck*. The package of files Alex sent sat in my Mac for years untouched, fermenting, like one of his notorious hard cider vintages distilled at his home in Petrolia. As the tenth anniversary of his death approached, I dug back into the bulging folder and began axing, slashing and trimming it down to a manageable thicket. What remains, I hope, gives a taste of the range of stories we covered about the wreckage inflicted by the policies of the so-called "New Democrats" of the 90s and the 2000s: the Clintons, Gore, Kerry, Obama and Biden. For continuity's sake, I've included a few pieces that I've written since Cockburn's death. But the brutal rhythms of our most recent history would be entirely familiar to him. Still he would have been cheered by the dramatic acts of resistance, from Standing Rock to the streets of Portland, that have sprung up in defiance of the merciless system of profit and repression that has been imposed upon us. **JSC**

Prelude: Mornings With Cockburn

My last talk with Alexander Cockburn was like so many others. It wandered around from topic to topic in an easy, freestyle way. His voice was a little weaker than usual, a little scratchy in the throat. He was in Germany, talking on a cell-phone, in a hotel room near the clinic where he was being treated for cancer. We talked about how dreary American politics had become, about the spinelessness of Obama and his liberal supporters, the insanity of the Republican ultras, and the stuffiness of Mitt Romney. "Is this all there is?" he asked. "Politics used to be so much more fun."

Then his voice livened up. He described an online photo essay on Brigitte Bardot, then vividly recalled his stroll through the Pompidou Center in Paris with his daughter Daisy to view the vast Matisse retrospective. "No question, Matisse was the greatest." Matisse had deposed Samuel Palmer, Edouard Vuillard, Turner, Hokusai, Bruegel the Elder, Morris Graves and Giorgioni, in Alex's ever-changing retinue of favorite painters.

He asked what I'd been listening to. I told him Howlin' Wolf and John Lee Hooker, as usual, reigniting a long-running debate between us. Alex was a Muddy Waters man. I emailed him a video clip of our mutual hero Ike Turner, playing at some odd venue in Italy, with the Ikettes high-stepping it in white mini-skirts and go-go boots. We watched it together online, laughing at the way the dancers seemed to mock Turner. "Ike's headed for trouble," Alex said.

Then Alex asked if the trout were rising in the Deschutes River in central Oregon. He said when he got back to the states we should ring up old Doug Peacock in Montana and spend a couple days tossing dry flies at the rainbows. I told him to count on it.

"Can you bring sausages? I can't believe I'm in the heart of Germany and can't even eat sausages."

I told him I'd order some garlic sausages from Taylor's down in Cave Junction, pack some goat cheese and a dozen bottles of Cotês du Rhône.

"Thanks, Buddy."

That was the last time I heard his voice.

The first time I heard his voice was in the fall of 1992, after the presidential elections. I was editing the environmental magazine *Wild Forest Review* at the time. The phone rang. I picked up. "Jeffrey, hullo, Jeffrey, is that you? This is Alexander Cockburn at *The Nation*."

Even though I'd long given up reading the tedious, East Coast-biased prose of *The Nation*, the name was familiar from the *Village Voice*, which I used to read assiduously in the 1970s, and his marvelous books *Corruptions of Empire* and *Fate of the Forest*, with Susanna Hecht, both of which had fractured spines. The voice was sweetly accented, seductive almost. "That was a helluva piece you wrote on Clinton's environmental record in Arkansas. You know, we may be the only two people in the country to the left of David Broder who see Bill for the corporate whore that he is."

We talked for an hour or so about Clinton, Weyerhaeuser, Tyson Chicken and the poisoning of the White River. Turns out, Alex was not "at" *The Nation*, geographically anyway. I was surprised to learn that he lived on the Lost Coast in a little hamlet along the Mattole River called Petrolia. He'd left Manhattan behind to the consternation of many of his readers, friends and editors. But most of them had never seen the Mattole Valley or that wild stretch of California coast that runs from Shelter Cove north to Cape Mendocino.

A few days later, the fax machine began to spit out Alex's column. It was pretty much a verbatim transcript of our talk—though I didn't make an appearance. And that was vintage Alex, too. If there was a deadline, he would run right up to it and often past it. This wasn't because Alex had writer's block, it was because he had better things to do, like feed the horses, teach his cockatiel Percy to whistle the Internationale, fix—or try to fix—the septic, prune the apple trees, tweezer out a deer tick from Frank the cat's black dreadlocks, distill hard cider, check the progress of the pit barbecue, negotiate a complex Persian rug deal with Lawrence of La Brea or find his glasses. Alex could write faster than anyone I've ever met and the faster he wrote the sharper his prose. And Alex wrote very sharp prose. His old partner at the *Village Voice,* James Ridgeway, called him "the Master."

Two months later Alex was writing for me. After his first column appeared in *Wild Forest Review,* Alex rang me up. "Jeffrey, nice looking issue. But didn't you forget something?"

"What's that?" I said, fearing that I'd mangled one of his paragraphs.

"My payment. I'm a professional writer, you know. Just a little something to make me feel I'm not giving it away."

We weren't paying writers then. We could barely pay the rent. I scrambled for a plan.

"Can I send you a bottle of Scotch?"

"I hate Scotch. Make it Irish whiskey. Jameson's."

Alex had a reputation as a heavy drinker. But that wasn't my experience with him. In the last few years, he tended to drink wine more than hard liquor. He flirted with hard cider and often came into possession of exotic distillations of dubious legality. But he didn't get rip-roaring drunk very often. Instead, he revealed a predisposition toward narcolepsy. He could simply fall asleep, often at surreal times. Once his ex-girlfriend Barbara Yaley had gotten us tickets to see Little Richard perform in San Francisco as a birthday present. Twenty-minutes into a raucous performance, Alex's head was nodding on my shoulder, snoring in sync to the beat of "Good Golly Miss Molly."

A few years earlier we gave a book talk at Powell's in downtown Portland. As usual, Alex drove his precious white Plymouth Valiant. After the gig we enjoyed a nice dinner at Jake's Famous Crayfish, drained a couple glasses of wine and headed back to Oregon City on Highway 99. We'd barely reached the swank community of Eastmoreland, near Reed College, when Alex muttered, "Jeffrey, can you take the wheel? Now...." His chin dropped to his sternum, the tiny car veering toward the Willamette. I leaned over, grabbed the steering wheel with one hand, pounded the brake with the other. I negotiated the car to the side of the highway, heaved Alex into the passenger seat, then sat befuddled at the control panels wondering how to get the car into gear. It was my first, though not last, encounter with the Valiant's infamous push-button transmission.

Then there was the notorious incident in North Richmond, California. Our book *Whiteout: the CIA, Drugs and the Press* had recently been published, greeted by what was perhaps the most hostile review ever printed by the *New York Times Book Review*. We were speaking to a big and boisterous crowd in this largely black community in the East Bay Area detailing the CIA's role in abetting cocaine trafficking during the Contra wars. I was about halfway through my talk when I was distracted by a delicate purring sound to my left. It was Alex, glasses perched on his forehead, hypnotized by the sedative power of my voice into a somnatic state. So, yes, even Cockburn nods.

Nearly every morning for the past 20 years, the phone would ring in our house at 7 am. "Jeffrey, this is Alex." As if it could be anyone else. We talked an hour each morning. Several hours a day when we were writing books together. Those calls oriented my days. Now there is a strange lacunae, as I wait for those early morning calls and find only silence. I feel lost without them.

These weren't business calls. They weren't "about" *CounterPunch*. They were notations on our lives. We talked about car mechanics and fishing; French cinema and the best way to bake salmon; the architecture of Barcelona and the merits of free jazz; surrealist poets and the proper way to stack hay; Kimberly and Daisy's adventures with the, yes, Alexander Technique; Roman emperors (we were intent on reclaiming the reputation of Nero) and the harvesting of mussels; the paintings Tintoretto and the dancing of James Brown; the plot of *Tron Legacy* ("Jeffrey, what's it all about? I've got to talk with Olivia later and I couldn't make heads or tails of it, could you?"); Becky Grant's dazzling ceramics and Greg Smith's latest project at Rancho Cockburn. One morning he called up and said, "Jeffrey, we have to rethink our opposition to journalism prizes. It seems my brother Patrick has just won the Gellhorn Prize for war reporting. And he's going to accept it!" Who says Alex refused to change his mind?

Increasingly, we didn't talk much about the political scene: too dull, too predictable, too dreary. We taunted each other on the phone with jokes and pop quizzes: identify this painting, this singer, this line from Joyce, Wodehouse, Ruskin, Edward Gibbon or Henry Miller. We played these games right up to the end. On Bastille day, a week before he died, I sent Alex this stanza under the subject heading: "?"

> Now was it that both found,
> The meek and lofty did both find,
> Helpers to their heart's desire,
> And stuff at hand, plastic as they could wish,

Both were called upon to exercise their skill—
Not in Utopia, subterranean fields, or some secreted island,
Or heaven knows where!
But in the very world, which is the world of all of us—
The place where in the end we find our happiness—
Or not at all.

Five minutes later an email skids into my Mac from Germany. "Wordsworth!"

And so he won again. Those are the closing lines of "The French Revolution as it Appeared to Enthusiasts at its Commencement." The young Wordsworth was something of an armchair revolutionary, cheering on the French radicals from his cottage in the Lake District. But those were dangerous sentiments, even coded in verse, and Wordsworth was hounded by the secret police and broke under the pressure.

Alex never broke, never retreated, but always moved forward, toward greater liberation, toward justice and sometimes toward vengeance for grievous wrongs. His favorite line from Lenin was "Be as radical as reality." This became *CounterPunch*'s motto. Alexander Cockburn's politics weren't static and they weren't theoretical. They were geared toward the circumstances of our daily lives, the weekly confrontations with the neoliberal orthodoxy we charted in these essays over two decades of writing together.

In the hundreds of interviews I've given since Alex's death, I've taken to calling him "our Voltaire." He shared Voltaire's wide-ranging mind, his hatred of oppression, his rapier wit and astounding productivity. Alex wrote with breath-taking speed. I think he wrote as fast as Jean-Paul Sartre, but without the amphetamines. And the prose emerged, from the Underwood and later (thank god) his Mac, with a vicious lucidity. His columns deepen and expand with re-reading, because, like Voltaire, they are studded with inside jokes, puns, secret insults and allusions. It's one of the reasons his friend Edward Said called him, "Alexander the Brilliant."

The last email Alex sent chastised me: "Jeffrey, why haven't you posted my diary! I sent it to you three DAYS ago!" I chuckled when I read it. He had actually sent the essay a few hours earlier and I had edited it and put it online only a few minutes later.

By that point Alex was apparently exploring Zeno's Paradox, he was surfing other waves of time, subdividing the seconds into infinite segments, as if he was hot on the trial of Schroedinger's Cat (the one that might be dead and alive at the same moment), a cat which, when he finally catches up with him, will be big and black and fluffy. Alex will call out: "Frankie!" And he will come…

Jeffrey St. Clair

An Orgy of Thieves

ALL THROUGH THE 1980s and 1990s, professorial mountebanks like James Q. Wilson and Charles Murray grew plump from best sellers about the criminal, probably innate, propensities of the "underclass," about the pathology of poverty, the teen predators, the collapse of morals, the irresponsibility of teen moms.

There was indeed a vast criminal class coming to full vicious potential in the 1990s: a group utterly vacant of the most elementary instincts of social propriety, devoid of moral fiber, selfish to an almost unfathomable degree. This class appeared in the form of our corporate elite.

Given a green light in the late 1970s by the deregulatory binge urged by corporate-funded think tanks and launched legislatively by Jimmy Carter and Ted Kennedy, by the 1990s, America's corporate leadership had evolved a simple strategy for criminal self-enrichment.

First, lie about your performance in a manner calculated to deceive investors. This was engineered by the production of a "pro forma" balance sheet freighted with accounting chicanery of every stripe and hue, willingly supplied by Arthur Andersen and others. Losses were labeled "capital expenditures"; losing assets were "sold" to co-conspirators in the large banks for the relevant accounting period.

Later, using Generally Accepted Accounting Principles, slightly more realistic balance sheets would be presented to the SEC and the IRS.

Flaunting the "pro forma" numbers, corporations would issue more stock, borrow more money from some co-conspiratorial bank, buy back the stock for the chief executives (who would further inflate its value by dint of bogus accountancy), sell the stock to the chumps and then finally bail out with their millions before the roof fell in, leaving pension funds like CalPERS holding the bag. The fortunes amassed by George W. Bush and Dick Cheney are vivid illustrations of this technique.

The scale of the looting? Prodigious. This orgy of thievery, without parallel in the history of capitalism, was condoned and abetted year after year by the archbishop of the economy, Alan Greenspan, a man with a finely-honed sense of distinction between the degree of reproof merited by the very rich and those less powerful. When Ron Carey led the Teamsters to victory way back in 1997, Greenspan rushed to denounce the "inflationary" potential of modestly improved wage packets. Even though declared innocent by a jury of his peers, Carey was forbidden ever to run in a union election again. And so it goes now with the drumbeats about raising the minimum wage.

Where were the sermons from Greenspan or his successor Ben Bernanke about the inflationary potential of stock-option fortunes lofted on the hot air of crooked accountancy and other kindred conspiracies?

Let someone die in gang-banger crossfire in South Central and William Bennett will rush to indict an entire generation, an entire race. Where are the sermons from Bennett, Murray and the Sunday Show moralists about CEOs scuttling off with their swag, leaving their employees to founder amid wrecked pensions and destroyed prospects? A street kid in Oakland is in the police database by the time he's 10. There are no "criminal propensity" profiles for grads of the Wharton or Harvard business schools.

You have to go back to Marx and Balzac to get a truly vivid sense of the rich as criminal elites. These giants bequeathed a tradition of joyful dissection of the morals and ethics of the rich, carried on by Veblen, John Moody, C. Wright Mills, William Domhoff, and others. But by the mid-1960s, disruptive political science was not a paying proposition if you aimed for tenure. A student studying Mills would be working nights at the soda fountain, while the kid flourishing Robert Dahl and writing rubbish about "pluralism" would get a grad fellowship.

Back in the 1950s, people were reading stuff about the moral vacuum in affluent suburbia by writers like Vance Packard and David Riesman. Presumably, inner loneliness soon became inner joy and there was nothing wrong with putting one's boot on a colleague's neck and cashing in. Where are the books now about these proving grounds for that great corporate criminal cohort of the 2000s which had come of age in the Reagan years?

In fact, it's nearly impossible to locate books that examine the class of corporate executives through the lens of cool scientific contempt. Much of the current writing on CEO culture is published in magazines like *Fortune*, *Businessweek* or *Forbes*. And though there are a few authors—like Robert Monks (*Power and Accountability*)—who focus their attention on executive culture, nowhere will you find empirical studies on the sociobiological roots of the criminal tendencies of the executive class.

Why? The rich bought out the opposition. Back in the mists of antiquity, you had communists, socialists and populists who'd read Marx and who had a pretty fair notion of what the rich were up to. Even Democrats had a grasp of the true situation. Then came the witch-hunts and the buyouts, hand in hand. The result was that a Goldman Sachs trader could come to maturity without ever once hearing an admonitory word about it being wrong to lie, cheat and steal, sell out your co-workers and defraud your customers.

The finest schools in America had educated a criminal elite that stole the store in less than a decade. Was it all the fault of Ayn Rand, of the Chicago School, of Hollywood, of God's demise?

+++

Hope walks arm in arm with fear and so naturally, in the midst of the 2008 financial crisis, liberal elitists like Barack Obama and Bill and Hillary Clinton admonished us, a la Roosevelt, that we have nothing to fear but fear itself and we must all pull together in the spirit of bipartisanship to bail out Wall Street. Wrong. We have many identifiable things to be frightened of, starting with a program designed to bail out the thieves running our financial system and then stick Middle America with a price-tag heftier than you can imagine. Why pull together with the licensed thug who just stole your money and then pledges to do it again to your kids?

When it comes to fingering the perpetrators, it is crucial to recall that the financial crisis is indeed truly bipartisan. What exploded in the late summer of 2008 was an economic credo that has been rolling along since the early 1970s: neoliberalism.

By all rights, this last crisis has brought us to the crossroads where neoliberalism should be buried with a stake through its heart. We've had thirty years' worth of deregulation—the loosening of government supervision. This has been the neoliberal mantra preached by both major parties, the whole of the establishment press and almost every university economics department in the country. It is central to all the current disasters. And if you want to identify symbolic figures in the legislated career of deregulation, there are no more resplendent culprits than Phil Gramm and Robert Rubin.

Take Gramm first.

In 1999 Gramm, then a senator from Texas, was the prime Republican force pushing through the Gramm-Leach-Bliley Act. It repealed the old Glass-Steagall Act, passed during the Great Depression, which prohibited a commercial bank from being in the investment and insurance business. President Bill Clinton cheerfully signed it into law.

A year later Gramm, chairman of the Senate Banking Committee, attached a 262-page amendment to an omnibus appropriations bill, voted on by Congress right before a recess. The amendment received no scrutiny and duly became the Commodity Futures Modernization Act, which allowed deregulation of investment banks and exempted most over the counter derivatives, credit derivatives, credit defaults and swaps from regulatory scrutiny. Thus were born the scams that produced the debacle of Enron, which boasted Gramm's wife Wendy as a member of its board. She had earlier served on the Commodity Futures Trading Commission from 1983 to 1993 and devised many of the rules coded into law by her husband in 2000.

Somewhat stained by the Enron debacle, Gramm quit the senate in 2002 and began to enjoy the fruits of his deregulatory efforts. He became a vice chairman of the giant Swiss bank UBS' new investment arm in the US, and lobbied Congress, the Federal Reserve and the Treasury Department about banking and mortgage issues in 2005 and 2006. He urged Congress to roll back strong state rules designed to crimp the predatory tactics of the subprime mortgage industry. UBS took a bath of about $20 billion in write offs from bad real estate loans in 2006.

Long acknowledged as one of the most mean-spirited men ever to reach Congress, Gramm is a prime exhibit on any roster of the architects of the current economic mess. At the behest of the banking industry, he wrote the laws that enabled the huge balloons of funny money debt that exploded in 2008. The deregulatory statutes bearing his name prompted Wall Street's looting orgy in subprime thievery.

But is he Exhibit A? No. That honor should surely go to Robert Rubin and to the economic course he set for his boss, the eagerly complicit Bill Clinton. Gramm has been the hireling of the banking industry. Rubin is at the beating heart of Wall Street finance, and he and Lawrence Summers were the guiding forces for financial deregulation at Clinton's Treasury.

The Republicans hoped that the roof wouldn't fall in on their watch, and that the crisis could be deferred to 2009 and then blamed on the Democrats. But their insurance policy was that if the roof did cave, as indeed it did, the rescue policy would be identical in either case. That's why Obama collected more money than McCain from the big Wall Street houses.

The gang that successfully got out of Dodge in time was the Clinton-Rubin-Summers gang, just before the last bubble—the stock market bubble—burst in March of 2001. They knew what was coming.

For a full appraisal of the mechanics of the looting, it is useful to pull off the shelf Robert Pollin's invaluable economic history of the Clinton years, *Contours of Descent*.

> The second major component of Clinton administration policy in this area was supporting the successful repeal of the Depression-era Glass-Steagall framework of financial regulation through the 1999 Financial Services Modernization Act, otherwise known as Gramm-Leach-Bliley. Dismantlement of Glass-Steagall, *de facto* and *de jure*, had been long in the making. Innovative financial market players were easily circumventing this old regulatory apparatus, with its focus on creating firewalls between segments of the financial services industry, and preventing commercial banks from operating in more than one state. But the point is that an alternative to both Glass-Steagall and complete deregulation could have been devised, through some combination of policies such as taxing speculative financial transactions and establishing lower reserve requirements for loans that finance productive, as against speculative, investments. But the Clinton administration never considered such an approach. Quite the contrary. The 2001 Economic Report of the President, the last one written under Clinton, was unequivocal in dismissing Glass-Steagall and touting the virtues of financial deregulation:
>
> 'Given the massive financial instability of the 1930s, narrowing the range of banks' activities was arguably important for that day and age. But those rules are not needed today, and the easing of interstate banking rules, along with the passage of the Financial Services Modernization Act of 1999 have removed them, while maintaining appropriate safeguards. These steps allow consolidation in the financial sector that will result in efficiency gains and provide new services for consumers.'
>
> Moreover, Robert Rubin, a major Clinton administration force behind Glass-Steagall repeal, was also among the first to benefit personally from it, in moving from his Treasury position to co-direct

the newly merged investment/commercial banking conglomerate Citigroup. Under any reasonable interpretation of Glass-Steagall, the former commercial bank Citicorp and the former investment banking firm Travelers would not have been permitted to merge.

Amid the embers of the meltdown on Wall Street—one of the most devastating in the nation's history—as Lehman went broke, as Merrill Lynch was swallowed up by Bank of America and AIG tottered to the Fed, begging bowl in hand—the orchestrators of the collapse insisted that "the fundamentals of our economy are strong." The system requires blind obedience.

Over the past quarter century, the US manufacturing economy went offshore. Lately the so-called New Economy of the "Information Age" has been moving offshore too. Free trade has left millions without a decent job or the prospect of ever getting one above the $15 an hour tier.

Below a thin upper crust of the richest people in the history of the planet the rest of America, in varying degrees of desperation, can barely get by. Millions are so close to the edge that an extra 25 cents per gallon of fuel is a household budget-breaker.

Wages have stagnated. Decade after decade the bargaining power of workers has dwindled. We've seen the macabre spectacle of American-based workers ordered to train their overseas replacements before being fired.

Bipartisan ruses like the Clinton-inspired exclusion of energy and food costs from the measures of "core inflation" ensure that social security payments don't keep up with real inflation, which—if you take in the soaring costs of groceries and fuel for heat and transport—is double the official rate. In the same way, real employment—now officially just above 6 per cent—is actually around 12 per cent.

The system is in dire trouble and nowhere is it more balefully manifest than in present and scheduled Pentagon spending, a figure barely mentioned in these days of crisis. Stick it to the imprudent homebuyers, not to the arms manufacturers and their gigantic pigsty, seeping its sewage across the planet.

But then, as the cranky German in the British Museum liked to point out, the capitalist system is always in crisis. Crisis is integral to the system. In too many ways, over the past twenty-five years, brooding on its own crises, the left has forgotten this. In the low contour of radical ideas and of radical political organization since the rise of the Clintons, we now suffer the consequences.

The Curious Case of Stephen Breyer

ANY MAN ADMIRED by both Senators Ted Kennedy and Orrin Hatch couldn't be all good. And, in fact, Stephen Breyer's elevation to the highest bench in 1994 illustrated concisely how, across the 80s and 90s, Kennedyesque liberalism and Hatchian conservatism merged into a unified, pro-corporate posture.

Put more nastily, Breyer's ascent to the Supreme Court offers an unpleasing paradigm for the utter bankruptcy and degradation of that liberal tradition of which Kennedy was erroneously supposed to be the custodian and stout defender. Those with short memories often ascribe certain familiar features of the socio-economic landscape to the "Reagan Revolution." Such features center on the erosion of government regulations unwelcome to big business.

But the intellectual and political groundwork was done by Teddy Kennedy's people back in the 1970s. And Stephen Breyer, who still shows no sign of relinquishing his seat, was one of them. This was the launch time for the deregulation of airlines, trucking and for the erosion of environmental victories won in the previous decade. Breyer and Alfred Kahn, another Kennedy man, predicted that in the bracing combat of the unregulated free market, the inefficient and unproductive would go to the wall, airline services would become more flexible, cheaper and, above all, more profitable.

Any student of the real world could have told them-and many did-the true consequences of deregulation would be greater business concentration and higher prices. Consumers paid the price and so did Kennedy's core constituency, organized labor. The same thing happened in trucking, deregulated in 1980 on Kennedy's initiative. In the next decade, freight-workers' wages fell more than 25 percent.

In January of 1979, Breyer, then Kennedy's chief legislative counsel, published an extremely influential article in *Harvard Law Review*, in which he argued an old business favorite: Environmental hazards could best be dealt with by market mechanisms in which "rights" to pollute would be traded.

In other words, the country would be divided into zones and pollution index would be established for each zone, with companies allowed a certain amount of pollution within the overall permissible limit. But if Company A used only 25 percent of its "pollution rights," it could trade or sell the remaining 75 percent to Company B in the same area that had already reached its limit. On paper, Company B would not be exceeding regulatory limits, though of course the people living next to Company B's plant would be dealing with higher levels of poisons.

To put it crudely, the Kennedy neoliberals wanted to organize a market in Cancer Bonds, offering relief to the Business Roundtable, which was screaming that in 1977 the operations of six regulatory agencies caused $2.65 billion in "incremental costs" to 48 major companies, about ten percent of their total capital expenditure.

Thus out of Kennedy's office came the initiative to replace environmental law compliance with "cost effective reforms," including pollution taxes and credits, effluent charges and markets for pollution rights. As environmental economists Jim O'Connor and Daniel Faber put it, the scheme is designed to "increase capital's flexibility to meet regulatory requirements but continue polluting in a profitable manner."

The regulatory theory promoted by Breyer was transmuted into law in the Clean Air Act of 1990. In May of 1992, the Tennessee Valley Authority bought an estimated $2.5 million worth of credits from Wisconsin Power and Light, which didn't need them. This credit allowed TVA to exceed its limit of sulfur dioxide and other toxic emissions. As Benjamin Goldman shows in his useful book, *The Truth About Where You Live*, among those on the receiving end, Shelby County, Tennessee, ranks twenty-second among all counties in the nation for excess deaths from lung cancer. Sheboygan County, Wisconsin, ranks twenty-eight from the bottom in the same category-an almost perfect reverse, mirroring the transfer of poisons from north to south, comfortable to poor, white to minority.

For Breyer, equity and the unregulated play of market forces move in harmony. His ascent to the Supreme Court owed everything to his patron, Ted Kennedy, in truth was one of the most effective foes of the real interest of labor and environmentalists during his interminable tenure in the U.S. Senate. Small wonder Orrin Hatch played along.

For the environmental movement there are lessons in this history. The legislative triumphs of the late 1960s and early 1970s, many of them coming to pass in Nixon time, had indeed imposed constraints on corporate profitability. By the end of the 1970s, Congress had passed more than 20 major laws regulating consumer products, the environment and workplace conditions. Hence the corporate counterattack described above and ongoing to this day.

In the early and mid-1970s, environmentalists played the game of rising liberal expectations, assuming that their pluralist conception of the political economy would in turn permit, at level of both popular awareness and state policy, a new, environmentally aware attitude toward cost and regulation.

In the late 1970s, the corporate titans bit back and successfully set labor and environmentalists at each other's throats. Since a good many greens are middle class and essentially anti-labor in philosophical outlook, the antagonism was real. Also, by the end of the 1970s, mainstream environmentalism had moved from popular activism to managerial caution, with some groups, such as the Environmental Defense Fund, gladly endorsing and promoting the market-based theory of environmental regulation offered by Breyer in his chilling 1979 tract.

The Making of Hillary Clinton

HILLARY CLINTON HAS always been an old-style Midwestern Republican in the Illinois mode; one severely infected with Methodism, unlike the more populist variants from Indiana, Wisconsin and Iowa.

Her first known political enterprise was in the 1960 presidential election, the squeaker where the state of Illinois notoriously put Kennedy over the top, courtesy of Mayor Daley, Sam Giancana and Judith Exner. Hillary was a Nixon supporter. She took it on herself to probe allegations of vote fraud. From the leafy middle-class suburbs of Chicago's west side, she journeyed to the tenements of the south side, a voter list in her hand. She went to an address recorded as the domicile of hundreds of Democratic voters and duly found an empty lot. She rushed back to campaign headquarters, agog with her discovery, only to be told that Nixon was throwing in the towel.

The way Hillary Clinton tells it in her *Living History* (an autobiography convincingly demolished by Jeff Gerth and Don Van Natta in their *Her Way: The Hopes and Ambitions of Hillary Rodham Clinton*, an interesting and well researched account) she went straight from the Nixon camp to the cause of Martin Luther King Jr., and never swerved from that commitment. Not so. Like many Illinois Republicans, she did have a fascination for the Civil Rights movement and spent some time on the south side, mainly in African Methodist churches under the guidance of Don Jones, a teacher at her high school. It was Jones who took her to hear King speak at Chicago's Orchestra Hall and later introduced her to the Civil Rights leader.

Gerth and Van Natta eschew psychological theorizing, but it seems clear that the dominant influence in Hillary's life was her father, a fairly successful, albeit tightwad Welsh draper, supplying Hilton hotels and other chains. From this irritable patriarch Hillary kept secret her outings with Jones and her encounter with King. Her public persona was that of a

Goldwater Girl. She battled for Goldwater through the 1964 debacle and arrived at Wellesley in the fall of 1965 with enough Goldwaterite ambition to become president of the Young Republicans as a freshman.

The setting of Hillary's political compass came in the late Sixties. The fraught year of 1968 saw the Goldwater girl getting a high-level internship in the House Republican Conference with Gerald Ford and Melvin Laird, politicians without an ounce of the Goldwater libertarian pizzazz. Hillary says the assassinations of King and Robert Kennedy, plus the war in Vietnam, hit her hard. The impact was not of the intensity that prompted many of her generation to become radicals. She left the suburb of Park Forest and rushed to Miami to the Republican Convention where she fulfilled a lifelong dream of meeting Frank Sinatra and John Wayne and devoted her energies to saving the Party from her former icon, Nixon, by working for Nelson Rockefeller.

Nixon triumphed, and Hillary returned to Chicago in time for the Democratic Convention where she paid an afternoon's visit to Grant Park. By now a proclaimed supporter of Gene McCarthy, she was appalled, not by the spectacle of McCarthy's young supporters being beaten senseless by Daley's cops, but by the protesters' tactics, which she concluded were "not viable". Like her future husband, Hillary was always concerned with maintaining viability within the system.

After the convention Hillary embarked on her yearlong senior thesis, on the topic of the Chicago community organizer Saul Alinsky. She had successfully persuaded Wellesley to keep this under lock and key, but Gerth and Van Natta got hold of a copy. So far from being an exaltation of radical organizing, Hillary's assessment of Alinsky was hostile, charging him with excessive radicalism. Her preferential option was to seek minor advances within the terms of the system. She did not share these conclusions with Alinsky who had given her generous access during the preparation of her thesis and a job offer thereafter, which she declined.

What first set Hillary in the national spotlight was her commencement address at Wellesley, the first time any student had been given this opportunity. Dean Acheson's granddaughter insisted to the president of Wellesley that youth be given its say, and the president picked Hillary as youth's tribune. Her somewhat incoherent speech included some flicks at the official commencement speaker, Senator Edward Brooke, the black Massachusetts senator, for failing to mention the Civil Rights movement or the war. Wellesley's president, still fuming at this discourtesy, saw Hillary skinny-dipping in Lake Waban that evening and told a security guard to steal her clothes.

The militant summer of 1969 saw Hillary cleaning fish in Valdez, Alaska, and in the fall she was at Yale being stalked by Bill Clinton in the library. The first real anti-war protests at Yale came with the shooting of the students at Kent State. Hillary saw the ensuing national student upheaval as, once again, a culpable failure to work within the system. "I advocated engagement, not disruption."

She finally consented to go on a date with Bill Clinton, and they agreed to visit a Rothko exhibit at the Yale art gallery. At the time of their scheduled rendezvous with art, the gallery was closed because the museum's workers were on strike. The two had no inhibitions about crossing a picket line. Bill worked as a scab in the museum, doing janitorial work for the morning, getting as reward a free tour with Hillary in the afternoon.

In the meantime, Hillary was forging long-term alliances with such future stars of the Clinton age as Marian Wright Edelman and her husband Peter, and also with one of the prime political fixers of the Nineties, Vernon Jordan. It was Hillary who introduced Bill to these people, as well as to Senator Fritz Mondale and his staffers.

If any one person gave Hillary her start in liberal Democratic politics, it was Marian Wright Edelman who took Hillary with her when she started the Children's Defense Fund. The two were inseparable for the next twenty-five years. In her autobiography, published in 2003, Hillary lists the 400 people who have most influenced her. Marion Wright Edelman doesn't make the cut. Neither to forget nor to forgive. Peter Edelman was one of three Clinton appointees at the Department of Health and Human Services who quit when Clinton signed the Welfare reform bill, which was about as far from any "defense" of children as one could possibly imagine.

Hillary was on Mondale's staff for the summer of '71, investigating worker abuses in the sugarcane plantations of southern Florida, as close to slavery as anywhere in the U.S.A. Life's ironies: Hillary raised not a cheep of protest when one of the prime plantation families, the Fanjuls, called in their chips (laid down in the form of big campaign contributions to Clinton) and insisted that Clinton tell Vice President Gore to abandon his calls for the Everglades to be restored, thus taking water Fanjul was appropriating for his operation.

From 1971 on, Bill and Hillary were a political couple. In 1972, they went down to Texas and spent some months working for the McGovern campaign, swiftly becoming disillusioned with what they regarded as an exercise in futile ultraliberalism. They planned to rescue the Democratic Party from this fate by the strategy they have followed ever since: the pro-corporate, hawkish neoliberal recipes that have become institutionalized in the Democratic Leadership Council, of which Bill Clinton and Al Gore were founding members.

In 1973, Bill and Hillary went off on a European vacation, during which they laid out their 20-year project designed to culminate with Bill's election as president. Inflamed with this vision, Bill proposed marriage in front of Wordsworth's cottage in the Lake District. Hillary declined, the first of twelve similar refusals over the next year. Bill went off to Fayetteville, Arkansas, to seek political office. Hillary, for whom Arkansas remained an unappetizing prospect, eagerly accepted, in December '73, majority counsel John Doar's invitation to work for the House committee preparing the impeachment of Richard Nixon. She spent the next months listening to Nixon's tapes. Her main assignment was to prepare an organizational chart of the Nixon White House. It bore an eerie resemblance to the twilit labyrinth of the Clinton White House 18 years later.

Hillary had an offer to become the in-house counsel of the Children's Defense Fund and seemed set to become a high-flying public interest Washington lawyer. There was one impediment. She failed the D.C. bar exam. She passed the Arkansas bar exam. In August of 1974, she finally moved to Little Rock and married Bill in 1975 at a ceremony presided over by the Rev. Vic Nixon. They honeymooned in Acapulco with her entire family, including her two brothers' girlfriends, all staying in the same suite.

After Bill was elected governor of Arkansas in 1976, Hillary joined the Rose Law Firm, the first woman partner in an outfit almost as old as the Republic. It was all corporate business, and the firm's prime clients were the state's business heavyweights Tyson Foods, Wal-Mart, Jackson Stevens Investments, Worthen Bank and the timber company Weyerhaeuser, the state's largest landowner.

Two early cases (of a total of five that Hillary actually tried) charted her course. The first concerned the successful effort of Acorn, a public interest group doing community organizing, to force the utilities to lower electric rates on residential consumers and raise rates on industrial users.

Hillary represented the utilities in a challenge to this progressive law, the classic right-wing claim, arguing that the measure represented an unconstitutional "taking" of property rights. She carried the day for the utilities.

The second case found Hillary representing the Coca-Cola Bottling Company of Arkansas in a lawsuit filed by a disabled former employee who had been denied full retirement benefits by the company. In earlier years, Hillary had worked at the Children's Defense Fund on behalf of abused employees and disabled children. Only months earlier, while still a member of the Washington, D.C., public interest community, she had publicly ripped Joseph Califano for becoming the Coca Cola company's public counsel. "You sold us out, you, you sold us out!" she screamed publicly at Califano. Working now for Coca Cola, Hillary prevailed.

Hillary and the Arkansas Elite

In 1990, the *National Law Journal* ran profiles of "the 100 Most Influential Lawyers in the United States". Hillary Clinton was on the list, and for years she would publicly boast that the *Journal* had named her one of "the nation's 100 top lawyers". Finally, the editor of the *National Law Journal*, Patrick Oster, wrote to Arkansas' first lady—as she still was in 1991—testily pointing out that the word "influential" is not synonymous with "top" or "best"—the latter two words used by Mrs. Clinton interchangeably.

By "influential" the *Journal's* profile writer, Peggy Fisk, had meant a lawyer plentifully endowed with corporate and political connections, which Mrs. Clinton certainly enjoyed in Arkansas where she had become a partner of the Rose Law Firm in 1977, amid the dawn of her husband's political career as he began his terms as governor of the state. By the late 1980s, Hillary Clinton was sitting on the board of Wal-Mart, with the rest of Arkansas' business elite crowding her Rolodex. Hillary ignored Oster's letter of correction, instructing her staff to continue to use the word "best" in invoking the *Journal's* profile. She continued to do so for years. Oster was still writing her a decade later about her misuse—including an editorial column in the *Journal* in 2000, when she was running for the U.S. Senate.

In fact, Mrs. Clinton was not a particularly good lawyer and would have had trouble making any honest list of the 100 best lawyers in Little

Rock. In their political biography, *Her Way: The Hopes and Ambitions of Hillary Rodham Clinton*, Jeff Gerth and Don Van Natta Jr. tell the story about the *National Law Journal* and also probe her lawyerly skills when she was at Rose Law. She only tried five cases and confided to Vince Foster—another Rose Law partner—that she was terrified of juries. So Foster had to accompany her to court. Because of her lack of prowess in the courtroom, she had to make her way at Rose Law by working her connections as the State's first lady to bring in clients, and even then her annual partner's share was mostly below $100,000—the lowest in the firm and very small potatoes for one of the hundred most influential lawyers in America.

The Clintons' joint income—at least the visible portion—was not substantial: the state paid Bill $20,000 a year, no doubt under the assumption he'd even up the score with kickbacks. So money was on Mrs. Clinton's mind. Her search for extra income led her into associations that were later to cause endless trouble.

First came the ties with Jim McDougall that were to flower into the Whitewater property speculation and later a huge federal investigation into that deal, unprofitable to the Clintons who had hoped—like many Americans—to make a big score in real estate and solve their money problems at a single stroke.

When things were looking bleak for the Clintons after the Arkansas voters threw Bill out in 1980 after his first term as governor (Arkansas had two-year gubernatorial terms until 1986), she fanned her friendship with James Blair, general counsel of Tyson Foods. Bill Clinton's Little Rock chief of staff, Betsey Wright, recalled that Hillary "loved Jim Blair. Blair was her money man". It was Blair who set up an account for Hillary Clinton with Refco, a small brokerage firm run by Robert "Red" Bone, Don Tyson's former bodyguard and a professional poker player. "Red" Bone got her into cattle future trades. She put up $1,000 and left the trading to Mr. Bone who's often assumed to have arranged the trades with Blair, to Mrs. Clinton's advantage. Nine months later, the $1,000 had swollen with miraculous speed into a profit for Mrs. Clinton of $99,000.

When Bill Clinton ran for the presidency in 1992, reporters noted a mysterious spike in the couple's net worth in the early 1980s and quizzed Mrs. Clinton about it. Her first untruthful explanation was that there had been a windfall in the form of an unexpected gift of cash from her parents.

But, aware that the questions wouldn't stop, she issued ferocious order to her staff about any leakage of her tax records. She told them that if they released the tax records showing the commodity trades, they'd "never work in Democratic politics again".

The records were stored in the Clinton Campaign headquarters in Little Rock, in a locked room for which only Hillary, Bill and Betsey Wright had keys. Also in "the Box Room" under lock and key were details of Bill's sexual capers and Hillary's dealings at Rose Law. An internal '92 campaign memo, quoted by Gerth and Van Natta, cited 75 "problem files" in the materials in the Box Room, two-thirds of which related to them as a couple or to Hillary alone. When David Ifshin, the campaign's legal counsel, asked for the key to the room to assess the likely problems, Bill Clinton told him: "We can't open our closet, we'll get crushed by the skeletons".

But two reporters in particular kept pressing: Gerth of the *New York Times* and James Stewart of the *Wall Street Journal*. Gerth finally got evidence of the $99,000 profit on a $1,000 trade and confronted Mrs. Clinton. Shorn of the family gift story, Mrs. Clinton avowed that she'd spent her days poring over cattle prices in the *Wall Street Journal*, that the $99,000 was the fruit of these studies and that she'd quit commodity trading in 1980, after she'd got pregnant with Chelsea, because the trading "was too nerve-wracking". Unfortunately for this story, details later surfaced amid prosecutor Kenneth Starr's investigation during the Clinton presidency, showing that in 1981 Hillary had made a trade netting her $6,500 and she hadn't reported the profit to the IRS.

Amid the Starr probe, the Clintons encouraged the *Wall Street Journal's* Stewart to do a book on what they saw as their unfair persecution on the Whitewater deal. As he researched this work, published as *Blood Sport*, Stewart took a hard look at the commodity trades and pressed Mrs. Clinton for an explanation for all the contradictory stories. Hillary blamed everything on her staff and told Stewart that her own statements should simply be "accepted at face value".

In the mid-1990s, federal special prosecutor Kenneth Starr's investigative team in Little Rock was headed by a veteran of the courtroom, Hickman Ewing Jr. Grilled by Ewing before a grand jury on July 22, l995, Mrs. Clinton used the words "I can't recall" in answer to 50 questions. Later, Ewing told Starr that he rated Mrs. Clinton's testimony as deserving an F Minus, and he wanted to indict the nation's first lady. He was contemplating a number of counts, headed by two major lines of enquiry. First came her handling of the commodity trades and her failure to report her profits to the IRS. Second came her conduct amid the collapse of Madison Guaranty Savings and Loan, owned by Jim McDougal. Relevant to this affair were Hillary Clinton's billings as a legal counsel to Madison Guaranty. These were germane to the question of whether Hillary was being truthful in denying she'd done any legal work for the bank. After many adventures, the records finally came into the hands of Starr's team and showed that Hillary Clinton had billed Madison Guaranty at the rate of $150 an hour, with a total of 60 hours of supposed work on the Castle Grande deal. The prosecutors had the billings but were never able to look at Hillary's time sheets. Her secretary had removed them from the Rose Law Firm in 1992, and it's generally assumed the first lady destroyed them.

Webb Hubbell, a partner at Rose Law and one of Hillary's closest friends, fell from his eminence as deputy attorney general in Clinton's first term and was convicted and imprisoned on charges of padding by $394,000 his legal billings at Rose Law. Ewing was convinced that Hillary had been doing the same thing. He prepared an indictment. It was the most serious brush with disaster that Hillary ever faced. Paradoxically, she was saved by the indiscretions of her faithless mate. Even as Ewing was urging Hillary's indictment, Starr was delightedly fingering what he conceived to be the object that would doom Bill Clinton, the semen-stained dress retrieved from Monica Lewinsky's closet by Starr's team. The only thing the prurient Starr cared about was nailing Clinton for sexual misconduct, and so he told the disappointed Ewing that there would be no indictment of Hillary.

Even as Hillary Clinton was making trouble for herself and Bill in her legal and business dealings, she was reinventing Bill as a politician. Defeat in 1980 after his first two-year gubernatorial term was a cataclysmic event. Bill called it a "near death experience". According to Gerth and Van Natta, it was "the only time anyone has seen Hillary Clinton cry in public". Bill was inclined to throw in the political towel and go back to being a law professor in Fayetteville, where he would doubtless be roosting in tenured bliss to this day, plump and pony-tailed, fragrant with marijuana and still working his way through an endless roster of coeds. But in 1980, over a funereal breakfast of instant grits, Vernon Jordan brokered a deal: Bill Clinton would give up being a southern populist in the mold of Orval

Faubus, six-term governor of Arkansas. Southern populism involved offending powerful corporations. Bill lost in 1980 because not only had he taken the un-populist course of hiking the rate on car registration, he'd angered Weyerhaeuser and Tyson Foods. So, for his comeback he would remake himself as a neoliberal. Hillary Rodham would give up insisting on keeping her maiden name and become Hillary Clinton. The man charged with supervising the Clintons' makeover was selected by Hillary: Dick Morris, a political consultant known for his work for Southern racists like Jesse Helms. Morris ultimately guided President Bill Clinton into the politics of triangulation, outflanking the Republicans from the right on race, crime, morals posturing and deference to corporations. As Hillary said in 1980, "If you want to be in this business, this is the type of person you have to deal with".

Bill Clinton duly pushed aside the *Playboy* centerfolds and pored over Dick Morris' polling data, trimming his positions to suit. He recaptured the governorship in 1982 and as a reward appointed his wife to head a special task force charged with reforming Arkansas' education system, at that time widely regarded as the worst in the country. The plan Mrs. Clinton came up with showcased teacher testing and funding the schools through a sales tax increase, an astoundingly regressive proposal since it imposed new costs on the poor in a very poor state while sparing any levies on big corporations. The plan went through. Arkansas' educational ranking remained abysmal, but Hillary won national attention as a "realistic Democrat" who could make "hard" choices, like taxing welfare mothers.

While enjoying this limelight, Mrs. Clinton was invited onto the board of Wal-Mart as the first woman director, the only Rose Law partner at that time to have accepted an outside position. She was also asked by Robert MacCrate, the president of the American Bar Association, to head up a commission on how to implement a resolution by the ABA to increase the profile of women and minorities in the legal profession. Mac Crate told Gerth and Van Natta that Mrs. Clinton declined, saying that she didn't want gender equity to be linked with race. She prevailed. Two years later, she agreed to head an ABA commission examining the status of women in the legal profession. Issues of race were not to be scrutinized.

By 1987, Hillary was wearying of life as first lady of Arkansas and began to press her husband on the 20-year plan they had made long before, whose consummation would be a successful run by Bill for the U.S. presidency. Dick Morris was assigned the task of running polls on Bill's chances. Betsey Wright was charged with sizing up the "problems". Morris' news was grim. The Democratic Party was not sold on the prospect of the governor of Arkansas as their nominee in 1988. Betsey Wright sat down with Bill and Hillary and read out to both of them a list of dozens of women Wright believed Bill had had some kind of fling with during his gubernatorial years. Bill's head sank into his hands, and he mumbled, "I'm not going to run for president and I don't want to run for re-election as governor either". As Wright recalled later, Hillary stood up and yelled, "If you're not gonna run for re-election, I'm gonna run". "Okay", said Bill, he'd run again. It was Hillary's call.

The next four years were spent gearing up for the White House run and trying to bury Bill's past. Amid these efforts Hillary made two huge mistakes, which haunted the Clintons throughout the 1992 campaign and their White House years. Clinton's opponent in the 1990 governor's race was Sheffield Nelson, a Little Rock lawyer. Nelson had accumulated a sleaze file on Bill, detailing his sexual escapades and the couple's Whitewater real estate transactions. But he never used this material in the campaign. Nonetheless, in 1990 Hillary Clinton publicly excoriated Nelson, calling him "a vindictive and very bitter man". The reason for Hillary's assault was that Nelson, in the climactic weeks of the race, had saturated the airwaves with a series of campaign ads charging Clinton with being a tax-and-spend Democrat. The ads had some effect, and the Clintons had to borrow $100,000 from the Jackson Stephens-controlled Worthen Bank to mount a counteroffensive ad campaign of their own. Nelson, seething at Hillary's onslaught, duly became bitter and vindictive and, as Clinton's presidential campaign got under way, he began to leak ripe details from the file he had kept closed in 1990.

Her second mistake also came in 1990, when Jim McDougal was facing trial over the collapse of Madison Guaranty Savings and Loan. In his hour of need, he asked Bill to testify as a character witness in his trial. Though Bill was willing to do so, Hillary was adamant that he should avoid any association with McDougal. She successfully persuaded Bill to decline. McDougal was acquitted, but he never forgave the Clintons for their disloyalty. He too began to leak damaging stories about Whitewater to Gerth and other reporters from his rusting trailer in Arkadelphia. Thus, even as she kindled her husband's presidential bid, Hillary helped spark the fires of financial and sexual scandal that almost destroyed his presidency.

The Vices of Hillary Clinton

Hillary Clinton's propensity for overkill earned her and Bill the enmity of people capable of inflicting serious damage, as the Whitewater and cattle futures scandals duly attested. And soon, as they embarked on the 1992 presidential campaign, the same overkill reflex produced a perfect storm of bad publicity that came within an ace of finishing Clinton off altogether.

In January 2002, America was introduced to the Gennifer Flowers scandal, courtesy of the *National Enquirer*. Flowers was a former Little Rock newscaster with whom Governor Clinton had an extended love affair for five years in the 1980s, as pleasingly chronicled in Flowers' entirely credible memoir, *Gennifer Flowers: Passion and Betrayal*.

After the *Enquirer* broke the Flowers story while Clinton was campaigning in New Hampshire, his campaign advisors went into crisis mode, trying to figure out the best defense. Seasoned tacticians like Betsey Wright and David Ifshin suggested that the best course would be to shrug the story off as unsubstantiated gossip mongering by a supermarket tabloid. The national press corps was already taking this tack, since the reporters on the campaign bus were loath to admit they had been scooped by the Enquirer—whose story was in fact a piece of well-researched investigative reporting, backed up by taped phone calls and messages to Gennifer from Bill.

It was Hillary who instructed the campaign to put the ruthless private investigator Jack Palladino on the case. In her memo to Palladino, she ordered him to "impeach Flowers' character and veracity until she is destroyed beyond all recognition." Thus primed, Palladino went into action, seeking to portray Flowers as a prostitute, a shakedown artist and career scamster.

While Palladino was trying to finish off Flowers, Hillary urged Bill to follow the high-risk strategy of both of them going on CBS's 60 Minutes for an interview conducted by Steve Kroft. In front of a vast national audience Bill, visibly ill at ease, admitted to causing pain to his family while denying that their marriage was merely an arrangement. "This is a marriage" he asserted. Hillary broke in. Years of effort in burnishing Bill's image as a Son of the South went up in smoke as she declared, "You know, I'm not sitting here like some little woman standing by my man like Tammy Wynette."

The polls promptly showed Bill's numbers plummeting south of the Mason-Dixon line. An affair with Flowers was one thing, but insulting Tammy Wynette? The nation's number one country star had been watching the program and was furious. She immediately called her publicist to vent her outrage, and the publicist relayed this to the press. For three days the Clinton campaign tried to talk to Wynette. She declined all calls until finally they got Burt Reynolds to call her, and she relented, releasing the news she would accept Hillary's apologies.

The next storm the Clintons had to face was the matter of his avoidance of the draft during the Vietnam War. James Carville, the campaign manager, advocated forthright admission that this is what he had done. Clinton agreed with Carville's plan to go on ABC's Nightline with Ted Koppel, bringing with him his famous letter to Colonel Eugene Holmes frankly discussing the conflict between his desire to go and fight in Vietnam and his concomitant eagerness to "maintain my political viability". But Hillary was adamant. Bill should not admit that he wanted to avoid the draft. On the other hand, he should not be forced to apologize for being against the war. The entire file of documents and letters should be concealed. Her view prevailed, and the inevitable consequence was the draft-dodging issue stayed alive as a steady stream of compromising documents was leaked to the press over the next five months.

The desire for secrecy is one of Mrs. Clinton's enduring and damaging traits, which is why these campaign imbroglios are of consequence. Clinton dug himself into many a pit, but his greatest skill was in talking his way out of them in a manner Americans found forgivable. Befitting a Midwestern Methodist with a bullying father, repression has always been one of Mrs. Clinton's most prominent characteristics. Hers has been the instinct to conceal, to deny, to refuse to admit any mistake. Mickey Kantor, the Los Angeles lawyer who worked on the 1992 campaign, said that Hillary adamantly refused to admit to any mistakes.

It's clear from Gerth and Van Natta Jr.'s very revealing book *Her Way* that Mrs. Clinton played a major role in driving White House lawyer Vince Foster to suicide. After the Clintons arrived in the White House, it became Foster's role to guard their secrets. It was one thing to lock documents into a secret room during the campaign. It was quite another to play hide-and-seek with files in the White House, as Mrs. Clinton required Foster to do. Now there weren't nosy reporters but special prosecutors with subpoenas, looking for documents relevant to Whitewater, to Mrs. Clinton's billing records at Rose Law, her tax records relevant to the commodity trades. Foster was tasked with hiding all these documents: some in his house, some in his office and some—the most damaging files—back in his Little Rock home.

There were additional burdens for Foster. He was trying to douse another fire started by Mrs. Clinton. This was her instruction to fire the White House travel staff, on a trumped-up rationale. There were six separate investigations into these firings, all of which Foster had to deal with. Finally, the wretched man had to listen to Mrs. Clinton publicly blame the whole "Travelgate" mess on him, even as he was concealing documents making it clear she had been the person initiating the mess. On top of that, Mrs. Clinton demanded Foster be the principal liaison with Congress on her health reform plan. For the last month of his life, she refused to communicate with him, even though their offices were thirty feet apart.

Health reform was Mrs. Clinton's assignment in her husband's first term. The debacle is well known. In early 1993, 64 per cent of all Americans favored a system of national health care. By the time Mrs. Clinton's 1342-page bill, generated in secret, landed in Congress, she had managed to offend the very Democratic leadership essential to making health reform a reality. The proposal itself, under the mystic mantra "Managed Competition", embodied all the distinctive tropisms of neoliberalism: a naïve complicity with the darker corporate forces, accompanied by adamant refusal to even consider building the popular political coalition that alone could have faced and routed the insurance and pharmaceutical lobbies—two of the most powerful forces on the American political scene. Mrs. Clinton's rout on health reform remains one of the great avoidable disasters of the last century in American politics, and one with appalling human and social consequences

This disaster was compounded by the fact that after the collapse of health reform, on the advice of Dickie Morris (summoned by Mrs. Clinton), the Clintons swerved right, toward all the ensuing ghastly legislative ventures of their regime—the onslaughts on welfare, the crime bill, NAFTA. With Morris came the birth of "triangulation"—the tactic of the Clinton White House working with Republicans and conservative Democrats and actively undermining liberal and progressive initiatives in Congress. Money that could have given the House back to the Democrats in 1996 was snatched by the White House purely for the self-preservation of the Clintons.

After health care went down the tubes, Hillary adopted a very low-key political profile, in part because Leon Panetta, the new White House chief of staff, banned her from political meetings. But, she outflanked him in two ways: by secret strategizing with Morris every two weeks and by nightly strategy sessions with Clinton and Al Gore. She swung back into a crucial public role with the Lewinsky affair, ironically enough, standing by her man. Gerth and Van Natta establish that she knew the full extent of her husband's relations with the woman she called "Elvira" (the mid-'90s horror queen) on January 21, 1998, eight months before the official narrative claims that Bill informed her of his treachery the night before he gave his deposition. She ordered a full-bore attack on Lewinsky as "a stalker with a weight problem" and shoved Bill toward the doomed posture of total denial. He himself had initially been trending toward a stuttering half-admission that hanky-panky might have taken place. But after he returned from the Lehrer show where he had taken this non-combative route, Hillary lashed him into the categorical denial—"I did not have sexual relations with that woman, Ms. Lewinsky"—that exploded so disastrously in the months and years ahead. (Only months earlier, Hillary had been the one who insisted that no deal be made with Paula Jones, who could have been bought off with the modest settlement her lawyer was requesting. Hillary said she didn't want Jones to get "a single dollar".)

Bill had his Tammy, and he knew the price. "Whatever Hil wants, Hil gets," he told his staff in 1998, and he began to read books about the campaigns of successful female politicians—Margaret Thatcher, Indira Gandhi, Benazir Bhutto, Golda Meir. As Clinton headed toward impeachment, Hillary set her course for the New York Senate seat.

+++

Since Vietnam, there's never been a war that Mrs. Clinton didn't like. She argued passionately in the White House for the NATO bombing of Belgrade. Five days after September 11, 2001, she was calling for a broad war on terror. Any country presumed to be lending "aid and comfort" to al-Qaeda "will now face the wrath of our country." Bush echoed these words eight days later in his nationally televised speech on September 21. "I'll stand behind Bush for a long time to come", Senator Clinton promised, and she was as good as her word, voting for the Patriot Act and the wide-ranging authorization to use military force against Afghanistan.

Of course she supported without reservation the attack on Afghanistan and, as the propaganda buildup toward the onslaught on Iraq got underway, she didn't even bother to walk down the hall to read the National Intelligence Estimate on Iraq before the war. (She wasn't alone in that. Only six senators read that NIE.) When she was questioned about this, she claimed she was briefed on its contents, but in fact no one on her staff had the security clearance to read the report. And her ignorance showed when it came time to deliver her speech in support of the war, as she reiterated some of the most outlandish claims made by Dick Cheney. In this speech, she said Saddam Hussein had rebuilt his chemical and biological weapons program; that he had improved his long-range missile capability; that he was reconstituting his nuclear weapons program; and that he was giving aid and comfort to Al Qaeda. The only other Democratic senator to make all four of these claims in his floor speech was Joe Lieberman. But even he didn't go as far as Senator Hillary. In Lieberman's speech, there was conditionality about some of the claims. In Senator Clinton's, there were no such reservations, even though a vehement war hawk, Ken Pollack, advising Senator Clinton prior to her vote, had told her that the allegation about the al-Qaeda connection was "bullshit".

Later, as the winds of opinion changed, Senator Clinton claimed—and continues to do so to this day—that hers was a vote not for war but for negotiation. In fact, the record shows that only hours after the war authorization vote she voted against the Democratic resolution that would have required Bush to seek a diplomatic solution before launching the war.

These days, Hillary Clinton says she supports the "surge" in Iraq and claims it's working. From candidate, maybe president Hillary Clinton, Iran can expect no mercy.

The NAFTA Saga

REALLY BIG DECISIONS about the nation's economic destiny are considered much too important to run the risk of any popular, democratic input. When you see the word bipartisan, know that the fix is in and democracy is out of the loop.

Take monetary policy. In the first presidential debate between Bill Clinton, Poppy Bush and Ross Perot, Sander Vanocur asked Bill Clinton how he proposed to deal with the chairman of the Federal Reserve, a man with more power over the economy than the President, yet accountable to no one. Clinton hastened to assure the vast television audience that he had no problem with the Fed. Bush and Perot chorused agreement that there be "separation" between the Federal Reserve and elected government.

That was it. Nothing more about Alan Greenspan, chairman of the Fed at the time; nothing about the impending banking crisis. No one could find room for a harsh word about Greenspan, appointed by Reagan in 1987 and distinguished since 1990 by his spectacularly inaccurate yet frequently repeated predictions before Congress that economic recovery was under way.

So much for Fed-bashing, which used to be a decent national sport. If you can't beat up on Greenspan, a fanatic follower of Ayn Rand, what can you do, other than admit that the people are the servants of the Fed, rather than the other way around?

Here's another area where the fix is in. America is on the edge of a free trade treaty with Mexico, following an earlier one with Canada. With democratic procedures and sovereignty annulled, workers in all three countries will be locked into a downward spiral of low-wage, low-skill jobs, with uninhibited movement of capital and a ratcheting down of social welfare provisions and environmental standards.

Elaborate mechanisms have been devised to minimize popular input and circumvent any democratic roadblocks that could be thrown up in the path of this outrageous agreement. The unions' Labor Advisory Committee, which has a congressional mandate to review trade matters, was only given a complete draft of the North American Free Trade Agreement (NAFTA) provisions on Sept. 8; nearly a month after agreement was announced.

So far as we know, the Labor Advisory Committee's report got no attention in the press.

The committee put the issues well. "The central objective of the NAFTA is providing security for private investment and reducing the role of government in regulating or directing that investment to promote the public interest." But the detailed scrutiny that accompanied this verdict will be shoved peremptorily aside. The agreement is to be raced on its undemocratic way through Congress on the notorious "fast track," which permits no amendment, merely an up-or-down simple majority vote by both houses of Congress within 90 days of the introduction of enabling legislation.

Here's where bipartisan finesse has been at its most elegant in the 1992. Of the two realistic candidates for the White House, Bush was of course in favor of the agreement and its "fast track" passage. So was Clinton, even though you have to read his lips very carefully.

Clinton, as a Democratic candidate avowedly sensitive to business, has always been for fast-track passage. Even in the wake of the Agency for International Development disclosures at the end of September, which highlighted the way the US government finances job flight to cheap, terrorized labor in Central America, Clinton stayed with that position, reiterating his support for NAFTA.

Being no fool and needing blue-collar support, Clinton, after prolonged shilly-shallying, now says the pact has "serious omissions" and promises that as President he would ask Congress to supplement the trade deal by passing legislation to safeguard the environment.

But NAFTA's whole purpose is precisely to lower the costs of production so that ultimately US wages and environmental protection will slide down to meet Mexican levels. To oppose this intent is to oppose the agreement. Both Canada and Mexico have said the agreement is a done deal, and that direct or indirect changes are impermissible.

+++

Under the terms of NAFTA, workers in all three countries will be locked into a downward spiral of low wages, low-skill jobs, and the ratcheting down of social and environmental standards that come with the uninhibited movement of capital.

The function of states like Arkansas has been to maintain the bludgeon of a low-cost nonunion workforce on the labor movement in the northern tiers. And as we stand on the threshold of NAFTA, Arkansas represents not the past but the future. From the point of view of capital, Bill Clinton has spent his political life thus far in the rehearsal room.

Among the Business Leaders for Clinton is Robert Haas, Chairman and CEO of Levi Strauss, supposedly one of America's more enlightened firms. On January 16, 1990, 1,500 textile-workers at the Levi Strauss plant in South Zarzamora Street in San Antonio, Texas were told that the plant was closing. The first group of about 300 workers was to clear out that afternoon: within three months the rest would be on the street. The Zarzamora Plant, which had record profits in 1989 and which overwhelmingly employed Mexican-American women, was Levi's largest operation in Texas. Its closing was the last in a series of at least twenty-six Levi plant closures nationwide since 1985.

The company moved its Zarzamora operation to Costa Rica, where it benefitted from reduced US import tariffs on goods re-entering the country. Conditions at Zarzamora were familiar: nonunion low-wage workers (one woman employed for eighteen years was earning an average of $5.24 an hour), paid on a piecemeal basis, performing repetitive actions at high speeds (at the time of the shutdown, at least 10 percent of the workers suffered from carpal tunnel syndrome) and deterred from reporting injures for fear of being assigned to slower, lower-paying jobs.

"Our sense is we do more than anyone in our industry and more than almost anyone in American industry," a Levi spokesman said later. This may be true. Levi had paid severance—one week for every year worked. But in October of 1989, even as managers assured worried workers the plant would stay open, its engineers went around to every sewing machine and added a task that slowed down the operators and thus lowered their pay. When it came time for calculating severance pay, the rate was set on the basis of the average from October to December, reflecting the lower amount after the machines were rigged.

The company claims it has paid out more than $1 million for retraining, education, social services and emergency assistance. But $770,104 of that came as general charitable payments in San Antonio, stretching back more than two years before the plant closed. As you might expect from the neoliberal pact between business and government, volunteer organizations are left to pick up the pieces (which was also Clinton's basic reaction to the L.A. riots). The city of San Antonio, which lost 10,000 jobs in 1990, received $460,000 for general support services.

Even then an officer at the Department of Economic and Education Development said it was a "drop in the bucket." Money for tuition, books and other materials for retraining came through federal programs. Not all the workers were eligible for these classes, which in any case were conducted only in English—a problem for Levi workers, 90 percent of whom spoke only Spanish. As for training for "high-skill, good-wage" jobs—the Clintons' mantra—only thirty-five of the workers were able, with federal assistance, to attend college. Most of the others languished in English and high school equivalency classes, both prerequisites for job retraining. "The few that received retraining, such as cosmetology people," Fuerza Unida, the laid-off workers' organization, reports, "were put to work cleaning the floors and bathrooms. When they completed their training, they had not learned what they needed." About 700 people have found some sort of work, most of them at lower pay.

And every Thanksgiving, the women stage a hunger strike in front of Levi Strauss headquarters in San Francisco.

+++

As with so many momentous economic debates, the fight over the North American Free Trade Agreement is mostly about something that already happened.

Jobs have been going south for decades. Ask any older worker from the shoe or apparel industries in New Hampshire and Massachusetts. Cheap assembly with low-cost Mexican labor has been going full-tilt for years now in the *maquiladora* plants along the US-Mexican border.

The effects of ratification of NAFTA have similarly been exaggerated. NAFTA will not resolve the problems of the US economy, even though lurid prophecies are issued on a daily basis about the horrors or blessings contingent upon its passage.

The Canadian experience offers a vivid illustration of the folly of seeing everything through a NAFTA perspective. Conflating the 1988 trade agreement between Canada and the United States with the poor performance of the Canadian economy, voters north of the border recently destroyed the Conservative Party, which they held responsible for signing the agreement. But the real dagger plunged in the heart of the Canadian economy is not wielded by the signatories to the trade treaty: it is in the hands of John Crow, who has run Canada's central bank since 1987.

Like his US counterpart, Alan Greenspan, chair of the Federal Reserve Board, Crow is a zero-inflation zealot, and has held to a tight-money policy with catastrophic consequences for Canadian employment. NAFTA has certainly contributed to economic hard times in Canada, but Crow is the major villain of the piece.

The same faulty deductions will be drawn in the United States. The main event in the US economy is not NAFTA, but monetary policy and the deflationary strategy of the Federal Reserve.

Much of the NAFTA debate has been shadowboxing or misrepresentation. How many jobs will the United States lose or gain? Line up the various models and it's obvious that economists are dealing in wildly varying assumptions, based on predictions that verge on necromancy.

From the US point of view, job losses will be bad. But trade agreements always favor the stronger party. From the Mexican perspective, the prospect is even more dire.

With cheap corn imports from the United States and Canada, Mexican peasants by the million face the prospect of ruin and displacement from the countryside to the cities. There, they will swell the cheap labor pool or head north.

Divide Mexico into three income categories and you have a third reasonably well-off, a third poor and a third poor to the level of destitution. NAFTA will favor the top third, and indeed here is where the true long-term effects of NAFTA would be felt most: in the cultural-economic annexation of the Mexican middle class, watching English-language TV, shopping in look-alikes of US and Canadian malls, running the local outposts of the northern businesses.

NAFTA is centrally about protecting the rights of US and Canadian investors in Mexico, locking Mexico into a dependency path, and foreclosing any radical option.

Indeed, some Mexican leftists argue that Mexico got locked onto that course amid its debt crisis of the 1980s. It was then that US banks forced the privatization of Mexico's state enterprises. Wages fell with the ensuing attacks on labor rights. The stage was set then for the Salinas-NAFTA model. Mexico must have investment or it will perish. There's no going back.

Here in the North, pro-NAFTA forces charge the left with narrow nationalism and a vision of Fortress America, courtesy of Ross Perot.

But this has not been the left's argument. The left does not say that all trade or trade agreements are bad, but that NAFTA is bad. It protects investors but not labor. It favors low-cost assembly but not the environment. It ratchets working rates and conditions in three countries not up but down. It is not about free trade but about the protection of the North American economy from Germany and Japan.

The left says that this is a political battle about sovereign democratic rights. The line is clearly drawn between progressive coalitions anchored in the labor movement against the Fortune 500 and their representative in the White House. The latter have mounted one of the most expensive lobbying campaigns in US history.

Clinton's broadsides against labor are all part of the idea that there is only one valid opinion. Labor has been written out of the definition of "the public" for so long that when it organizes against something that's deemed "good" for that public, it is painted as thuggish, beyond the pale, employing "real roughshod muscle-bound tactics" and "naked pressure," as opposed to the well-clothed bribes and agitations of Clinton and his corporate allies.

Clinton is the ultimate distillation of neoliberalism. With Clinton, it all boils down to that dreadful phrase "investing in people," as in "investing in people, challenging the private sector to organize in new ways to increase productivity by putting business and labor, education and government on the same side, and making an intense commitment to be competitive in the global economy." This particular slab of Clintonspeak was served up at the Economic Club of Detroit, but he says the same sort of thing ten times a day. Harness "investing in people" to its equally repulsive stablemate, "policy wonk," and you experience the bleak mental landscape of the Clinton class.

Clinton thinks of human liberation in terms of asset management. Asked about poor education or lousy heath care, he speaks only of "competitiveness," never about how such blights keep people from living happier lives. Asked about the debt crisis in Third World countries, he says it's a problem because it "has lessened their capacity to buy American goods and probably cost us 1.5 million jobs."

Despite this, people who should know better are hailing Clinton's surrender to Wall Street as somehow an augury of liberal renewal and of Rooseveltian commitment to social reform. When Ronald Reagan fired the PATCO workers, there were howls of protest. Clinton proposes to layoff 100,000 federal employees (maybe they'll end up as his new national police corps) and cut the wages of all federal workers (numbering almost 3 million) by around 7 percent over four years, and no one even bleats, except for the AFL-CIO, which has emitted a sheepish cough of tender reproach.

The fact that Clinton systematically betrayed every economic pledge of his campaign doesn't seem to bother liberals, which only shows how much they despise ordinary people. Wait a couple of years and you'll find these same liberals deploring apathy and cynicism among the electorate.

Clinton's proposals were entirely traditional. Nothing truly dangerous—economic populism with teeth as well as bark—was on offer. No suggestion of limiting home mortgage interest deductions, a notorious gift to the better off. (The better off are now refinancing their houses to take advantage of this famous bolt-hole.) Nothing dismaying to Wall Street, like a securities transaction tax, an idea ardently endorsed at various times by economic advisers to Clinton such as Joseph Stiglitz, but also an idea presumably unappetizing to powerful financiers in the Clinton court, such as his chief economic coordinator, Robert Rubin of Goldman Sachs. And indeed Clinton's plan pivoted on Wall Street's demand that the new administration be concerned first and foremost with deficit reduction.

"If there's anything this program is directed at," Rubin told reporters, "it's interest rates." The theory here is one beloved by Wall Street: that the prime inhibition to economic growth is the deficit, and that with an attack on the deficit, interest rates will fall and rosy times return. The theory does not require anything as raffish as the promotion of growth via consumer demand. The answer to Wall Street would be that the relationship between interest rates and investment growth is weak and that there are cheaper ways of getting interest rates down than by cutting demand. But Wall Street and the deficit cutters won the day. It was clear that they had from the moment Clinton announced his economic team. Actually, the

Clinton program is deflationary, will fail and will discredit the idea of liberal programs for years to come, just as Carter's did.

We're paying the penalty for fifteen years' worth of Chamber of Commerce propaganda about the deficit, which ordinary Americans now conceive to be as big a threat as cancer. As a percentage of gross domestic product, the deficit is currently far below levels associated with periods of great economic expansion. Clinton's approach to military conversion is merely gestural. A timid, shriveled jobs-and-infrastructure plan barely dares lift its head above the rubble of urban America. On a day when it was announced that housing starts had dropped 7 percent nationally, and when the National Guard was rehearsing how to put down the next riot in Los Angeles, the dominant tone was one of belt-tightening and austerity.

Alexander Cockburn

NAFTA and the Shameful Seven

AS SPRING TURNED to summer in 1993, President Bill continued with his divinely-appointed mission of trying to secure Congressional ratification of the North American Free Trade Agreement initialed by George Bush. It's a measure of Clinton's devotion to the Fortune 500 that he persisted in an enterprise that spells political ruin for the Democrats. As Jeff Faux of the Economic Policy Institute wrote in a memo to the White House, "The president is making NAFTA his program. And after it passes, Bill Clinton will be blamed for every factory that closes down whether NAFTA closes it down or not. That is exactly what happened to Mulroney in Canada." Polls for March showed that 63 percent of Americans opposed the treaty and, incidentally, 60 percent agreed that the environment must be protected even if jobs "in your community" are eliminated.

The pro-NAFTA forces lost the economic argument. Lobsters take note: Clinton is trying to bail out a business scheme hatched by Reagan and Bush to protect Mexican elites, perpetuate Mexican underdevelopment, lower wages on both sides of the border, destroy American private sector unions, shore up multinational capital and defend the hemisphere's market against European and Asian penetration. "Free trade" has nothing to do with it, as Melvin Burke, an economist at the University of Maine, pointed out in an excellent paper presented at a January conference on NAFTA in Mexico City.

Exactly at this fraught moment, with pro-NAFTA forces in increasing disarray, some environmental groups rallied to Clinton's side. On May 4, seven of them outlined their conditions for supporting NAFTA. In a letter to US Trade Representative Mickey Kantor, the groups indicated their readiness to back the treaty if a supplemental agreement on the environment included the provisions they set forth. The groups are: World Wildlife Fund, the National Wildlife Federation, the National Audubon

Society, the Natural Resources Defense Council, the Environmental Defense Fund, Defenders of Wildlife and the Nature Conservancy.

The letter was silly enough. The signatories did not discuss the environmental implications of NAFTA's rules in the areas of natural resource development (i.e., forests, fisheries, and water and energy resources), trade, agriculture, intellectual property rights and government purchasing practices. On this last point, NAFTA rules forbid the use of technical performance specs as a condition for government procurement. In an excellent analysis of the letter, Steven Shrybman of Greenpeace USA points out that this would nix efforts by the US government to use purchasing policies to stimulate technical innovation in the areas of energy efficiency, recycling and clean technology. It would also nix performance criteria favoring local or domestic suppliers of green products or technologies.

As a fig leaf for their support of NAFTA, the seven groups requested a North American Commission on the Environment (NACE), which would plainly end up like those two useless international commissions already dealing with environmental problems between the United States, Canada and Mexico—the International Boundary Waters Commission and the International Joint Commission. The IJC was given the specific environmental task of overseeing progress toward zero discharge of persistent toxic substances into the Great Lakes. Thus far, after years of "oversight," the Canadians have not even completed their toxic release inventory and, in 1990 alone, US industries discharged no less than 300,000 tons of toxic waste into the Great Lakes. Shrybman pointed out that NACE wouldn't even have a mandate as specific as that of the IJC.

The letter from the Shameful Seven was stimulated by the World Wildlife Fund. Its president, Kathryn Fuller, had participated in consultations on NAFTA with the Bush White House and had been installed by Bush on the Advisory Commission on Trade Policy, an eco-reservation for apex predators. The Clinton trade strategists paraded bigwigs from the Shameful Seven around Washington as evidence that the environmental "community" had come aboard. Indeed, on June 9, the Seven went to Mexico to furnish similar services for President Salinas. Out of the Seven, only Audubon has any sort of grassroots base, and local officials in some Audubon chapters were vigorously anti-NAFTA. The other groups have no field presence and are East Coast in migratory habits. They nest in corporate suites and are recognizable by a mellow "whorp-whorp" sound, a cross between a warble and a chirp, emitted whenever the glint of the corporate dollar is detected.

To give an idea of the whoring that's been going on:

- World Wildlife received $2.5 million in a single donation from Eastman Kodak, whose C.E.O., Kay Whitmore, is co-founder of USA-NAFTA, the big corporate lobby for the treaty. The $2.5 million was the largest single gift World Wildlife (known as Woof Woof by Beltway public-interest folk) had ever received. Other donors included such NAFTA boosters as Hewlett-Packard and Waste Management, both in the $100,000–$250,000 range; also Du Pont and Philip Morris (whose chairman emeritus, Joseph Cullman III, sat on World Wildlife's board), each in the $50,000–$100,000 range.

- The National Wildlife Federation, according to its 1992 annual report, got support from such NAFTA boosters as Dow, Du Pont, Monsanto, 3M, Shell, Duke Power, Pennzoil and Waste Management.

- Audubon got big bucks from General Electric, a member of the NAFTA lobby. Audubon also received support from treaty booster Procter & Gamble and, of course, that friend of all living things, Waste Management.

- Corporate, pro-NAFTA support for the Nature Conservancy is exhilarating, with Coca-Cola giving more than $2 million, and Canon USA and Tenneco puffing along behind in the $250–$500,000 range. Among the Conservancy's "corporate associates" are such old friends as Cargill, Du Pont, Philip Morris, Procter & Gamble and Waste Management.

Environmental groups deeply critical of NAFTA include, importantly, the Sierra Club, Friends of the Earth, Greenpeace USA and the most powerful organization on earth outside the Vatican, the Humane Society of the United States.

The Seven had the corporate bucks. The Four had the grassroots. In the end, the money won and John Adams, CEO of NRDC, gloated about "breaking the back of the environmental opposition to NAFTA."

How NAFTA Ate the West

IN THE TWO years following the enactment of NAFTA, the price of beef dropped by as much as 50 percent. If hamburger eaters exulted at the news, they should have also been aware that with this fall in beef prices has come a crisis for the nation's small ranchers as grave as that which put 80,000 of them out of business in the early 1980s.

As the small ranches go under, their land is either picked up by agribusiness giants like J.R. Simplot or billionaires playing cowboy like David Packard, or subdivided for the dreary ranchettes that disfigure southern Colorado.

Blame NAFTA. With the signing of the trade agreement came truckloads of Mexican calves, headed for the feedlots and slaughterhouses north of the border. The influx of these Mexican calves produced a meat glut in the United States, driving the prices down to levels disastrous for marginal operations on the arid grasslands of the Interior West.

In an effort to help out the beleaguered ranchers the Interior Department lowered the fees it charges ranchers to graze their cows on federal lands from $1.97 per cow per month in 1993 to $1.37 in 1996—the lowest level in 20 years. This fee amounts to a generous $100 million a year subsidy to public-lands ranchers, and is roughly one-fifth the amount charged on private lands. But in the wake of NAFTA even these subsidies won't save many of the small ranchers, who have always faced dire financial pressures.

The economics of small ranching on federal lands work as follows: In order to graze cattle or sheep on federal lands, ranchers must own what's called a base property. The base property must be at least 40 acres in size and situated adjacent to lands held by the Forest Service or Bureau of Land Management. The grazing permit allows the rancher to lease hundreds of thousands of acres of public lands at below-cost rates. The value of the ranch—and hence the approval of the bank or insurance company financing his mortgage—depends entirely on his access to publicly owned grass and water. Even if the rancher wants to reduce the number of cattle he's running to ease the stress on the grasslands, the banks will insist that he continue with the highest stocking rates permitted by the feds, since he will thus be a better risk. This is a primary reason America's rangelands are in such an impoverished ecological condition.

When the feds have tried to reduce the number of cattle on the public range to protect fragile riparian habitat for endangered trout and salmon, the U.S. government has been sued for breach of contract by the banks, notably the Farm Credit Bank of Texas, which holds half a billion dollars in loans that are tied to federal grazing permits.

As the falling beef prices beset small ranchers, the banks will simply foreclose on their property, either subdividing it or selling entire parcels to agribusiness or to mining companies. Even though the whole purpose of subsidized range-leasing was to help the small rancher, these days only 3 percent of the leasers hold 40 percent of all the grazing land leased from the U.S. government. The small rancher is giving way to the big corporation. This has yielded huge concentrations for companies such as Simplot, which holds a million acres in grazing rights on public lands, or the Metropolitan Life Insurance Company, which control 800,000 acres of public land, or Sierra Pacific Resources, an oil company, which has 600,000 acres in California and Nevada.

This trend toward consolidation is accelerating rapidly. It recalls the days of the American Cattle Trust of the 1870s, a ranching syndicate modeled on John D. Rockefeller's Standard Oil Trust. The American Cattle Trust consisted of a handful of ranchers and meatpackers backed by the railroads and English banking houses. Their goal was to strip western lands away from the small ranchers and homesteaders. Before succumbing to internal conflicts, a string of extremely harsh winters, and relentless overstocking of the ranges, the American Cattle Trust ended up controlling 80 percent of the grazing lands in states like Wyoming, Colorado, and Montana. The trust ran their vast herds hard on the land, leaving behind a permanently degraded range.

The new combination of interests consists of industrial agriculture giants such as Agribeef, Inc.; real estate developers; oil companies such as Chevron; and mining corporations such as Phelps Dodge. The key resource here is water. It has always been so. In the arid West, all political power flows from those who control the water. Traditionally, this power has resided with the rancher, whose grazing allotments encompass the mountain headwaters of the great rivers of the West. This is the main reason ranchers—who account for less than 1 percent of the population of western states—have received such devout attention from Congress. Watching the impending ruin of many small ranchers with a keen anticipation are the mining companies. As the fortunes of the ranchers decline, those of the gold companies are on the rise. Small ranchers were always the mining companies' most irksome foes. Gold mines, in particular, consume enormous quantities of water. But ranchers have held the water rights on public lands, and have represented the most effective grassroots opposition to the mining companies and their noxious practices. Ranchers can certainly ravage the land, but big mining companies make even worse messes and end up with title (at $5 an acre, courtesy of the 1872 Mining Law) in the bargain.

Ironically, ranchers, under assault from environmentalists for destructive grazing practices, reflexively aligned themselves with some of the more vicious incarnations of the property rights movement, such as the Colorado-based People for the West!, long funded by mining and oil interests. These companies were glad to have the ranchers on their side, since the rancher puts a publicly pleasing, almost mythological face on the nefarious motives of their political movement.

Many of the big ranchers and the corporations that back them fanatically pushed for passage of NAFTA in 1993. It is worth noting that many of the mining companies now preying on western mountains, rivers, and deserts are Canadian firms (such as Echo Bay, Noranda, and Barrick) devoted to unrestricted transborder operations.

Some of the big environmental groups are also cheering. Anything that does down a rancher is okay with them. That's one of the reasons groups like the National Wildlife Federation and Natural Resources Defense Council shilled for NAFTA—they said the agreement would push inefficient industries out of business. Let them wait until the Interior West vanishes under ranchette driveways, toxic cyanide piles from heap-leach gold mining, or ends up in the hands of J.R. Simplot Company.

So the bills for NAFTA are finally coming due. Under its stipulations polychlorinated biphenyls (PCBs) are now being trucked into the U.S. from Canada and Mexico for the first time. Imported Mexican tuna, caught with fishing techniques deadly to dolphins, will lead to the probable destruction of the dolphin-safe tuna labeling legislation passed in the

U.S. in 1989. Canadian forests are being logged at a vicious pace at subsidized rates by multinational corporations such as James River, Champion International, and MacMillan Bloedel. This lumber is being dumped on already depressed U.S. markets, resulting in the loss of 35,000 mill jobs. Lead-spewing trucks from south of the border are now legal, thanks to a ruling from the GATT tribunal.

Claims of job gains north of the border are transparent fictions. South of the border two-thirds of the Mexican population are far worse off than they were four years ago. The environment? It has been ravaged from the Yukon to Chiapas.

The Neoliberal War on the Poor

IN NOVEMBER OF 1994 two years of ramshackle government, breached pledges and the Clinton administration's frequently manifested contempt for its traditional base, exacted their price. In the midterm elections Republicans seized control of both the House and the Senate for the first time since the Eisenhower era. The rout extended to governors' mansions across the country, where the Republicans captured the majority of governorships for the first time in a quarter-century. Newt Gingrich, the new Speaker of the House, became the nation's political wunderkind.

Yet for Bill Clinton the Democratic defeat held its paradoxical allure. The old-line Democratic Congressional leadership no longer held sway on the Hill. Tom Foley and Dan Rostenkowski were gone altogether— one back to the Inland Empire of the Pacific Northwest and the other to a federal penitentiary. The White House no longer had to dicker with hostility to its agenda from New Deal-oriented Democrats. Without the threat of a presidential veto to lend clout to their resistance, the liberal Democrats on the Hill were impotent against the Republicans flourishing their Contract with America. Thus unencumbered, the Clinton administration could cut deals with the Republican leadership.

All this strategy needed was a name, and soon after the election Bill Clinton summoned in the man who would introduce "triangulation" into the lexicon of the late 1990s.

Dick Morris, a man of elastic political scruple, had enjoyed a fluctuating relationship with Clinton. He'd bailed out the young governor of Arkansas after the latter's first comeuppance at the hands of the voters in 1980. Since then Morris had served many masters, ranging from the millionaire socialist from Ohio, Howard Metzenbaum, to Bella Abzug of New York, to Trent Lott of Mississippi ("I love his feisty, shit-on-the-shoes style") and Jesse Helms of North Carolina. Morris worked as a consultant for Helms in 1990, in a particularly foul campaign against the black Democratic challenger, Harvey Gantt.

Morris came to the White House with the purpose of providing new ideas and a new strategy. He says Clinton told him, "I've lost confidence in my current team." Morris commenced his mission of refreshment under conditions of secrecy, code-named Charlie, his function at first known only to the Clintons. His advice: steal the Republicans' thunder, draw down the deficit, reform welfare, cut back government regulation and "use Gore's reinventing government program to cut the public sector's size." The president should demonstrate toughness, Morris counseled, with decisive action overseas.

As the new Republican leadership took over in January of 1995, Clinton summoned Gore to the Oval Office, disclosed the hiring of Morris and instructed the vice president to work with him. "Charlie" then laid out the new agenda for Gore. Morris later wrote, "He grasped what I was saying at once and offered his full support Gore told me that he had been increasingly troubled by the drift of the White HouseHe said he had tried, in vain, to move the administration toward the center, but the White House staff had shut him outGore said, 'We need a change here, a big change, and I'm hoping and praying that you're the man to bring it.' We shook hands on our alliance."

Soon Morris, Gore and Clinton came to two fateful decisions. As part of the strategy of stealing the Republicans' thunder, Morris urged an intensive fundraising drive, aimed at amassing "soft money" for TV spots designed to boost the new Clinton agenda, trump the Republicans and detour the old-line concerns of the Democrats at the other end of Pennsylvania Avenue. Soft money earns that much-abused name because it can be raised in amounts not limited by campaign spending laws; it can be procured directly from corporations, labor unions or other institutions so long as the money is used to promote "issues" rather than specific candidates. That at least is how the law supposed soft money would work. Morris knew very well that the issue ads would be identified directly with Clinton, because they would sound themes Morris himself had prescribed. To execute these ads Morris and Gore turned to the latter's longtime media consultant, Bob Squier. Down the road lay many a funding scandal, not least the Buddhist temple imbroglio that found Al Gore on the receiving end of thousands of dollars in contributions from monks and nuns supposedly ennobled by the spiritual distinction of poverty. But such things were still a year away.

The time had come to go public with the new line. Morris drafted a speech for Clinton in which the president would announce that he was ready to work with the Republicans. It laid out the grounds on which the President was prepared to meet Newt Gingrich. Within the White House there was a storm of protest, led by Leon Panetta, Clinton's chief of staff and onetime California congressman, who was aghast at what he correctly perceived to be the betrayal of his former colleagues on the Hill.

As Panetta presented his case, Clinton began to tilt toward his position. Morris sensed crisis at hand. At the crucial moment, so he relates, Gore, who had been silently following the debate, made a decisive intervention. "I agree with Dick's point, that we need to emerge from the shadows and place ourselves at the center of the debate with the Republicans by articulating what we will accept and what we will not in a clear and independent way." It was music to Morris's ears, and he cried, "Bravo!"

For Morris, as for his employer, polls were everything. He developed what he called a "neuro-psychological profile" of the American voter, and established an iron rule that no initiative could be undertaken by the White House unless polling showed an approval rating of 60 percent. By constant polling he concocted what he called a "values agenda". At the top of the list was affirmative action. "Mend it, don't end it" was the mantra, which meant, in practice, destroy affirmative action from the inside while professing support for the general principle.

Next came TV violence. Intimidate the networks, Morris advised, into adopting a "voluntary" system of ratings for TV shows and movies. Soon media executives were summoned to the White House for a session with Clinton and Gore. Simultaneously Clinton pushed for installation of the so-called V-chip in all new TV sets, which would allow parents to block all offensive material. Next came teen pregnancy, an issue pounded on by the Clinton White House, even though the rate had been falling. Education: go after tenured teachers, an attack increasingly popular in Morris's focus groups, and demand that at least they be tested. Youth: advocate school uniforms and curfews for teens. Gay marriage: on Morris's advice Clinton and Gore embraced the Defense of Marriage Act, a purely grandstanding piece of legislation which preemptively bars gay marriages from recognition under federal law for any purpose. Immigration: the poll numbers were off the chart, and the Clinton White House duly set a goal to double the number of turn-backs by the Immigration and Naturalization Service—among other things, enlisting the Labor Department to help speed the pace and breadth of workplace raids. Taxes: Morris believed that Main Street America was now playing the market, so that a 20 percent reduction in the capital gains tax rate would be hugely popular.

But there were two issues that towered above the rest in Morris's assaying of public opinion: welfare and crime. In the 1992 campaign, Clinton had pledged to "end welfare as we know it." In 1993, Gore had urged Clinton to declare war on welfare as part of the first 100 days and had implored the president to let him lead the charge. After all, Gore argued, he was one of the few Democratic senators to have supported a welfare-to-work law narrowly approved in 1988, forcing states to require parents getting welfare checks to work at least 16 hours per week in unpaid jobs. But Hillary thought an attack on welfare would divert energy from her health care package, and Gore lost the battle.

By 1995 the welfare rolls were shrinking, from a peak of 18 million in the recession of 1991 to about 12.8 million. Defenders of the system in Clinton's cabinet, Labor Secretary Robert Reich and Donna Shalala of Heath and Human Services, argued that the total budget for Aid to Families with Dependent Children was a tiny fraction of the federal budget; indeed, it was only 14 percent of the amount devoted to Medicare, a middle-class entitlement. The real problem, they argued, was lack of training for the chronically underemployed and unemployed.

Reflexively hostile to welfare and fortified by Morris's polls, Clinton pressed ahead. The administration began granting waivers to states to implement their own onslaughts on welfare, feature "workfare" requirements, time limits and "family caps", a punishment for women who dared to have more than the approved number of children the government would help support. Through 1995 and early in 1996 the Republicans had passed and sent to Clinton two bills to dismantle the federal welfare system. He vetoed both, but in his veto messages he stressed that he agreed with much of their content in principle. Peter Edelman, a high level official at HHS, described this as "the squeeze play", whereby Clinton would reap approval from Democratic New Dealers for standing up for poor kids while at the same time signaling that in the long run he'd throw the mothers of those kids off the rolls altogether.

As they approached the Democratic convention in the summer of 1996, Clinton was floating on Morris's magic carpet. Assisted by staggering blunders by Gingrich and a lackluster opponent in Bob Dole, Clinton was ahead by no less than 27 percent in the polls. The Republicans were eager to wrap up their legislative work before the conventions in July and August. They pushed through a welfare bill arguably worse than the ones Clinton had vetoed previously. Many Democrats on the Hill believed that Clinton would veto this bill too. But Senator Daniel Patrick Moynihan of New York had more sensitive political antennae. He warned, "I've heard that the leaders of the cabinet recommended a veto but that the president remains under the sway of his pollsters."

On July 30, 1996, Clinton mustered his cabinet to hear arguments on whether or not he should sign the Republicans' bill. One by one his advisers said he should not. No's from people like Shalala and Reich came as no surprise. But similarly disapproving were not only Leon Panetta but Laura Tyson, his chief economic adviser, Henry Cisneros of HUD and even Treasury Secretary Robert Rubin, who said that too many people would be harmed by the bill and that it show an act of political courage to veto it.

Not trusting Shalala's department to produce objective assessments of the consequences of the bill, the White House staff had commissioned a survey from the Urban Institute, a DC think tank. The numbers were dire. The bill would push 2.6 million people further into poverty—1.1 million of them children. In all, the Institute predicted that 11 million families would lose income. That was the best-case scenario. In the event of a recession (which would come in 2001), the numbers would be far, far worse. In that fateful cabinet meeting Rubin invoked this study, and the numbers seemed to find their mark with Clinton, while Gore remained mute.

The meeting came to an end and Clinton, Panetta and Gore headed for the Oval Office for a private session. All accounts agree that, first, Panetta again made the case for a veto, laying particular emphasis on an appalling provision in the bill that would deny legal immigrants federal assistance, such as food stamps. Finally Gore broke his silence and urged Clinton to sign.

Clinton, Morris and Gore prepared a press statement, delivered by the president later that same day. Clinton admitted that the bill contained "serious flaws" but went on to say, "This is the best chance we will have in a long time to complete the work of ending welfare as we know it." No one at the press conference quizzed Clinton on this curious claim. After all, the election was only about three months away. By early fall of 1996 it was clear: the Democrats had a chance of regaining the House. Would not that recapture afford a better chance of crafting a welfare bill not compromised by Gingrich and the others?

To this day many Democrats in Congress become incensed on the topic of what Clinton and Gore did. One the eve of a Democratic convention, with Gingrich already ensconced in the national imagination as the Bad Guy, Clinton had just made common cause with him, thus undercutting all plans to campaign against the Gingrich Congress. As for Al Gore, the consensus was that he was looking ahead to a possible challenge in 2000 from his old rival Dick Gephardt. With Morris's polls showing that an attack on welfare scored well over the 60 percent bar, Gore would have the advantage over Gephardt or any other liberal challenger.

Suspicions about Gore deepened as the fall campaign proceeded. The president and vice president argued that it was crucial that they be re-elected so that they fix the problems with the welfare bill they had just signed. The problems here concerned not the welfare bill itself but the denial of federal services to legal immigrants and a slash in the food stamp program. In October of 1996, with the presidential election no longer in doubt, Democratic candidates came to the Democratic National Committee urgently seeking infusions of cash to help them in the crucial final weeks. Finally, Senator Christopher Dodd of Connecticut, then the general chairman of the DNC, organized a meeting with Clinton and Gore. Dodd explained that the two were home safe and there was a chance to recapture the House. Clinton seemed amenable to a release of funds. Gore adamantly disagreed. On one account, Gore was the only person in the White House to oppose this transfer of funds from the presidential campaign to congressional races. It's a measure of how a number of Democrats view Al Gore that some participants in that meeting felt that the only explanation for his conduct was that he did not want the Democrats to re-take control of the House because victory would elevate Gephardt to Speaker of the House.

The cynicism may not have stopped there. Why did Clinton and Gore decide to sign on to that third Republican welfare bill? The only major difference from the previous ones came in the form of the denial of federal services to legal immigrants and a $2.5 billion cut in the food stamp program. It's likely that these two Republican add-ons were what allured the White House, because (as noted above) Clinton could then turn to the liberals saying they needed him to be re-elected so he could repair part of the damage wrought by the very bill he had just signed. In fact the White House probably could have insisted the riders be dropped, because Dole desperately wanted a legislative victory under the Republicans' belt.

The welfare bill ended a federal entitlement that had been a cornerstone of the New Deal. It caps the federal contribution to welfare programs at $14.6 billion a year and hands the money over in block grants to the states to distribute as they see fit. The main requirement is that the states agree that welfare recipients can spend no more than a total of five years in their lifetime on welfare. It allows states to adopt even harsher standards. Finally, under the old system, welfare money came to the recipient as cash. Under the new system, the money can be given to intermediaries, for possible conversion to other services such as housing or food. Al Gore particularly liked this provision. In Atlanta in May of 1999, he told an audience why: "It allows faith-based organizations to provide basic welfare services. They can do so with public funds—without having to alter the religious character that is so often the key to their effectiveness. We should extend this approach to drug treatment, homelessness and youth violence prevention. People who work in faith-and values-based organizations are driven by their spiritual commitment. They have done what government can never do: provide compassionate care. Their client is not a number but a child of god." In other words, treat welfare payments like school vouchers. Gore had just laid out the welcome mat for Bush's faith-based initiatives.

Not long after Clinton signed the welfare bill, judgment came from Senator Moynihan, who had begun his service to the state back in the sixties with sermons about the "pathology" of the black family and now, bizarrely, was defending the system he'd denounced for years. Even this man of all seasons and all masters was shocked: "It is a social risk no sane person would take, and I mean that. If you think things can't get worse, just wait until there are a third of a million people on the streets. It's not welfare reform; it's welfare repeal."

Hugh Price, president of the National Urban League, called the bill "an abomination for America's most vulnerable mothers and children" and accused Clinton, Gore and the Congress of defecting from a war on poverty and "waging a war against poor people instead."

Within weeks three high-ranking officials in the Department of Health and Human Services had resigned: Mary Jo Bane, Walter Primus and Peter Edelman. That was it. Across the length and breadth of the Clinton administration, only these resignations were tendered in principle against this abandonment of the New Deal and the shafting of America's poor. Since that time Edelman has missed no opportunity to denounce the bill as a punitive strike against defenseless people. "The bill closes its eyes to all the facts and complexities of the real world and essentially says to recipients: find a job."

The edict "find a job" was central to the bill and to the mythology nourished by opponents of welfare-that freeloaders with jobs available to them were abusing the system. Of course, there is always some abuse, but study after study had shown that most welfare recipients had looked for jobs and couldn't find a suitable one or had been on welfare for a limited period, then found a job and got off the rolls. In 1999 a University of Michigan study making an assessment three years after the welfare bill went into effect found that the welfare population faces "unusually high barriers to work: such as physical and mental health problems, domestic violence and lack of transportation." More than 30 percent of the families on welfare are constrained by disability, a sick child, no child care or an infirm relative. Those that want to find work are faced with narrow options even in an economy hyped as in mid-boom. In 1996 the Congressional Budget Office offered some bleak realities about the reserve army of the unemployed. With an official unemployment rate of four percent (the unofficial rate is roughly twice that, since government figures don't count frustrated people who have given up looking for work), there are still three to five people needing work for each available job. In the Bush recession, this ratio rose to more than 10 to one.

In urban areas the job market is even more constricted. A 1998 study in Harlem showed just how brutally competitive the low-wage job market is. Over a five-month period, an average of fourteen people applied for each job opening at a local McDonalds. A year later researchers from the University of Chicago found that 73 percent of those same job searchers still hadn't found even minimum wage level work.

In many states, there's the last resort of workfare, which compels welfare recipients to accept public jobs, such as highway clean-up or garbage picking with the Parks Department, in return for benefits. Nationally the average benefit for workfare jobs is $381 per month, which works out to $4.40 an hour, or 80 percent of the minimum wage. But in some places it's much worse. Mississippi, for example, requires single mothers to work twenty hours a week at $1.38 an hour, and a two-parent household to work fifty-five hours at 50 cents an hour.

On top of this the people in the workfare labor force are denied such basic rights as collective bargaining, unemployment insurance, the earned income tax credit and Social Security credit. States are finding it to their budgetary advantage to fill job vacancies with these "slavefare" workers. A Senate study in 1996 estimated that the consequences of welfare reform would depress the wages of the working poor by 12 percent.

Allowing the states to freelance their welfare programs has resulted in some particularly cruel policies and inequities. Minnesota spends $50 million a year on child care for single mothers receiving welfare benefits who are working or looking for work. New York spends $54 million to serve a population six times as large. Clinton and Gore repeatedly touted the approach taken by Indiana, where welfare reform was instituted by a Democratic governor, Evan Bayh, and his successor in the governor's mansion, Frank O'Bannon. The pair presided over the shrinking of the welfare rolls in the Hoosier state by 30 percent. There's no way to know if those people actually found work. It's possible that the conditions of supervision of welfare recipients simply became unbearable and they left the program and perhaps the state. Under Indiana's scheme, one missed job-training course means the loss of a welfare check for two months. A second infraction means loss of benefits for a year. A third strike and you're out for good.

The Clinton welfare bill also included a provision that allows states to begin drug testing welfare recipients. In theory the provision was aimed at people suspected of having drug problems. Oregon, for example, initiated a testing policy but soon reversed course when recipients began dropping out of the welfare program to avoid testing. The state found that it was better to stop drug testing, keep people in the program and steer addicts into treatment. Michigan took a different approach. In 1999 the state adopted a mandatory drug-testing policy for all welfare recipients, which prompted a lawsuit by the ACLU. A federal judge ruled in 1999 that the policy was unconstitutional. He noted that in the five weeks of the program's operation there were positive drug tests in only eight percent of the cases, and all but three of those were for marijuana.

In his 2000 campaign, Al Gore pushed for what he called "Welfare Reform 2", saying that more remained to be done to weed out cheats and freeloaders. He was particularly vehement in attacking dads behind on child support, vowing that he would make it easier for credit card companies to deny credit to such fathers. This would have come on top of a program, initiated by Janet Reno in her Florida years, whereby fathers behind on their payments get their driver's license lifted, meaning that they can't drive to work. In 1995, Clinton, Gore and Morris put into operation a program that saw these father's mug shots put up in Post Offices, their federal benefits garnished and the IRS sent on their trail. This pattern of inflicting administrative conviction outside the court system and due process is integral to the Clinton/Gore philosophy on crime.

The Clinton crime bill of 1994 introduced mandatory life imprisonment for persons convicted of a third felony in certain categories. It maintained the 100-to-1 disproportion in sentencing for crimes involving powder and crack cocaine, even though the US Sentencing Commission had concluded that the disparity was racist. It expanded to fifty the number of crimes that could draw the death penalty in a federal court, reaching even to crimes that did not include murders—the largest expansion of the death penalty in history. Pell grants giving prisoners an avenue to higher education were cut off. Federal judges were stripped of their powers to enforce the constitutional rights of prisoners and the power of states to set sentencing standards for drug crimes was greatly diminished.

The curtailment of states' rights went further. Grants for new prisons contained the provision that receipt of the money was dependent on the states ensuring that prisoners served at least 85 percent of their sentences. These inmates, remember, had been convicted in state, not federal, courts so this was simply federal blackmail to curtail parole at the state level. The Clinton administration also pressed the states to try juvenile offenders as adults. Gore articulated the administration's position: "When young people cross the line, they must be punished. When young people commit serious, violent crimes, they should be prosecuted like adults." Nonviolent offenders were to be sent to boot camps. Not, it should be noted, his own kids, who evaded punishment for nonviolent infractions such as smoking pot and having an open alcohol container in the car.

The Clinton/Gore administration was particularly assiduous in its assaults on the Fourth Amendment, protecting citizens against unreasonable searches and seizures. In 1994, they successfully pressed for a bill providing all communications providers to make existing and future communication systems wiretap ready. They also pushed hard for the so-called Clipper Chip, an encryption device that makes it easy for law enforcement and intelligence agencies to snoop on private messages.

The high-water mark in the Clinton administration's attack on the Bill of Rights came in 1996 with the Counter-Terrorism and Effective Death Penalty Act, which among other horrors allowed the INS to deport immigrants without due process, and denied prisoners the right to appeal to the federal bench based on habeas corpus petitions. "When historians write the story of civil liberties in the twentieth century," said Ira Glasser, head of the ACLU, "they will say that the Clinton administration adopted an agenda that has everything to do with weakening civil rights and nothing to do with combating terrorism."

In May of 2000, Gore outlined his campaign posture on crime and drugs in another speech in Atlanta. The erstwhile dope-smoker from Tennessee evidently feared that the man who refused to discuss cocaine use in his early years, George W. Bush, had the edge on the crime issue. Gore proclaimed he wanted to swaddle communities in "a blanket of blue". He swore that the minute he settled in the Oval Office, President Gore would call for 50,000 more cops (i.e., more half-trained recruits like the ones who shot Amadou Diallo forty-one times in the Bronx) and would allow off-duty cops to carry concealed weapons (which they almost all do anyway).

Gore promised prisoners what he called a simple deal: "Before you get out of jail you have to get clean. If you want to stay out, then you better stay clean. We have to stop that revolving door once and for all. First we have to test prisoners for drugs while they're in jail". Gore was so blithe in his disregard for elementary rights that he was unable to see a distinction between a prison sentence fully served and a further punitive add-on: "We have to insist on more prison time for those who don't break the habit". Even after prisoners are released the eye of the state would still follow them: "We should impose strict supervision on those who have just been released—and insist they obey the law and stay off drugs".

Another feature of Al Gore's prospective war on crime was the especially vigorous targeting of minority youth. "I will fight for a federal law that helps communities establish gang-free zones with curfews on specific gang members, a ban on gang-related clothing and the specific legal authority to break violent teen gangs once and for all".

Both parties have eagerly conjoined in militarizing the police, extending police powers and carving away basic rights. Often the Democrats have been worse. It was Republican Representative Henry Hyde of Illinois who led the partially successful charge in 1999 against the seizure of assets in drug cases. It was Democrat Senator Charles Schumer of New York who played the role of factotum for the Justice Department in trying to head off Hyde and his coalition.

The rise of the Jackboot State has marched in lockstep with the insane and ineffective War on Drugs. This has been an entirely bi-partisan affair. Its consequences are etched into the fabric of our lives. Just think of drug testing, now a virtually mandatory condition of employment, even though it's an outrageous violation of personal sovereignty, as well as being thoroughly unreliable. In an era in which America has been led by three self-confessed pot smokers—Clinton, Gore and Bush—the number of people held for drug crimes in federal prisons has increased by 64 percent.

No-knock raids are becoming more common as federal, state and local politicians and law enforcement agencies decide that the war on drugs justify dumping the Fourth Amendment. Even in states where search warrants require a knock on the door before entry, police routinely flout the requirement.

The Posse Comitatus Act forbidding military involvement in domestic law enforcement is rapidly becoming as dead as the Fourth Amendment. Because of drug war exceptions created in that act, every region of the United States now has a Joint Task Force staff in charge of coordinating military involvement in domestic law enforcement. The involvement has now expanded to include anti-terrorism investigations.

In many cases, street deployment of paramilitary units is funded by "community policing" grants from the federal government. The majority of police departments use their paramilitary units to serve "dynamic entry" search warrants. The SWAT Team in Chapel Hill, North Carolina, conducted a large-scale crack raid of an entire block in a predominantly black neighborhood. The raid, termed Operation Redi-Rock, resulted in the detention and search of up to 100 people, all of whom were black. (Whites were allowed to leave the area.) No one was ever prosecuted for a crime. In Albany, New York, not long before the change-of-venue trial there of the four white cops who had killed Amadou Diallo in the Bronx, police in camouflage uniforms went on a ransacking spree in the black neighborhood of Arbor Hill, beating down doors house-to-house in search of a black suspect.

Where there is no social program, there's always a violence program. For the Clinton/Gore administration welfare reform and expansion of the police state were not only means to trump the Republicans; they were also essential to economic policy. Intense competition for jobs at the lowest rungs would depress wages, pit poor and working-class people against each other and, where workfare recipients displace municipal workers, weaken labor unions. The spectre and reality of incarceration would have the traditional effect of suppressing the dangerous classes, at a time when the wage gap between the rich and the poor grew wider than at any time in recent history.

When Democrats Ran the Culture Wars

GRANDSTANDING ABOUT THE entertainment industry was a specialty of Al and Tipper Gore since Al first entered Congress in 1977 (the year the couple were formally "Born Again"). Tipper was part of a Congressional wives' club agitating against violence and sex on TV, and then in the mid-eighties came Tipper's famous campaign, abetted by her husband, against explicit rock and rap music, revving up a culture war far more sinister than anything proposed by Dan Quayle.

In early June of 1985 Tipper's group PMRC (Parents' Music Resource Center) sent a letter to Stanley Gortikov, president of the Recording Industry Association of America, demanding a ratings code. The group called for an X to be put on records that contained profanity, violence, or sexually explicit lyrics, including "topics of fornication, sado-masochism, incest, homosexuality, bestiality and necrophilia." The inclusion of homosexuality harked back to Al's comment in 1976 as he campaigned for Congress that he considered homosexuality to be "abnormal" behavior.

Back then Tipper swore up and down that she and her group were against censorship. This was false. In a memo to Gortikov the PMRC wrote that it wanted the record labels to "reassess contracting artists who engage in violence, substance abuse and/or explicit behavior in concerts where minors are admitted." So much for Al's favorite band, the substance-abusing Beatles. So much too for Tipper's Rolling Stones or Grateful Dead, whom she welcomed into her office in 1993, thus honoring a group that had introduced two generations to the joys of drugs.

From the start, Tipper's PMRC worked hand in glove with right-wing fundamentalist Christian groups. One of her partners in the PMRC was Susan Baker (wife of James Baker, a Cabinet officer in the Reagan/Bush years), who was also a board member of the Rev. James Dobson's Focus on the Family. This outfit, now based in Colorado, is notoriously antigay and antiabortion. Dobson, who argued that serial killer Ted Bundy had been driven to murder by an addiction to pornography, served on Attorney General Ed Meese's 1985 commission to eradicate smut.

This was not the only group touted by Tipper's PMRC. Take the Missouri Rock Project, an outfit run by an associate of Phyllis Schlafly, which distributed information packets, prepared by the Victory Christian Church of St. Charles, Missouri, claiming that the Holocaust was overblown, that Hitler didn't write *Mein Kampf* and that Hollywood shamelessly advocates race-mixing. The church described the slain civil rights leader, whose memory is often invoked by Al Gore, as "Martin Lucifer King." Enthusiastically plugged by the PMRC as a useful resource were the writings of David Noebel, author of *Rhythm, Riots and Revolution,* whose essays in music criticism include the following: "The full truth is that [the origin of rock] goes still deeper-to the heart of Africa, where it was used to incite warriors to such a frenzy that by nightfall neighbors were cooked in carnage pots!"

Contrary to Tipper's repeated suggestions that the PMRC wanted to act only as an agent of consumer information, the rock "porn" crusade quickly transmuted into a spate of legal proposals and criminal trials of musicians, songwriters, and record retailers. In Maryland a bill that would have made it a crime to sell "obscene" music to minors was only narrowly defeated. Similar measures were proposed in eighteen other states. In 1986 Jello Biafra, lead singer of the anarcho-punk band the Dead Kennedys, was charged with producing "material harmful to minors." Tipper applauded the prosecution and lamented that she hadn't personally been responsible for the charges being brought. For Tipper, the band's "tastelessly styled" name may have been enough. But Biafra had enclosed in one album a poster of a painting by Swiss artist H.R. Giger titled Landscape #20, depicting, as Tipper excitedly put it, "multiple erect penises penetrating vaginas".

The Gores and PMRC were prudent about one sector of the recording industry, headquartered in their occasional home port of Tennessee. Country music, despite its obsession with despair, drinking, adultery, suicide, and revenge, was spared their scrutiny. Ed Meese was successfully ridiculed by liberals for his censorship campaign. The Gores survived intact, and their concerns became Clinton Administration policy in 1993, with the successful drive for the V-chip, the war on teenage mothers (often linked to the one against music and MTV) and kindred moral campaigns.

How Goldman Sachs Killed the Peace Dividend

GOLDMAN SACHS'S TIES to the Clintons date back at least to 1985, when Goldman executives began pumping money into the newly formed Democratic Leadership Council (DLC), a kind of proto-SuperPAC for the advancement of neoliberalism. Behind its "third-way" politics smokescreen, the DLC was shaking down corporations and Wall Street financiers to fund the campaigns of business-friendly "New" Democrats such as Al Gore and Bill Clinton.

The DLC served as the political launching pad for the Clintons, boosting them out of the obscurity of the Arkansas dog-patch into the rarified orbit of the Georgetown cocktail circuit and the Wall Street money movers. By the time Bill rambled through his interminable keynote speech at the 1988 Democratic Convention in Atlanta, the Clintons' Faustian pact with Goldman had already been inked, their political souls cleansed of any vestiges of the primitive southern populism Clinton had exploited so effortlessly during his first term as governor.

In 1991, the Clintons traveled to Manhattan, where they tested the waters for Bill's then rather improbable presidential bid. At a dinner meeting with Goldman's co-chair Robert Rubin, Clinton made his case as a more pliant political vessel than George H.W. Bush, who many of the younger Wall Street raiders had soured on. Rubin emerged from the dinner so impressed that he agreed to serve as one of the campaign's top economic advisors.

More crucially, Rubin soon began orchestrating a riptide of Wall Street money into Clinton's campaign war chest, not only from Goldman but also from other banking and investment titans, such as Lehman Brothers and Citibank, who were eager to see the loosening of federal financial regulations. With Rubin priming the pump, Clinton's campaign coffers soon dwarfed his rivals and enabled him to survive the sex scandals that detonated on the eve of the New Hampshire primary.

After his election, Clinton swiftly returned the favor checking off one item after another on Rubin's wish list, often at the expense of the few morsels he'd tossed to the progressive base of the party. In a rare fit of pique, Clinton erupted during one meeting of his National Economic Council, which Rubin chaired, in the first fraught year of his presidency by yelling: "You mean my entire agenda has been turned over to the fucking bond market?" Surely, Bill meant this as a rhetorical question.

When the time came to do the serious business of deregulating the financial sector, Rubin migrated from the shadows of the NEC to become Treasury Secretary, where he oversaw the implementation of NAFTA, the immiseration of the Mexican economy, imposed shock therapy on the struggling Russian economy, blocked the regulation of credit derivatives and gutted Glass-Steagall. When Rubin left the Treasury to cash in on his work at Citigroup, Clinton called him "the greatest secretary of the Treasury since Alexander Hamilton," as all of Bill's airy promises about remaking America with a "peace dividend" lay around him in smoldering ruins.

The Clintons and the Rich Women

Hillary Clinton has never addressed her role in the midnight pardon of billionaire fugitive Marc Rich. In fact, she's rarely been asked her opinion on the free pass given to one of the world's most wanted fugitives, a man who violated embargoes against Iran and South Africa and fled the country rather than face trial in what was billed as "the biggest tax evasion case in history." HRC has variously said that she was "unaware" of the decision and "surprised" by it. When pressed, she merely cackles.

Even though 300 pages of core documents relating to the pardon decision remain under seal at the Clinton Library, a review of the available record tells a much different story. In fact, the Rich legal team viewed Hillary as a secret weapon, and as one door after another closed on their search for a pardon, they focused more and more on invoking what Rich lawyer Robert Fink called the "HRC option."

Who is Marc Rich? And why did he need a presidential indulgence?

Born in Belgium to Jewish parents, Marc Rich moved with his family to the United States to escape Hitler. Young Marc soon went to work for a commodity firm in New York called Phillip Bros, later acquired by Salomon Brothers. He soon made his mark as an oil trader and, along with his friend Pincus "Pinky" Green, he is credited with inventing spot market trading in oil, ferrous metals and sugar. Billions flowed into the firm, and the European press took to calling Rich "the Aluminum Finger."

But Rich and "Pinky" Green felt underappreciated and underpaid. They bolted the firm, and Rich angrily vowed to "grind Phillip Bros. into oblivion." In 1974, the pair started their own holding company, eventually known as the Marc Rich Group, and began making oil deals with Iran, Iraq and wildcatters in Texas. He and Pinky soon became billionaires and big shots in the global petrochemical trade.

Around this time, Rich courted a buxom young Jewish singer/songwriter from Worcester, Massachusetts, named Denise. He whisked her off to his seaside villa in Marbella, Spain, where the couple were married and rapidly assumed the life of international jet-setters and art collectors. It is said that Rich owns one of the largest private collections of Picasso paintings and sculptures in the world. Rich began referring to himself as a "business machine." The years passed. Denise bore Rich three daughters and honed her songwriting skills on transcontinental flights on the family's private jet. Saccharine pop flowed off her micro recorder, including minor hit "Frankie." The bank accounts swelled.

Then in 1983 crisis hit the Rich family. The U.S. Attorney's office for the Southern District of New York notified Rich and Pinky that they were under investigation for fraud, illegal oil deals with Iran and the apartheid regime in South Africa, as well as tax evasion. Documents were subpoenaed. Indictments were in the works. Rich hired D.C. heavy-hitter Edward Bennett Williams to fend off assaults of a vicious young prosecutor—none other than Rudy Giuliani.

When Giuliani requested that Pinky and Rich turn over their passports and post a large bond, Williams acted indignant and personally avowed to the federal judge overseeing the case that his client was not a flight risk. Two days later, Pinky and Rich were on a plane bound for Europe. As expected, the indictments came: a 65-count charge alleging fraud, trading with the enemy (Iran), and tax evasion.

Humiliated, Williams resigned in a huff, and Rich hired a succession of new lawyers over the next decade, including former Nixon attorney Leonard Garment and Lewis Scooter Libby, who would later find refuge in the awesome power of presidential privilege.

Rich's escape from Giuliani's clutches is the stuff of spy novels, made even more thrilling due to the fact that he almost certainly had several moles inside Giuliani's office, U.S. law enforcement and intelligence agencies who kept him apprised of the schemes to nab him. He evaded the U.S. marshals on his tail at Heathrow Airport in England, and then later his plane bound for Finland mysteriously turned at the last moment for Sweden, once again narrowly avoiding landing in custody. Years later, Rich would also escape capture in Germany and Jamaica, courtesy of anonymous tips to the fugitive billionaire.

The tycoon's eventual passage to safe harbor in Switzerland went from Sweden through East Germany, aided by the notorious Wolfgang Vogel, an East German lawyer who specialized in shuttling spies into and out of Eastern Europe.

Rich dropped millions at every stop, especially in Switzerland. He and Pinky Green choose the town of Zug to establish their new headquarters in a blueberry-colored office tower. Entreaties were made to Swiss officials, and money liberally dispensed.

"He bought Swiss loyalty," says Shawn Tulley, a financial crimes reporter for *Fortune* magazine, who covered the Rich case. "He really put out the charm and the money." When the U.S. Marshals finally tracked Rich down in Switzerland, they immediately petitioned the Swiss government for his extradition. Request denied. As far as the Swiss were concerned, financial crimes, especially involving taxation, were trivial matters unworthy of governmental consideration.

When the Swiss refused to turn Rich over, the Marshals tried to kidnap the world's most famous tax evader under the extraordinary rendition program, which has since become a staple of the Bush regime.

The Marshals set up snatch teams outside of Rich's mansion and his offices. But again, there was a fortuitous leak. The Swiss police approached the would-be kidnappers and told them to shut down their operation or they would be the ones sitting in jail. The Marshals retreated. Rich had found his sanctuary. He summoned Denise and the children to join him in a sprawling mansion near Lucerne and then renounced his U.S. citizenship. This freed him from the nagging obligation of ever again having to worry about entanglements with the IRS over tax obligations. But it also threw the validity of his eventual pardon into question.

The exile of Marc Rich was not an idle one. Indeed, from 1983 to 1996 Rich's fortune ballooned from a mere billion dollars to more than $7 billion. He and Pinky struck oil deals in Russia and Bulgaria (prompting accusations of fraud and thievery in both countries) and mining operations in central Asia, Africa and South America. Along the way, he sharpened the art of the political gratuity. Rudy Giuliani alleges that during this period Rich tried to bribe the state of New York, offering millions to the State Department of Education in exchange for a withdrawal of the pending charges.

In order to buy alumina from the new leftist government of Jamaica for less than half the market price, Rich wired $50 million to Jamaican President Michael Manley in an hour of acute distress for the embattled ruler.

Even as he neared the top of the FBI's Ten Most Wanted list, Rich didn't see any reason to abandon his operations in the United States. In fact, his hand is seen orchestrating one of the most savage crackdowns on organized labor in recent decades. In 1989, Rich secretly acquired the controlling interest in a West Virginia-based company called Ravenswood Aluminum. Ravenswood was embroiled in a tumultuous battle between management and workers at the plant when in 1990, under Rich's long-distance orders, the company tried to bust the union. On a bitterly cold night, a private security force arrived at the plant, set up armed guards at the gates, and deployed surveillance cameras around the perimeter of the facility, and locked out 1,700 workers, all members of the Steelworkers Union. Over the ensuing weeks, the armed guards repeatedly clashed with picketing union members, fogging the air with tear gas and beating skulls with their police clubs. Soon Rich made the call to hire permanent replacement workers, for less pay and reduced benefits. The lockout went on for two more years. "It was a brutal affair," says Dan Stidham, president of the Ravenswood union local at the time of the lockout. "I'm still pretty upset with Clinton for pardoning that guy after all we went through."

Meanwhile, back in Lucerne, Rich was beginning to cultivate the Israeli government. He established the Rich Foundation in Tel Aviv, which would distribute more than $100 million to Israeli causes over the next decade. To oversee the foundation, Rich selected a former high-ranking Mossad official named Avner Azulay, whose ties to the intelligence agency probably never totally evaporated. Azulay was a useful conduit to Israel's political elite. He was close to Yitzak Rabin, Ehud Barak, Shimon Peres and Ehud Olmert. A decade later, Azulay would play a key role in securing Rich's pardon from the Clintons.

Through Azulay, Rich offered his services to the Israeli government, especially the Mossad. Indeed, according to letters from Israeli officials, Rich played the role of a "Say-Ayon," or unpaid asset of the Mossad. In fact, Rich was subsidizing Israeli intelligence operations. He financed numerous covert missions and allowed Mossad operatives to work covertly in his offices around the world.

With experience as an international spook now added to his C.V., Marc Rich reached out through intermediaries to both the FBI and the CIA. He offered his services to both agencies in exchange for dropping the charges against him. The CIA's response is unknown, but the FBI was intrigued and sent the request to the Justice Department, where it was quashed.

Around this time, Rich launched into a public liaison with a glamorous Italian widow by the name of Gisela Rossi. He flaunted the affair in front of Denise, the tycoon's wife who had followed him into his luxurious life on the lam. Denise filed for divorce and prepared to return to New York. But Rich, whose net worth now neared $10 billion, was offering her only a tiny settlement. So Denise took matters into her own hands. She removed a Van Gogh painting from the wall of their palace in Lucerne and warned her estranged husband that unless he ponied up more money, she would take the masterpiece with her. Ultimately, Rich offered her a settlement of $200 million. Although the amount is far less than she would have gotten in most U.S. courts, Denise signed the papers and took her daughters with her back to Manhattan.

Rossi and Rich soon married and divided their time between St. Moritz and Marbella, Spain.

A year after the Rich's divorce, their oldest daughter, Gabriella, was diagnosed with a rare and terminal form of leukemia. She died within the year. Marc Rich made no effort to visit Gabriella in her final months. Denise Rich seethed.

Pardon Me

The machinations to secure a pardon from Bill Clinton for Marc Rich began in earnest in the fall of 1998, when Rich's public relations flack in the U.S., Gershon Kekst, squirmed his way into a seat next to Eric Holder, the number two in the Clinton Justice Department, at a gauche D.C. party thrown by Daimler/Chrysler. Without mentioning Rich by name, Kekst asked Holder how a man of considerable resources might be relieved of the burden of being "unproperly indicted by an overzealous prosecutor."

Holder took a sip of wine and told Kekst that such a man would need to hire a D.C. lawyer who knows the ropes and has deep connections inside the Clinton administration. "He comes to me and we work it out," confided Holder.

"Can you recommend such a person?" Kekst inquired.

Holder pointed to a man sitting at a nearby table. "There's Jack Quinn," Holder whispered. "He's a perfect example."

Kekst dutifully wrote down Quinn's name, conducted background research on the former lawyer for the Clintons, and transmitted the joyful news to the Rich camp.

There is every indication that Holder was trying to drum up business for Quinn, a partner at the powerhouse firm of Arnold and Porter, as well as a top advisor for Al Gore's presidential campaign. Holder was desperate to have Quinn's backing in his doomed bid to become attorney general.

Back in Switzerland, Rich ordered up a dossier on Quinn. His initial response was not favorable. Rich believed Quinn to be merely a "pretty boy" with little experience and "more connections than clout." He decided to stick with Scooter Libby's team. But Scooter, who had represented Rich since 1985, produced no results, and in the summer of 1999, with the clock ticking down on Clinton time, the desperate tycoon reached out to Jack Quinn.

Quinn formally became Rich's lawyer on July 21, 1999. His fees were stiff: an initial retainer of $355,000, plus a minimum payment of $55,000 each month. Quinn's firm, Arnold and Porter, reserved the right to represent clients suing Rich on a range of matters. Rich consented.

Initially, Quinn intimated to the Rich team that securing the pardon would be a relatively easy matter. A few calls to his good friend Eric Holder, and that would be that. Quinn was wrong. When Holder contacted the prosecutors in Manhattan about the Rich case, they vowed to oppose any deal until Rich returned to the U.S. and entered a plea in the case. Rich refused.

From that point on, the Rich team, including his sympathizers inside the Clinton administration, hid their maneuvers from federal prosecutors. After discussions with White House aides Bruce Lindsey and Beth Nolan, Quinn sent out an email calling for a new approach: "It's time to move on the GOI [Government of Israel] front but we have to get the calls initiated over there."

Letters and calls soon flooded the White House from Israeli officials and high profile Jews, including Shimon Peres, Ehud Barak, Ehud Olmert and Elie Weisel. In one way or another, each had received benefits from Rich or one of his foundations. But a problem soon developed. When presented the opportunity to discuss presidential pardons with Clinton, many of these leaders, anxious perhaps to legitimize Israeli penetration of the U.S. government, choose to plead the case of convicted spy Jonathan Pollard instead of the fugitive billionaire.

Quinn scrambled comically for a solution. The DC fixer sent an urgent email to Robert Fink, Rich's longtime New York lawyer.

> From: Jack Quinn. To: Fink, Robert, NY.
> Hope you're checking email; I don't have access here to avner's email address, or marc's, and wonder if you can inquire whether there is a possibility of persuading Mrs Rabin to make a call to POTUS [President of the United States]. He had a deep affection for her husband.

Fink leapt into action with an email to Avner Azulay, the former Mossad officer, now heading the Rich Foundation in Tel Aviv.

> From: Fink, Robert, NY. Sent: Saturday. To: Avner Azulay
> … Jack asks if you could get Leah Rabin to call the President; Jack said he was a real big supporter of her husband…

Azulay wrote back with distressing news.

> From: Avner. To: Fink, Robert, NY.
> Bob, having Leah Rabin call is not a bad idea. The problem is how do we contact her? She died last November …

Eventually, Quinn secured a letter and congenial phone call to Clinton from Rabin's daughter, who didn't really know Rich. Their best hopes seemed to be evaporating. Perhaps Rich was right about Quinn, after all.

First Catch Your Foxman

The scene shifts to a crowded restaurant in Paris. It's Valentine's Day. Two men are having dinner and drinking wine. They know each other well. One man has just received a $100,000 contribution from the other man's boss. The man on the receiving end of the money is Abe Foxman, and the financial gift was for his group the Anti-Defamation League. The man picking up the hefty dinner tab is Avner Azulay—though Marc Rich will soon reimburse him.

Rich has one last shot, Foxman advises. They need to get directly to Bill and Hillary. And the key to unlocking the inner doors of the White House, Foxman told Azulay, is Denise Rich. Foxman confided that he and Denise had flown together on Air Force II to the funeral of Yitzak Rabin. There was just one problem. Denise Rich still loathed her husband. Entreaties are made to Denise, now a New York socialite and successful songwriter, by Quinn and others on the Rich teams. Three times Denise Rich declined to come to the rescue of her former husband.

Then suddenly, in November 2000, she agrees to help. What made her change her mind?

That remains open to speculation, but given Marc Rich's history and Denise's view that she was shortchanged in the divorce, it may well have involved a financial offering. This much is known. On November 16, Avner Azulay flies to New York and takes Denise to dinner. He pleads for her to back Rich's pardon to her friends Bill and Hillary. Two days later Denise consents.

Denise calls her close friend Beth Dozoretz for help in the best way to handle the matter. Another rich Manhattan socialite, Dozoretz had been the finance chair of the Democratic National Committee (DNC). She had contributed more than $1 million to Democratic coffers. Bill Clinton was the godfather of her daughter.

Dozoretz who, like Denise Rich, would later plead the Fifth at a Senate hearing in the matter, helped Rich craft her strategy. Almost immediately, a check for $25,000 was sent from Denise Rich's account to the DNC. This was soon followed by Denise Rich's first letter to the Clintons, imploring them to pardon her ex-husband. Dozoretz also helped Rich bundle a $450,000 contribution to the Clinton library fund. (A Democratic fundraiser told the *New York Times* in 2001 that Denise had also pledged another million in four installments over the next two years. This figure was disputed by Denise Rich. But the donor lists to the Clinton Foundation are kept secret.) In all, Denise Rich made at least $1.1 million in contributions to Democratic causes, including $70,000 to Hillary's Senate campaign and PACs, and at least $450,000 to the Clinton foundation.

For her part, Dozoretz kicked in another million of her own money to the fund. This is the same library that refused to release more than 300 pages of Clinton's records relating to the pardon. She later lavished gifts on the Clintons as they left the White House, including antique furniture for the new home and golf clubs for Bill.

As Beth Dozoretz and Denise Rich plotted their strategy, Quinn and Azulay sought another opening. In a December 19, 2000, email to Quinn, Azulay emphasized the importance of Hillary's role in the affair. She has just been elected senator from New York, where Rich was indicted. If there was to be fallout, it might backfire on Hillary. She would need reassurance. Dozoretz and Denise would provide financial aid, but HRC might also need political cover. Azulay recommends Abraham Burg, former speaker of the Knesset. "Burg is on very friendly terms with Hilary (sic) and knows POTUS from previous contacts."

The next night there's a party at the White House honoring Barbra Streisand, Quincy Jones and Maya Angelou. Dozoretz and Denise are invited, and Denise lands a plum seat at the presidential table. Denise is wearing a burgundy ball gown trimmed in fox fur. She eats little and talks less. After dinner, Denise espies Bill having an intimate conversation with Streisand. She rushes across the room, cuts in on Babs and whisks Bill away. She makes an impassioned plea for the ex-husband, who had humiliated her, stuffs a letter into Bill's hand and whispers, "I could not bear it were I to learn you did not see my letter." When Denise arrives home, she makes a call to Lucerne. It's the first time she has talked to Marc Rich since the divorce. She describes her meeting with Clinton. Her friends say she ended the conversation by telling Rich: "You owe me."

A week later the Rich team is getting antsy. There's still been no word on how Hillary feels. Rich's New York attorney Robert Fink sends an email to Quinn: "Of all the options we discussed, the only one that seems to have real potential for making a difference is the Hillary option."

Quinn, Dozoretz, Burg and, perhaps, Denise call Hillary's people. They are told that the senator needs cover. According to a December 26 email from Azulay titled "Chuck Schumer": "Hillary shall feel more at ease if she is joined by her elder sen. of NY, who also represents the Jewish population."

Gershon Kekst leaps at the opportunity, firing an email to Fink looking for Schumer's pressure points:

> Can Quinn tell us who is close enough to lean on Schumer?? I am willing to call him but have no real clout. Jack might be able to tell us who the top contributors are … maybe Bernard Schwartz??

Bernard Schwartz was a good guess. The former CEO of Loral (a friend of Bill and Marc Rich) was a top DNC contributor and had lavished money on both Schumer and Hillary. Schwartz also had donated $1 million to the Clinton library fund.

But Quinn had been around Washington a long time. He knew enough not to trust Schumer, a famous media hog who was already showing signs of being jealous of the attention Hillary was getting. Quinn notes: "I have to believe that the contact with HRC can happen w/o him after all, we are not looking for a public show of support from her."

Calls continue to flood the Clinton White House. The King of Spain. Sandy Berger. Ehud Barak.

Meanwhile, Denise and Beth are skiing in Aspen. Beth's phone rings. It's Bill Clinton. Clinton tells Dozoretz, "I want to do it and am trying to get around the White House counsel." Keep praying, Bill told the women. He also let them know that Michael Milken wasn't getting a pardon.

A few days later, the two women are back in Washington. It's now January 19, 2001. Jack Quinn is sitting at a board meeting of Fanny Mae. He quietly types a message to Denise on his Blackberry. (It's not known if he bills both clients for this hour of his time.) The text message urges Denise to make one last call to Bill. Quinn tells her not to "argue merits" but merely to explain to Clinton that "it is important to me personally."

Though both women will later dispute it, the Secret Service logs show that the next afternoon at 5:30, Beth and Denise were admitted to the private quarters of the White House. This was Denise's nineteenth visit to the White House. Beth had visited the White House 76 times in the last two years. The logs do not record when the women departed. This is the encounter that appears to have consummated the pardon.

At 2:30 in the morning on January 20, Clinton gets a call from his National Security Advisor. Marc Rich's name has surfaced in an intelligence file in connection with an international arms smuggling network. Clinton calls Quinn. Quinn says the allegations are bogus. Bill turns to his staff, all of whom oppose the pardon that is now being signed. "Take Jack's word," Clinton snapped. Later Clinton will claim to have been "sleep deprived" when he signed the pardon, an excuse that his wife would resurrect to explain her fabulous account of landing under sniper fire in Bosnia.

Marc Rich was free to fly the globe in his private jet, while Leonard Peltier was left to languish in prison with no hope of release. That pretty much sums up Clintonism.

Jeffrey St. Clair

Shattered Promises, Toxic Towns

THE FIRST ENVIRONMENTAL promise Al Gore made in the 1992 campaign, he soon shattered. It involved the WTI hazardous waste incinerator in East Liverpool, Ohio, built on a floodplain near the Ohio River. The plant, one of the largest of its kind in the world, was scheduled to burn 70,000 tons of hazardous waste a year in a spot only 350 feet from the nearest house. A few hundred yards away is East Elementary School, which sits on a ridge nearly eye-level with the top of the smokestack.

On July 19, 1992, Gore gave one of his first campaign speeches on the environment, across the river from the incinerator, in Weirton, West Virginia, hammering the Bush Administration for its plans to give the toxic waste burner a federal air permit. "The very idea is just unbelievable to me", Gore said. "I'll tell you this, a Clinton-Gore Administration is going to give you an environmental presidency to deal with these problems. We'll be on your side for a change." Clinton made similar pronouncements on his swing through the Buckeye State.

Shortly after the election, Gore assured neighbors of the incinerator that he hadn't forgotten about them. "Serious questions concerning the safety of the East Liverpool, Ohio, hazardous waste incinerator must be answered before the plant may begin operation", Gore wrote. "The new Clinton/Gore administration will not issue the plant a test burn permit until all questions concerning compliance with the plant have been answered."

But that never happened. Instead, the EPA quietly granted the WTI facility its test burn permit. The tests failed, twice. In one trial burn, the incinerator eradicated only 7 percent of the mercury found in the waste, when it was supposed to burn away 99.9 percent. A few weeks later the EPA granted WTI a commercial permit anyway. They didn't tell the public about the failed tests until afterward.

Gore claimed his hands were tied by the Bush Administration, which had promised WTI the permit only a few weeks before the Clinton team took office. But by one account, William Reilly, Bush's EPA director, met with Gore's top environmental aide Katie McGinty in January 1993 and asked her if he should begin the process of approving the permit. In this version of events apparently McGinty told Reilly to proceed. McGinty said later that she had no recollection of the meeting.

That evasion was demolished when former EPA administration Reilly testified before EPA's ombudsman Robert Martin that he was approached by McGinty and told that Gore had had a change of heart on the incinerator and wanted the test burn permit granted. "McGinty said it was the wishes of the new incoming administration to get the trial burn permit granted and get the decision made before they took office," Reilly testified. She [McGinty] said the vice president-elect has had second thoughts about his position, had concluded that he should not interfere in the regulatory process and that the transition team would be grateful, the vice president-elect would be grateful if I simply made that decision before leaving office."

Gore has persisted in maintaining that there was nothing he could do about it once the permit was granted. A 1994 report on the matter from the General Accounting Office flatly contradicted him, saying the plant could be shut down on numerous grounds, including repeated violations of its permit.

"This was Clinton and Gore's first environmental promise, and it was their first promise-breaker", says Terri Swearingen, a registered nurse from Chester, West Virginia, just across the Ohio River from the incinerator. Swearingen, who won the Goldman Prize in 1997 for her work organizing opposition to WTI, has hounded Gore ever since, and during the 2000 campaign she was banned by Gore staffers from appearing at events featuring the vice president.

The decision to go soft on WTI may have had something to do with its powerful financial backer. The construction of the incinerator was partially underwritten by Jackson Stephens, the Arkansas investment king who helped bankroll the Clinton-Gore campaign. According to EPA whistleblower Hugh Kaufman, during the period when the WTI financing package was being put together Stephens Inc. was represented by Webb Hubbell, who later came into Clinton's Justice Department and was indicted during the Whitewater investigation, and the Rose Law Firm, to which Hillary Clinton belonged. Over the ensuing years, the WTI plant has burned nearly a half-million tons of toxic waste, 5,000 truckloads of toxic material every year, spewing chemicals such as mercury, lead and dioxin out of its stacks and onto the surrounding neighborhoods. The inevitable illnesses have followed.

A Secret History of the Monarch

ON MAY 20 1999, *Nature* magazine sounded what might have been the death knell of the biotech food industry. A short paper in the respected British science magazine by John Losey, an assistant professor of entomology at Cornell University, reported the ominous results of his laboratory study on the effects of pollen from genetically modified corn on the Monarch butterfly. Losey found that that Monarch caterpillars fed on milkweed leaves dusted with genetically modified corn pollen ate less, grew more slowly and suffered a higher mortality rate than those fed on leaves with normal pollen, or with no pollen at all. Nearly half of the GM pollen-fed caterpillars in the study died.

The corn in question is "Bt" corn, modified by genetic engineers in corporate labs to produce *Bacillus thuringiensis,* a soil bacterium and natural pesticide that organic farmers have for years been spraying on crops, if and when threatened by insects. In contrast to the intermittent doses of the organic farmers, however, the GM variety exudes Bt all the time, at a level of toxicity 10 to 20 times that deployed by the organic sprayers and is distributed via wind-blown pollen. The target of this laboratory-bred plant is the dreaded European corn borer, pending the inevitable evolution of a Bt resistant borer.

By early 1999, Bt corn appeared to be fulfilling the wildest hopes of its developers. First approved for sale by Clinton's EPA in 1996 (without any requirement that it be tested for effects on "non-target" species, such as butterflies) the genetically altered seeds were being sown on 20 million acres in 1998. The companies hoped for a doubling in sales by the following year.

At the time, Cornell was a dangerous place for the untenured Losey to pursue his investigations, given that the university's agriculture school has long enjoyed carnal relations with agri-chemical corporations, such as Monsanto and Novartis. Indeed, one member of the faculty, apprised of its dangerous implications, sent a draft of Losey's paper to Monsanto. A tremulous executive rushed to Ithaca and issued a stern warning against publication of the research, exclaiming that the publicity would "ruin" the GM industry. Losey stood his ground.

Once the May 20 issue of *Nature* hit the stands, events swiftly justified the corporation's forebodings. Americans, who love their Monarch, reacted with outrage. Monsanto stock began a slide from which it has never recovered; Ohio Rep. Dennis Kucinich introduced a bill in Congress to compel labeling for all GM foods on sale; major environmental groups such as the Natural Resources Defense Council, hitherto hailed by Monsanto executives for an "understanding" attitude to GM, joined calls for restrictions on Bt corn; the European Commission cited the report as justification for a moratorium on approvals for sales of new GM products.

The bloodied biotech industry rallied and fought back. In June 1999, the leading biotech companies, including Monsanto, Novartis Seeds Inc, AgrEvo USA and others, carpentered together an entity called the "Agricultural Biotechnology Stewardship Working Group", which allotted $100,000, to a number of scientists across the US and Canada, urging them to hasten to their labs and computers and probe the relationship between Monarch and corn pollen. By fall, the results, or at least something that could be profitably passed on to the public, were in. On November 2, 1999, massed ranks of industry executives assembled for a symposium in Chicago under the joint banner of the Stewardship Working Group and the USDA's Agricultural Research Service (playing its traditional role as a handmaiden of agribusiness.) In attendance were Burson Marsteller and other sleek professionals of the PR industry.

Eight of the researchers at the symposium had been funded by the industry. For appearances sake, however, the organizers felt it necessary to invite other less predictable scientists, such as Dr. Lincoln Brower of Sweet Briar College, America's leading expert on the Monarch. Given that they could not therefore be assured of one hundred percent quiescence from the assembled egg-heads, the corporate overseers adopted a simple expedient. Even before the proceedings commenced, they issued a press release, buttressed by a conference call with selected scientists and reporters, headlined: "Scientific symposium to show no harm to Monarch butterfly". Journalists from most major metropolitan papers, including the *Los Angeles Times, Chicago Tribune, St Louis Post Dispatch* and others did their duty, assuring their readers that the Monarch is safe. The smooth operation was disrupted only by Carol Yoon of the *New York Times*, who had the ill grace to reveal the message of the press release to the meeting and asked if all researchers present agreed. Several voiced their dissent.

Reports from those scientists presenting an optimistic view of the Monarch's prospects in a biotech world did not inspire confidence among all concerned. A number had eschewed the messy business of actually scrutinizing butterflies in the field, opting instead for the more controllable environment of the laboratory and computer simulation. Thus, as Lincoln Brower noted in a tart report on the proceedings: "Several papers presented at the symposium indicated a lack of understanding of basic Monarch biology and ecology (even though most of this information has been published in peer-reviewed scientific journals, including methods for working with caterpillars in the field, life table studies, and fecundity data)." In Brower's scornful view, scientific research in this area is badly compromised by industry money

The system worked. Two months after the Chicago gathering, Gene Grabowski, senior flack with the potent Grocery Manufacturers of America, could claim that the threat of GM foods becoming as hot an issue here as they are in Europe has been beaten back "The fire caught on the edges", he crowed, "but it is under control." True, the EPA belatedly issued a requirement that Bt cornfields be abutted by "refuges" of non-GM corn to screen Monarchs from the deadly pollen, but such tactical victories did not outweigh the overall triumph of the biotech industry on the issue.

Meanwhile the poor Monarch, poised to begin its annual spring migration from central Mexico to the US, may find that come next fall there will be little left of the Oyamel fir forest to which these butterflies return for the winter. The forested mountain area in Michoacan to which all Monarchs east of the Rockies migrate is tiny, totaling less than 62 square miles. Alas, the vital forests are rapidly diminishing under the onslaught of local loggers.

The Mexican government, while decreeing that the core Monarch areas be protected, has unwisely followed US Forest Service practice by permitting a "buffer zone", where limited logging is allowed around the central and supposedly inviolate zones. The buffer zones are being clearcut and the central zones are rapidly thinning.

Tens of thousands of tourists flock to Mexico to witness the incomparable spectacle of Monarchs en masse, an economic boon esteemed by the locals. In hotel gift shops visitors can buy Monarch memorabilia, as well as toy lumber trucks laden with simulated Oyamel logs.

Once the forests are gone, the Monarchs will have no canopy to protect them from winter damp and frosts, and they will disappear forever from field and forest, eliminated by chainsaws and bioengineering.

The Political Economy of Dead Meat

THERE'S A SOUR irony to the fact that it's taken the extremely rare mad cow disease, which has thus far killed a very small number of people in England, to raise the alarm about the consequences of intensive meat and milk production. Over the past 150 years the demands of such production have destroyed much of the world's ecological balance and impoverished millions.

Start today with one giant U.S. corporation, Monsanto, which makes chemicals and agribusiness products. It has spent many years and a billion dollars or two developing recombinant Bovine Growth Hormone. The purpose of this product is to increase milk yield in dairy cattle. Inject BGH into cows twice a week and the milk yield goes up by some 10 to 20 percent. But crucially, with the artificially increased milk production, the cows need the infamous protein supplements made from rendered cows and sheep, thus opening the way to diseases such as bovine spongiform encephalopathy (BSE, or mad cow disease), which can transfer to humans.

There are other problems, of course. First, who needs higher productivity per dairy cow when there's a huge milk glut in the United States? Second, as happened with poultry and now with hogs, BGH accelerates the demise of small producers and the emergence of the industrial dairy conglomerates.

Like any junkie, cows hooked on BGH tend to get sick, mostly with mastitis, an infection of the udder. Treatment of mastitis requires liberal doses of antibiotics. The antibiotic injected into the cow passes on to the human consumer, and thus contributes to the process whereby more and more bacteria are building up greater resistance to antibiotics. Moreover, BGH also causes cows to produce more Insulin Growth-like Hormone-1 (or IGH-1), which has been linked to a number of disorders in humans, including acro-megaly (gigantism in the form of excessive growth of the head and extremities) and an increased risk of prostate, breast, and ovarian cancer. There is also research to suggest that IGH-1 reduces the body's ability to suppress naturally occurring

Mad cow disease—a degenerative brain disorder first detected in England in 1986—is a comparative trifle in some ways. Cattle apparently contracted BSE by eating protein supplements made from rendered sheep infected with scrapie, a form of spongiform encephalopathy. Infected cattle become disoriented, suffer seizures, fall down, and die. Scientists believe that consumption of meat from BSE-infected cattle leads to Creutzfeldt-Jakob disease (CJD), a fatal neurological disease. The virus may incubate for 30 years. There is no way to detect it or treat it.

The U.S. government, of course, maintains that no BSE-infected cattle have been discovered in the United States. But in fact, the disease may have appeared in the U.S. before the outbreak in England. According to a Jan. 24, 1994 story by Joel Bleifuss in *In These Times*, Richard Marsh, a veterinary scientist at the University of Wisconsin, was raising the alarm about BSE in American cattle back in 1985. Marsh discovered an outbreak of spongiform encephalopathy at a mink farm in Wisconsin. The mink had been fed a protein supplement made from rendered cows that had supposedly died from "downer cow syndrome." Marsh believes the cows had actually succumbed to a previously undetected form of BSE. (In 2012, a California dairy cow tested positive for Mad Cow Disease.)

"The signs that these cattle showed were not the widely recognized signs of BSE—not signs of mad cow disease," Marsh told Bleifuss. "What they showed was what you might expect from a downer cow." About 100,000 cows a year die from downer cow syndrome in the United States. Most of these dead cows are rendered into protein supplements to feed other cattle. If this is true, the U.S. cattle population may already be infected with BSE and American meat consumers may have already contracted CJD. Still, the U.S. government has done nothing to regulate the contents of animal feed.

Intensive meat production—these days mostly of beef, veal, pork, and chicken—is an act of violence: primarily, of course, an act of violence against the creatures involved. But it is also violence against nature and against poor people. David Wright Hamilton, a biologist at the University of Georgia, once wrote that an "alien ecologist observing... Earth might conclude that cattle is the dominant species in our biosphere." The modern livestock industry economy and the passion for meat have radically altered the look of the planet. Today, across huge swaths of the globe, from Australia to the western plains of the United States, one sees the conquest landscapes of the European mass-meat-producers and their herds of ungulates. Because of romantic ideas of "unchanging" landscapes it is hard to grasp the rapidity of this process, or the degree to which it leaves the land changed forever.

Take California. In the late 18th century, when the first cattle herds arrived in what the Spanish colonists called Alta California, the region presented itself as a Mediterranean landscape, but of a sort that had been extinguished in Europe for many centuries. There were meadows with perennial bunchgrasses, beardless wild rye, oat grass, perennial forbs: 22 million acres of such prairie and 500,000 acres of marsh grass. Beyond this, there were 8 million acres of live oak woodlands and park-like forests. Beyond and above these, chaparral.

By the 1860s, in the wake of the gold rush, some 3 million cattle were grazing California's open ranges and the degradation was rapid, particularly as ranchers had been overstocking to cash in on the cattle boom. Floods and drought between 1862 and 1865 consummated the ecological crisis. In the spring of 1863, 97,000 cattle were grazing in parched Santa Barbara County. Two years later only 12,100 remained. In less than a century, California's pastoral utopia had been destroyed; the ranchers moved east of the Sierra Nevada into the Great Basin, or north, to colder and drier terrain.

California is one of America's largest dairy states, and livestock agriculture uses almost a third of all irrigation water. It takes 360 gallons of water to produce a pound of beef (that's counting irrigation for grain, trough water for stock, and so on), which is why, further east in the feedlot states of Colorado, Nebraska, and Kansas, the Ogallala aquifer has been so severely depleted.

The answer? Drill deeper. Deep-drilling began as a response to the dustbowl disaster of the 1930s, itself a product of farming practices ill-suited to the natural conditions; intensive pumping of the high plains aquifer began after WWII. By 1978 there were 170,000 wells drawing off 23 million acre-feet of water each year. (An acre-foot represents the amount of water required to cover one acre with water one foot deep.) This is in large part a testament to the requirements of a livestock industry worth $10 billion a year.

And of course the gasoline, diesel fuel, natural gas, and electricity required to pump the water up several hundred feet from the shrinking aquifer are as finite as the water itself. Sometime in the next century, the high plains will be forced back to dryland farming, with such descendants of the present population as remain facing other environmental disasters—prominent among them the poisoning of the remaining groundwater by herbicides, fertilizer, and vast amounts of nitrogen and phosphorus from the manure excreted day by day in the feedlots. At the end of the 1980s, Frank and Deborah Popper of Rutgers University began arguing that an era of agricultural "pullback" lay ahead, and the future of the plains might include "buffalo commons" in which native animals such as the buffalo would roam over federally owned grasslands once more.

The pattern is the same the world round: Unsustainable grazing and ranching are laying waste to drylands, forests, and wild species. Brazil's military dictators, who came to power in the early 1960s, hoped to convert their nation's Amazonian rain forests, which cover more than 60 percent of the country, to cattle pasture and thus make Brazil a major beef producer on the world market. A speculative frenzy ensued, with big companies acquiring million-acre spreads that they promptly stripped of trees in order to get tax write-offs and kindred subsidies from the junta. Big ranchers accounted for most of the destruction. Within a decade or so, degraded scrubland had yielded money to the corporations but few cattle, and none of these could be sold on the world market because they were diseased. Indeed, the Amazon is a net beef-importing region. Meanwhile, many of the 2 or 3 million people who lived in the rainforest have been evicted with each encroachment of the burning season.

Such are the assaults on the environment and the poor. By 1990 about half of all American rangeland was severely degraded, with habitats along narrow streams the worst in memory. Australian pastures show the same pattern. In the drylands of South Africa, overgrazing has made over 7 million acres useless for cattle, and 35 million acres of savanna are rapidly becoming equally useless.

Over the past quarter-century many national governments—prodded by the World Bank—have plunged into schemes for intensive grain-based meat production. In Mexico the share of cropland growing feed and fodder for animals went from 5 percent in 1960 to 23 percent in 1980. Sorghum, used for animal feed, is now Mexico's second largest crop by area. At the same time, the area of land producing the staples for poor folk in Mexico—corn, rice, wheat, and beans—has fallen relentlessly. Mexico is now a net corn importer, with imports from rich countries such as Canada and the United States wiping out millions of subsistence farmers who have to migrate to the cities or to El Norte. Mexico feeds 30 percent of its grain to livestock while 22 percent of the population suffers from malnutrition.

Multiply this baleful pattern across the world. Grain-based livestock production inexorably leads to larger and larger units and economies of scale, in a kind of world beef gulag whose consequences are now causing such a panic.

Alexander Cockburn

From Mitch to Katrina: Nature is Politics

NATURE REALLY KICKS the door down once in a while, and let us know how humans have made a mess of things. A few years ago Hurricane Mitch laid waste much of Guatemala and neighboring countries. The hills crumbled and topsoil sluiced into the sea. There was politics, class politics, in that sluicing, same way there's politics in most "natural" disasters. The US had crushed land reform in Guatemala in the 1950s, with the CIA overseeing a coup against Arbenz and launching decades of savage repression. The peasants had to surrender the good flat land to the United Fruit Co and scratch small holdings for subsistence into ever steeper hillsides

Katrina the aftermath is payback time for decades of stupidity, greed, pillage, racism. The tempo towards catastrophe really picked up in the Reagan era. That's when the notion of this society being in some deep sense a collective effort, pointed towards universal human betterment the core of the old Enlightenment went onto the trash heap.

Once you stop believing in universal betterment, you stop investing in social defenses, like health care, or flood control. You build your shining condo on the hill, put a fence round it, and cancel the local bus service so the poor can't get at you. What was the final answer to the bus boycott in Montgomery, Alabama? Cancel the busses!

So collective effort goes out the window, and soon the society forgets how collective effort works. Tens of thousands of poor people standing on roofs in the Delta and they haven't the slightest idea how to get them off. The ones they have brought to dry land they dump on the highway, where they stand as the Army trucks roll by.

There are all sorts of bargains the rich and the powerful in any society make with the poor. But one way or another through bread, circuses, the dole, the promise that Anyone Can Make It there's the offer of a deal: Don't make trouble: we'll take care of you. Empires collapse when the offer of the "marginal rate of return" becomes empty: we won't take care of you. Or, we can't take care of you. We don't need you and we're not frightened of you.

We're at that point here. Malthus, a Christian, proposed locating the surplus poor next to unhealthy marshes, in the hope they would get sick and die. How much of a difference is there between that and the "emergency preparedness" and evacuation procedures before, during and after Katrina? How did Washington perceive New Orleans and most of the Gulf coast? Basically as a vast huddle of the mostly poor and the mostly black. So, year after year, they denied funds to shore up levees that all experts agree are bound to give way in more than a Force Three storm. They hollowed out every state economy so that in the end Mississippi's tax base was its cut of the gambling take, from floating casinos because the Christians said the Devil's Work couldn't take place on dry land.

Mainstream politics in America has ceased to deliver the goods in anything but the meanest terms. The bigger the hog, the bigger the bucket of slops. There's no worthwhile opposition at the established level. People are looking at the scenes along the Gulf coast and in the Delta with horror, at the realization of what our society has come to.

Fukushima and the Ring of Eternal Fire

AMERICANS READ THE increasingly panic-stricken reports of meltdown at the Fukushima Daiichi nuclear-power plant in Japan and asked: 'Can it happen here?'

They already knew the answer.

As the late great environmentalist, David Brower, used to put it, 'nuclear plants are incredibly complex technological devices for locating earthquake faults'. Along much of America's West Coast runs the Ring of Fire, which stretches all around the Pacific plate from Australia, north past Japan, to Russia, Alaska, and down the coast to Chile. Some 90 per cent of the world's earthquakes happen around the Ring.

Apparently acting predictively on Brower's piece of sarcastic wisdom, the US has deployed four nuclear plants near the Ring of Fire fault lines, two of them in Brower's home state of California. In Eureka, California forty miles up the road from CounterPunch headquarters in Petrolia, there was a boiling-water reactor that was closed in 1976 following an earthquake from a 'previously unknown fault' just off the coast.

In its place, there are now spent nuclear fuel rods—except one they now cannot find—in ponds, right on the shoreline; nicely situated for a tsunami, such as the one that disabled the relief diesel generators that were designed to pump emergency coolant in the Fukushima plant. Three plates meet at Triple Junction off Cape Mendocino. The region experienced a 7.1 earthquake in 1992.

Moral number one in the nuclear business: eyes wide shut at all times; deny the predictable.

Further south, halfway between San Francisco and Los Angeles, is the Diablo Canyon nuclear plant. It was planned in 1968 when no one knew about the Hosgri Fault, part of the Ring of Fire, a few miles from the coast. Further enquiry established that there had been a 7.1 earthquake forty years earlier, offshore from the plant, which was duly completed in

1973. The power company, Pacific Gas & Electric, said it would beef up defenses. In their haste, the site managers reversed the new blueprints for earthquake-proofing the two reactors, so the retro-fit was not a total success. Moral number two in the nuclear business, as in any other human enterprise: somewhere along the line people always fuck things up.

Diablo Canyon was supposedly built and retro-fitted to survive a 7.3 quake intact. In 1906, San Francisco was destroyed by a 7.7 quake, which ripped the San Andreas fault for 300 miles, north and south of the city. Back to the first moral, 'deny the predictable': Diablo Canyon authorities recently learnt of yet another fault and are now worried about 'ground liquefaction' in the event of a big quake. In 2008 there was an attack by a smack of jellyfish (Yes, the collective noun is correct), which blocked the cold-water intake; the plant was shut down for a couple of days. At the last count there were four identified fault lines offshore from Diablo Canyon.

Another 150 miles south lies the recently shuttered San Onofre plant, perched on the shoreline. It has been cited as 'the scariest workplace in America'. People swim in its shadow, in waters highly esteemed by anglers because fish gather there to enjoy the elevated temperatures; some also claim the fish there get bigger, faster. There are storage ponds for spent fuel in a decommissioned unit, a spherical containment of concrete and steel, the smallest wall being an adamantine six feet thick; just about the same as the ruptured containment at one of the collapsing Fukushima units.

Further illustration of moral number two, 'fucking up', is to be found in one of San Onofre's two sizzling units: the mighty engineering and construction firm Bechtel installed a 420-ton nuclear-reactor vessel here backwards. The nearest faultline is the Cristianitos, deemed inactive; see moral number one. The power company says San Onofre is built to withstand a 7.0 quake. There is a 25-foot sea wall, half the height of the walls that crumbled like sand along Japan's north-east coast, as the tsunami from the 9.0 Tohoku earthquake rolled in. San Onofre is seawater-cooled. Environmentalists didn't care for that, so they planned to build two cooling towers the other side of Interstate 5, California's main north—south road; immune to jelly-fish attack, but open to other methods of assault. The Uniform California Earthquake Rupture Forecast figures a 67 per cent probability of an earthquake 6.7 or higher for Los Angeles, 63 per cent for San Francisco. Up here in the Cascadia subduction zone—where one bit of a plate pushes under another, as happens off north-east Japan—we have a 10 per cent possibility of an 8 or 9 force quake; a Big One is a near certainty fairly soon.

The United States produces more nuclear energy than any other nation. It has 104 nuclear plants, many of them old, prone to endless leaks and kindred malfunctions: all of them dangerous. Twenty-four of them are the same design—by General Electric—as the Fukushima reactors.

Take the Shearon Harris power station in North Carolina, also a repository for highly radioactive spent fuel rods from two other nuclear plants. It would not even require a quake or tsunami, only a moderately ingenious terrorist to breach Shearon Harris's puny defenses and sabotage the cooling systems. A study by the Brookhaven Labs estimates that a pool fire there could cause 140,000 cancers, and contaminate thousands of square miles of land.

The reactions to Fukushima from the nuclear industry's shills have been predictable—if still scarcely believable—sallies into cognitive dissonance.

George Monbiot seized the opportunity of one of the worst disasters in the 'peacetime' history of nuclear power to announce his endorsement of atomic energy in the *Guardian*:

> You will not be surprised to hear that the events in Japan have changed my view of nuclear power. You will be surprised to hear how they have changed it. As a result of the disaster at Fukushima, I am no longer nuclear-neutral. I now support the technology. A crappy old plant with inadequate safety features was hit by a monster earthquake and a vast tsunami. The electricity supply failed, knocking out the cooling system. The reactors began to explode and melt down. The disaster exposed a familiar legacy of poor design and corner-cutting. Yet, as far as we know, no one has yet received a lethal dose of radiation.

Does Monbiot live on Fantasy Island? "Sound as the roots of the anti-nuclear movement are, we cannot allow historical sentiment to shield us from the bigger picture," he wrote. "Even when nuclear power plants go horribly wrong, they do less damage to the planet than coal-burning stations … The Chernobyl meltdown was hideous and traumatic. The official death toll so far appears to be 43–28 workers in the initial few months then a further 15 civilians by 2005."

The 1986 explosion in the fourth reactor at the Chernobyl power station in the Ukraine does indeed remain the benchmark catastrophe amid peacetime nuclear disasters. Denial that Chernobyl actually killed—and is killing—hundreds of thousands of people is crucial to the efforts of the nuclear lobby. Amid the Fukushima crises, Fergus Walsh, the BBC's medical correspondent, comforted his audience with the absurdity that by 2006, Chernobyl had prompted only sixty deaths from cancer; the same drivel has been repeated many times over since the Fukushima catastrophe, buttressed by a shameful report overseen by the UN's nuclear lobby.

In 2009 the New York Academy of Sciences published *Chernobyl: Consequences of the Catastrophe for People and the Environment*, a 327-page volume by scientists Alexey Yablokov, Vassily Nesterenko and Alexey Nesterenko, the definitive study to date with comprehensive health statistics. In the summary of his chapter 'Mortality After the Chernobyl Catastrophe', Yablokov demonstrates that 4 per cent of all deaths in the contaminated territories of Ukraine and Russia from 1990 to 2004 were caused by the Chernobyl catastrophe.

Set Fukushima next to Chernobyl and its ongoing lethal aftermath; think of southern California or North Carolina. Nuclear expert Robert Alvarez, an advisor to Clinton and *CounterPunch* contributor, wrote a few weeks after the meltdown that a single spent fuel-rod pool—as in Fukushima Number 4 or Shearon Harris—holds more cesium—137 than was deposited by all atmospheric nuclear-weapons tests in the northern hemisphere combined; an explosion in that pool could blast 'perhaps three to nine times as much of these materials into the air as was released by the Chernobyl reactor disaster'.

Pro-nuclear greens like Monbiot and the despicable James Hansen prattle on about "better safeguards." Can they not get it into their heads that nuclear power's entire history has been the methodical breaching of supposedly reliable safeguards? There are 40-foot sea walls around much of Japan's coastline. The Fukushima tsunami went through them like a wavelet through a child's sandcastle.

Monbiot writes as though the nuclear-industrial-academic complex— one of the most powerful lobbies in the world, in continuous operation for seventy years—did not exist. Yet its real-world effects are plain enough. President Obama, for example, took plenty of nuclear-industry money, specifically from the Exelon Corporation, for his presidential campaign. In his State of the Union address in January 2011, Obama reaffirmed his commitment to 'clean, safe' nuclear power, as insane a statement as pledging commitment to a nice, clean form of syphilis.

Post-Japanese earthquake, Obama's press spokesman confirmed that nuclear energy 'remains a part of the President's overall energy plan'. Even as Fukushima Daiichi threatened a runaway meltdown, Obama found time to record a tv interview for a news program in southwestern New Mexico on his 2010 proposal for nuclear-warhead development. The centerpiece of this plan is funding for a sprawling $6bn factory to produce explosive triggers for thermo-nuclear weapons at the Los Alamos nuclear compound, 50 miles from Santa Fe. Why choose the moment of Fukushima's collapse to address New Mexico? As the tv interviewer made clear, it is home to powerful potential donors of Democratic Party campaign funds: Lockheed Martin (which manages the Sandia National Laboratory, Bechtel, Babcock & Wilcox and the URS Corporation (which, along with the University of California, collectively administer Los Alamos).

In Germany and in France there have been huge turnouts against atomic energy in the wake of Fukushima. In the US only a handful of Greens have spoken out. Why have we not seen furious demonstrations outside every one of America's 104 nuclear plants? One reason: major environmental organizations long ago made a devil's pact with the nuclear industry, which since the early 1970s has worked to frame carbon dioxide as the real environmental problem and nuclear power as its only solution.

There has been no upsurge against nuclear power here because American progressives still mostly cram in under the toxic umbrella of Obama's energy plan. When the House of Representatives (though not the US Senate) voted for a climate bill in 2009, a "clean energy bank" to provide financial backing for new energy production, including nuclear, was part of the bargain.

In political terms, nuclear power has always been a war on the people, starting with the Japanese in Hiroshima and Nagasaki, going on to the Marshall Islanders, ranchers and kindred inhabitants of test sites across the West, Native Americans, poor Latinos and African Americans (the usual involuntary neighbors of waste dumps), people in the path of 'accidents' or deliberate secret experiments, and most recently Fukushima. Not the executives of the Tokyo Electric Power Company. They are in Tokyo or heading further south. It is 'worker heroes'—who know perfectly well they are doomed. It is the Board of TEPCO and the likes of Monbiot and Hansen that should be sent to the front lines.

Look at the false predictions, the blunders. Remember the elemental truth that Nature bats last, and that folly and greed are ineluctable parts of the human condition.

Why try to pretend that we live in a world where there are no force 8–9 earthquakes, tsunamis, dud machinery, forgetful workers, corner-cutting plant owners, immensely powerful corporations, permissive regulatory agencies, politicians and presidents trolling for campaign dollars?

Is that the shoal on which the progressive movement in America is beached?

This shameful pact between the nuclear industry and many big greens must end.

Fukushima Mon Amour

IS THE CRISIS in Fukushima over or just beginning? You might be forgiven for scratching your head at that one. Nearly five years after the nuclear meltdown triggered by the Tohoku earthquake and subsequent tsunami, one of the planet's worst radioactive catastrophes has almost completely faded from both the media and public consciousness. Amid that information void, the lethal history of those events has been swamped under pernicious myths being spread by nuclear hucksters.

In brief, the revised story of the Fukushima meltdown goes something like this: the Daiichi facility was struck by an unprecedented event, unlikely to be repeated; the failsafe systems worked; the meltdown was swiftly halted; the spread of radioactive contamination contained and remediated; no lives or illnesses resulted from the crisis. Full-speed ahead!

One of the first to squirm headlong down this rabbit hole of denial was Paddy Reagan, a professor of Nuclear Physics at the University of Surrey: "We had a doomsday earthquake in a country with 55 nuclear power stations and they all shut down perfectly, although three have had problems since. This was a huge earthquake, and as a test of the resilience and robustness of nuclear plants it seems they have withstood the effects very well."

For Reagan and other atomic zealots, the Fukushima meltdown did not represent a cautionary tale, but served as a real time exemplar of the safety, efficiency and durability of nuclear power. Call it Fukushima Mon Amour, or How They Stopped Worrying and Learned to Love the Atom.

Such extreme revisionism is to be expected from the likes of Reagan, and other hired guns for the Big Atom, especially at a moment of grave peril for their economic fortunes. More surreal is the killer compact between the nuclear industry and some high-profile environmentalists, which reached a feverish pitch at the Paris Climate conference. Freelance nuclear shills, such as the odious James Hansen and the clownish George Monbiot, have left carbon footprints that would humble Godzilla by jetting across the world promoting nuclear energy as a kind of technological deus ex machina for the apocalyptic threat of climate change. Hansen has gone so far as to charge that "opposition to nuclear power threatens the future of humanity." Shamefully, many greens now promote nuclear power as a kind ecological lesser-evilism.

Of course, there's nothing new about this kind of rationalization for the doomsday machines. The survival of nuclear power has always depended on the willing suspension of disbelief. In the terrifying post-Hiroshima age, most people intuitively detected the symbiotic linkage between nuclear weapons and nuclear power and those fears had to be doused. As a consequence, the nuclear industrial complex concocted the fairy tale of the peaceful atom, zealously promoted by one of the most devious conmen of our time: Edward "H-Bomb" Teller.

After ratting out Robert Oppenheimer as a peacenik and security risk, Teller set up shop in his lair at the Lawrence Livermore Labs and rapidly began designing uses for nuclear power and bombs as industrial engines to propel the post-World War II economy. One of the first mad schemes to come off of Teller's drafting board was Operation Chariot, a plan to excavate a deep-water harbor at Cape Thornton, near the Inuit village of Point Hope, Alaska, by using controlled (sic) detonations of hydrogen bombs.

In 1958, Teller, the real-life model for Terry Southern's character Dr. Strangelove, devised a plan for atomic fracking. Working with the Richfield Oil Company, Teller plotted to detonate 100 atomic bombs in northern Alberta to extract oil from the Athabasca tar sands. The plan, which went by the name Project Oilsands, was only quashed when intelligence agencies got word that Soviet spies had infiltrated the Canadian oil industry.

Frustrated by the Canadians' failure of nerve, Teller soon turned his attentions to the American West. First he tried to sell the water-hungry Californians on a scheme to explode more than 20 nuclear bombs to carve a trench in the western Sacramento Valley to canal more water to San Francisco, the original blueprint for Jerry Brown's Peripheral Canal. This was followed by a plot to blast off 22 peaceful nukes to blow a hole in the Bristol Mountains of southern California for the construction of Interstate 40. Fortunately, neither plan came to fruition.

Teller once again turned to the oil industry, with a scheme to liberate natural gas buried under the Colorado Plateau by setting off 30 kiloton nuclear bombs 6,000 feet below the surface of the earth. Teller vowed that these mantle-cracking explosions, marketed as Project Gasbuggy, would "stimulate" the flow of natural gas. The gas was indeed stimulated, but it also turned out to be highly radioactive.

More crucially, in 1957 at speech before the American Chemical Society Teller, who later helped the Israelis develop their nuclear weapons program, became the first scientist to posit that the burning of fossil fuels would inevitably yield a climate-altering greenhouse effect, which would feature mega-storms, prolonged droughts and melting ice-caps. His solution? Replace the energy created by coal and gas-fired plants with a global network of nuclear power plants.

Edward Teller's deranged ideas of yesteryear have now been dusted off and remarketed by the Nuclear Greens, including James Lovelock, the originator of the Gaia Hypothesis, with no credit given to their heinous progenitor.

There are currently 460 or so operating nukes, some chugging along far past their expiration dates, coughing up 10 percent of global energy demands. Teller's green disciples want to see nuclear power's total share swell to 50 percent, which would mean the construction of roughly 2100 new atomic water-boilers from Mogadishu to Kathmandu. What are the odds of all of those cranking up without a hitch?

Meanwhile, back at Fukushima, unnoticed by the global press corps, the first blood cancers (Myelogenous leukemia) linked to radiation exposure are being detected in children and cleanup workers. And off the coast of Oregon and California every Bluefin tuna caught in the last year has tested positive for radioactive Cesium 137 from the Fukushima meltdown. The era of eco-radiation has arrived. Don't worry. It only has a half-life of 30.7 years.

Jeffrey St. Clair

The Price America Paid for Madeleine Albright

MARTYRDOM IS HARD to beat. In the first few centuries after Christ the Romans tried it against the Christians, whose martyrdoms were almost entirely sacrificial of themselves, not of others. The lust for heaven of a Muslim intent on suicidal martyrdom was surely never so eloquent as that of St Ignatius in the second century who, under sentence of death, doomed to the Roman amphitheater and a hungry lion, wrote in his Epistle to the Romans,

> I bid all men know that of my own free will I die for God, unless ye should hinder me… Let me be given to the wild beasts, for through them I can attain unto God. I am God's wheat, and I am ground by the wild beasts that I may be found the pure bread of Christ. Entice the wild beasts that they may become my sepulchre… Come fire and cross and grapplings with wild beasts, wrenching of bones, hacking of limbs, crushings of my whole body; only be it mine to attain unto Jesus Christ.

Eventually haughty imperial Rome made its accommodation with Christians, just as Christians amid the furies and martyrdoms and proscriptions of the Reformation, made accommodations with each other.

What sort of accommodation should America make now? How about one with the history of the past hundred years, in an effort to improve the moral world climate of the next hundred years? We use the word accommodation in the sense of an effort to get to grips with history, as inflicted by the powerful upon the weak.

+++

What moved those kamikaze Muslims of September 911 to embark, on the training that they knew would culminate in their deaths as well of those (they must have hoped) of thousands upon thousands of innocent people? Was it the Koran plus a tape from Osama bin Laden? The dream of a world in which all men wear untrimmed beards and women have to stay at home or go outside only when enveloped in blue tents?

We doubt it. If one had to cite what steeled their resolve the list would surely include an exchange on CBS in 1996 between Madeleine Albright and then US ambassador to the United Nations and Lesley Stahl. Albright was maintaining that sanctions had yielded important concessions from Saddam Hussein.

When the US imposed sanctions on Iraq, they had a pretty good idea of what was going to happen. In July 1991, Doug Broderick, a professional aid worker who was sent to Baghdad by the US charity Catholic Relief Services, predicted that as a consequence of sanctions 175, Iraqi children would die because of the deteriorating health conditions. Broderick called it a "disaster in slow motion." It turned out his prophecy was badly off.

After five years of sanctions Iraq found itself in desperate straits. In May of 1996, the World Health Organization said that "the vast majority of the country's population has been on a semi-starvation diet for years." The sewage treatment plants either barely functioned or didn't work at all. Denis Halliday, who worked for the United Nations Development program in Iraq and who had issued many public denunciations of the sanctions, said that they were "in contradiction of human rights provisions in the UN's own charter."

The hospitals were filled with dying children, while medicines necessary to save them were banned by the US-officials in New York supervising the operations of the sanctions committee. By the end of 1995 alone, the United Nations Food and Agricultural Organization said that after careful investigation it had determined that as many as 576,000 Iraqi children had died as a result of sanctions. The mortality rates were soaring with terrifying speed. The infant mortality rate had gone from 47 percent per 1000 in 1989 to 108 per 1000 in 1996. For kids under five the increase in the rate was even worse, from 56 per 1000 in 1989 to 131 per 1000 in 1996. By 1996 the death count was running at 5,000 children a month.

By the late 90s, UN officials working in Baghdad explained that the root causes of child mortality and other health problems were no longer simply lack of food and medicine, but lack of clean water (freely available in all parts of the country prior to the Gulf War) and of electrical power, now running at 30 percent of the pre-bombing level. Of the 21.9 percent of contracts vetoed as of mid-1999 by the UN's US-dominated sanctions committee, a high percentage were integral to repair the water and sewage systems. The Iraqis submitted contracts worth $236 million in this area, of which $54 million worth—roughly one-quarter of the total value—were disapproved. "Basically, anything with chemicals or even pumps is liable to get thrown out," one UN official revealed.

The same trend was apparent in the power supply sector, where around 25% of the contracts were put on hold—$138 million worth, out of $589 million submitted. But the proportion of approved/disapproved contracts does not tell the full story. UN officials referred to the "complementarity issue," meaning that items approved for purchase were useless without other items that had been disapproved. For example, the Iraqi Ministry of Health ordered $25 million worth of dentist chairs, said order being approved by the sanctions committee—except for the compressors, without which the chairs were useless and consequently spent the next several years gathering dust in a Baghdad warehouse.

In February of 2000, the US moved to prevent Iraq from importing 15 bulls from France. The excuse was that the animals, ordered with the blessing of the UN's humanitarian office in Baghdad to restock the Iraqi beef industry, would require certain vaccines which, who knows, might be diverted into a program to make biological weapons of mass destruction.

We know that the big killers were the prohibitions the US placed on the import of medicines, medical equipment and parts for power plants and water treatment stations. But many of the items banned were absurd in their pettiness, marking a captious cruelty designed to have a demoralizing effect on the minds of Iraqi citizens. Here are few: baby food (because adults might eat it), ping pong balls, cotton swabs, syringes, bicycles, nail polish and lipstick, funeral shrouds, pencil sharpeners, erasers, school notebooks, computers, blood testing machines, pagers, ambulance sirens, heaters and tennis balls.

This, then, is the ghastly context for Lesley Stahl famous question.

Stahl: "We have heard that half a million children have died. I mean, that's more children than died in Hiroshima. And you know, is the price worth it?"

Albright: "I think this is a very hard choice, but the price? We think the price is worth it."

+++

Surely, the 9/11 hijackers read that exchange in the Middle East. It was infamous all over the Arab world. We'll bet the September 11 kamikazes knew it well enough, just as they could tell you the crimes wrought against the Palestinians. So would it have been unfair to take Madeleine Albright down to the ruins of the Trade Towers, remind her of that exchange, and point out that the price turned out also to include that awful mortuary. Was that price worth it too, Mrs. Albright?

Mere nit-picking among the ruins and the dust of the 3,000? Hardly. America has led a charmed life amid its wars on people. The wars mostly didn't come home and the press made as sure as it could that folks including the ordinary workers in the Trade Towers weren't really up to speed on what was been wrought in Freedom's name. In freedom's name America made sure that any possibility of secular democratic reform in the Middle East was shut off. Mount a coup against Mossadegh in the mid-1950s, as the CIA did and you end up with the Ayatollah Khomeini 25 years later. Mount a coup against Kassim in Iraq, as the CIA did, and you get the Agency's man, Saddam Hussein.

What about Afghanistan? In April of 1978 an indigenous populist coup overthrew the government of Mohammed Daoud, who had formed an alliance with the man the US had installed in Iran, Reza Pahlevi, aka the Shah. The new Afghan government was led by Noor Mohammed Taraki, and the Taraki administration embarked, albeit with a good deal of urban intellectual arrogance on land reform, hence an attack on the opium-growing feudal estates. Taraki went to the UN where he managed to raise loans for crop substitution for the poppy fields.

Taraki also tried to bear down on opium production in the border areas held by fundamentalists, since the latter were using opium revenues to finance attacks on Afghanistan's central government, which they regarded as an unwholesome incarnation of modernity that allowed women to go to school and outlawed arranged marriages and the bride price. Accounts began to appear in the western press along the lines of this from the *Washington Post* to the effect that the mujahedeen liked to "torture their victims by first cutting off their noses, ears and genitals, then removing one slice of skin after another."

At that time the Mujahedeen were not only getting money from the CIA but from Libya's Muammar Qaddafi who sent them $250,000. In the summer of 1979 the US State Department produced a memo making it clear how the US government saw the stakes, no matter how modern minded Taraki might be or how feudal the Muj. The memo was dispatched to US embassies around the world, including the one in Tehran.

A few months later the embassy was occupied by Iranian students and the occupants taken hostage. The diplomats and CIA residents shredded their secret files but the students laboriously reassembled them, and ultimately they were published in 68 paperback volumes. Among the documents was the following memo, written shortly after the Taraki coup:

The United States' larger interest would be served by the demise of the Taraki-Amin regime, despite whatever setbacks this might mean for future social and economic reforms in Afghanistan. The overthrow of the DRA [Democratic Republic of Afghanistan] would show the rest of the world, particularly the Third World, that the Soviets' view of the socialist course of history being inevitable is not accurate.

Taraki was killed by Afghan army officers in September 1979. Hafizullah Amin, educated in the US, took over and began meeting regularly with US embassy officials at a time when the US was arming Islamic rebels in Pakistan. Fearing a fundamentalist, US-backed regime in Afghanistan, the Soviets invaded in force in December 1979.

+++

Of course, sanctions weren't Albright's only method of enforcing the dictates of American power. She didn't hesitate to call in airstrikes, after sanctions had softened up a target population. Take Serbia.

As always, the initial predictions were optimistic and the rhetoric ebullient. The NATO bombing was to be of Serbian military units, and brief in duration. Milosevic would soon come to his senses. The committal of ground forces was out of the question. Public opinion was hesitant even on the bombing, and dead-set against any ground war.

The Serbian military in Kosovo was certainly behaving in a disgustingly brutal fashion. What army doesn't, when under attack by a rebel army, this one almost certainly supplied by NATO powers, in breach of the UN Security Council's embargo on arms imports into the territory of the former Yugoslavia.

Clinton and Albright wanted confrontation, which had been the US strategy with Serbia for close to a decade: the dismemberment of the former Yugoslavia, the heightening of ethnic tensions, economic siege and the supply of a client armed force: the KLA. They had no interest a peaceful diplomatic resolution. Otherwise they would have parleyed further with Milosevic on the Serb's final offer to countenance peacekeepers in Kosovo, if the latter were under the auspices of the UN, which seemed entirely reasonable.

Yes, Milosevic was a monstrous fellow, though a midget in thuggery when his deeds when compared to the records of those who orchestrated the bombing of his country.

So, the bombs and missiles started falling steadily. Soon there were even more refugees heading into Belgrade than out of Kosovo into Macedonia. Belgrade itself was going the way of Baghdad, on exactly the same US targeting strategy: bridges gone, power plants gone, sewage treatment plants destroyed. Missiles started on killing civilians as they did in Novi Sad. Shrapnel in the marketplace. High explosives on a hospital, and for good measure, NATO bombed Chinese sovereign territory in the form its embassy in Belgrade. On the latter blunder, NATO and the State Department flacks at first tried to argue that the embassy was inconveniently located amid "targets" in downtown Belgrade and it was all an understandable error. But the embassy's actual location was in a residential neighborhood and, as someone said, the "mistargeting" was like aiming for Newark and hitting Queens.

By May, Clinton and Albright's war had descended into straightforward terror bombing with cable news footage of explosions lighting of the night sky over Belgrade, in an eerie preview of Bush's "shock and awe" airstrikes on Baghdad four years later. "Lights out in Belgrade," as the deplorable opportunist John McCain shouted.

We were treated to pictures of a burned-out train in the Grdelica Gorge, where fifty-five Serbian passengers were blown to bits or burned alive and another sixteen wounded. There was the carnage amid the refugee columns.

But those snapshots alone don't paint the full-picture of what had been done to Serbia. The bombing put more than 500,000 Serbs out of work and plunged 2 million people in destitution. Roads were blown up. Railways gone. Bridges gone. Factories destroyed or damaged. More than 200 schools hit by bombs and missiles. Power plants bombed out. Phone lines cut. Refineries destroyed. In the first month of bombing alone, more than 1000 civilians killed and nearly 5000 maimed or seriously injured.

After the demolition of the Petrovardian Bridge, the water supplies to Novi Sad and Petrovardin were cut, leaving more than a million people without water.

The protocols of the Geneva Convention prohibit bombing not justified by clear military necessity. If there is any likelihood that the target has a civilian function, then bombing is prohibited. In other words, the vast majority of NATO targets in Serbia were criminally attacked. Both NATO supremo Wesley Clark and Madeleine Albright both publicly stated that they hoped the suffering of would prompt them to rise up against Milosevic. NATO, in other words, was waging war on Serbian civilians—and Kosovar civilians for that matter.

Before the war, many Serbs detested Milosevic and worked for his downfall. But as their country was being destroyed most rallied to the national flag. And who could blame them? For years, they had awaited invasion from the East. What a shock to be reduced to rubble by those liberals, like Clinton and Albright, who piously claimed the mantel of humanitarians.

+++

Well, the typists and messenger boys and back-office staffs throughout the Trade Center didn't know this history. There's a lot of other relevant history they probably didn't know but which those men on the attack planes did. How could those people in the Towers have known, when US political and journalistic culture is a conspiracy to perpetuate their ignorance?

Those people in the Towers were innocent portions of the price that Albright insisted, in just one of its applications, as being worth it. It would honor their memory to insist that in future our press offers a better accounting of how America's wars for Freedom are fought and what the actual price might include.

Serbia: the Neoliberals' War

STRANGE ARE THE ways of men! It feels like only yesterday that the *New York Times* was denouncing President Bill as a moral midget who deserved the harshest reprobation for fondling Monica Lewinsky's breasts. And now here's the *New York Times* doling out measured praise to the same president for blowing little children to pieces. In early March 1999, the *Times* ran pictures of those dead refugees on its cover, bombed by one of NATO's aviators. Editorial page editor Howell Raines staked out the *Times*' official view that "For now, NATO must sustain and intensify the bombing." What a weird guy Raines must be. Kiss Monica's tits and he goes crazy. Bomb peasants and he shouts for more.

Maybe some corner of Clinton's brain reckons that bombs on Serbia will extinguish Monica Lewinsky from popular memory. But what man of mature judgment and compassion would not prefer to be remembered by the Starr Report than by bomb craters and dead bodies?

Being a peacenik is definitely passé. Liberals are learning once again— did they ever truly forget?—that it's fun to be a warmonger and cheer each high explosive as it falls. After suffering indigestion towards the end of the Vietnam affair, they got the taste for war again in the mid-1990s with Bosnia. They became the "laptop bombardiers," a phrase coined by Simon Jenkins in the *Spectator* in 1995.

Back then, a week didn't go by without liberal columnist Anthony Lewis calling for the bombardment of Serbia. The Serbs became demons, monsters and Milošević the most demonic of all.

There were plenty of chances for agreement on a Bosnian settlement in the mid-1990s but the Americans always nixed them. There was the Lisbon Plan and then the Vance-Owen Plan, both not so different—after thousands of deaths—from the final Dayton Plan. But the trouble was that the US, amid the furious screams of the liberals, refused to admit the Serbs had legitimate grievances and rights.

In Britain in 1995. there was a coalition that spanned from Margaret Thatcher herself to the Labourite *New Statesman* in favor of bombing the Serbs. Ken Livingstone, the pinko firebrand of London, bellowed for bombs. So did Michael Ignatieff. In the US the laptop bombers crossed over from the *Wall Street Journal* editorial page, which likes to bomb anything (most of all Little Rock), to William Safire, to Anthony Lewis, to the Democratic Socialists of America.

The worst offender was the press, which carefully ignored detailed accounts of how Bosnia Muslims were manipulating Western opinion, most notoriously when they almost certainly lobbed a missile into a marketplace filled with their own people. When the Croats ethnically cleansed Krajina of hundreds of thousands of Serbs—the biggest such cleansing in the Balkans since World War II—with direction from US military and CIA officers, reporters and commentators mostly looked the other way or actually cheered.

Monitors for the European Union prepared a report on the Croat atrocities. Though it was confidential, Robert Fisk of the London *Independent* was able to get a copy:

> Evidence of atrocities, an average of six corpses a day, continues to emerge…the corpses—some fresh, some decomposed—are mainly of old men. Many have been shot in the back of the head or had throats slit, others have been mutilated…Serbian homes and lands continue to be looted. The crimes have been perpetrated by the HV (Croatian Army), the CR (Croatian Police) and CR civilians. There have been no observed attempts to stop it and the indications point to a scorched earth policy.

If American journalists had bothered to report this, then perhaps public opinion would have been prepared for the notion that there are no innocent political players in the Balkans. The better-informed the people are, the harder it is to demagogue them with the idea that the best way forward is—to get back to Raines and that editorial—"to sustain and intensify the bombing."

Well over 80 percent of the Democrats in the House cheered Clinton's bombs on Serbia, including that brass-lunged fraud from Vermont, Bernie Sanders. Neoliberals are discovering the joys of war. Consider Barbara Boxer, who marveled to the *Boston Globe*: "I never believed I'd go back and vote on air strikes!"

It's clear that the US and its NATO subordinates wanted a confrontation and they forced one. It's also clear that vocal and explicit charges by the Russians that the Kosovo Liberation Army (KLA) was supplied by the Germans and the CIA have merit. The KLA itself was roundly denounced—before the bombings—in the *Times* of London as a Maoist gang fueled by heroin trafficking. (This is standard operating procedure for a CIA operation, as any scrutiny of the recent histories of Afghanistan or Southeast Asia will attest.)

So Clinton's bombs began to fall and, predictably, the Serbian brutalities in Kosovo escalated and the tidal wave of refugees began. Everything went according to script. Clinton's bombs destroyed Serbian civilian infrastructure: power plants, sewage treatment, electricity, gas, oil supplies. Everything that was hit was hastily described by NATO spokesmen as "dual-purpose" (i.e., possibly also for Serb military use), unless it was obvious to all that only peasants, with no conceivable "dual purposes" had been blasted to bits, such as the column of Albanian refugees on tractors killed by Clinton's airstrikes.

Compared with Bill Clinton and his accomplices, Slobodan Milošević is a piker when it comes to war crimes. The protocols of the Geneva Convention of 1949 prohibit bombing that is not justified by clear military necessity. If there is any likelihood that the target has a civilian function, then bombing is prohibited. In other words, the vast majority of NATO's targets were criminally attacked. Clinton's bombers have attacked hospitals and health care centers, public housing, infrastructure vital to the well-being of civilians, refineries, warehouses, agricultural facilities, schools, roads and railways. NATO spokesmen have openly stated their hope that the suffering of Serbs will prompt them to rise up against Milošević. NATO, in other words, is waging war on Serbian civilians, and on Kosovar civilians too, for that matter.

Then there's the matter of Iraq. The sanctions imposed by the United States in 1991, and tightened by Clinton and his grim Secretary of State Madeleine Albright, have had a notoriously devastating effect on Iraq's civilian population, especially its children. In May of 1996, the World Health Organization reported that "the vast majority of the country's population has been on a semi-starvation diet for years." The hospitals have almost no medical supplies. The sewage treatment plants either barely function or don't work at all. Denis Halliday, who worked for the UN Development program in Iraq and who has issued many public denunciations of the sanctions, said that Clinton's sanctions are "in contradiction of human rights provisions in the UN's own charter."

In July 1991, Doug Broderick, a professional aid worker who was sent to Baghdad by the US charity Catholic Relief Services, predicted that as a consequence of sanctions at least 175,000 Iraqi children would certainly die because of the poor health conditions. He called it "a disaster in slow motion." It turned out that his prophesy was badly off. By the end of 1995 alone, the UN Food and Agriculture Organization said that after careful investigation it had determined that as many as 576,000 Iraqi children have died as a result of sanctions. Using figures from Iraq's Ministry of Health, the WHO estimated that 90,000 Iraqis were dying every year in Iraq's hospitals, over and above those who would have expired at the normal rate.

In sum, it is beyond argument that under the Clinton regime the US engineered a program of enforced scarcity that has caused the deaths of hundreds of thousands of Iraqi children. In 1996 Secretary Albright was asked on CBS's 60 Minutes by Leslie Stahl the following question: "We have heard that half a million children have died [in Iraq]. I mean, that's more children than died in Hiroshima. And you know, is the price worth it?" The repulsive Albright famously replied: "I think that this is a very hard choice, but the price—I think the price is worth it."

Back in the days of Nuremberg, Albright would certainly have been hanged if she had been on the losing side. And so would her commanding officer, Bill Clinton.

Hillary Rodham Clinton was an enthusiastic advocate for the cluster-bombs that now litter the Serbian and Kosovan landscapes, set to kill or cripple for the next half-century. But memories are short. Perhaps we will soon see Hillary clutching some Balkan infant, bent over the maimed tyke. Who will then recall that she bears some responsibility for that lost limb? "I urged Bill to bomb," Hillary confided to Lucinda Franks in *Talk*. "You cannot let this go on at the end of a century that has seen the major holocaust of our time. What do we have NATO for if not to defend our way of life?"

In fact it's scarcely surprising that Hillary should have urged the First Man to drop cluster bombs on the Serbs to "defend our way of life." The First Lady is a social engineer. She believes in therapeutic policing. And the duty of the state is to impose such measures. War is social engineering, fixitry via high explosives, social therapy via the nose-cones of cruise missiles.

It was the neoliberal's war, bombing a country from 30,000 feet for two-and-a-half months. It was the neoliberal's war waged by social democracy's best and brightest, intent on proving once again that wars can be fought with the most virtuous of intentions. The companion volume of Hillary's *It Takes a Village* turns out to be *It Takes an Air Force*.

There's not much of a Left any more. But there are plenty of therapeutic cops around and Hillary is their leader, the very quintessence of social worker neoliberalism. All it takes to usher in the New Jerusalem are counselors, community action programs and tougher gun laws, which is what Hillary called for after Columbine, not long after she gave Bill that bit of advice about bombing Serbian children.

As a tough therapeutic cop, Hillary does not shy away from the most abrupt expression of therapy: the death penalty, the last resort of social engineering. She comes from the liberal therapeutic tradition that sponsored the great sterilization boom earlier in the century, whose rampages in Vermont are only now coming to light. As in many other states, progressives with a devout belief in the ability of science to improve Vermont's gene pool lobbied successfully for passage of a sterilization law in 1931. The law targeted poor rural Vermonters, Abenaki Indians and others deemed "unfit" to procreate.

Hillary, never forget, is a Methodist, and that bleak creed of improvement is bedrock for her. She's a social cleanser. This is the cold steel that stiffens her spine and carries her forward, self-righteous amid the untidy mess of her contradictions.

Venezuela and the Imperial Script

YOU CAN SET your watch by it. The minute some halfway decent government in Latin America begins to reverse the order of things and give the have-nots a break from the grind of poverty and wretchedness, the usual suspects in El Norte rouse themselves from the slumber of indifference and start barking furiously about democratic norms. It happened in 1973 in Chile; we saw it again in Nicaragua in the 1980s; and the same show was on summer rerun in Venezuela, pending the August 15 2004 recall referendum of President Hugo Chávez.

Chávez was the best thing to happen to Venezuela's poor in a very long time. His government actually delivered on some of its promises; there were improved literacy rates and more students got school meals. Public spending quadrupled on education and tripled on healthcare, and infant mortality declined. The government promoted one of the most ambitious land-reform programs seen in Latin America in decades.

Most of this has was done under conditions of economic sabotage. Oil strikes, a coup attempt and capital flight resulted in about a 4 percent decline in GDP for the five years that Chávez was in office. But the economy grew at close to 12 percent soon after, and with world oil prices near $40 a barrel at the time, the government had extra billions that it put into social programs. So naturally the United States wanted him out, just as the rich in Venezuela did. Chávez was re-elected in 2000 for a six-year term. A US-backed coup against him was badly botched in 2002.

The imperial script called for a human rights organization to start braying about the irregularities of their intended victim. And yes, here's José Miguel Vivanco of Human Rights Watch. He was last seen helping to ease a $1.7 billion US aid package for Colombia's military apparatus. In 2004, he held a press conference in Caracas, and hollered about the brazen way Chávez was trying to expand membership of Venezuela's Supreme Court, the same way FDR did, and for the same reason: the Venezuelan court has been effectively packed the other way for decades with judicial flunkies of the rich. We don't recall Vivanco holding too many press conferences to protest that perennial iniquity.

The "international observers" recruited to save the rich traditionally include the Organization of American States and the Carter Center; in the case of the Venezuelan recall, they mustered dead on schedule. On behalf of the opposition, they exerted enormous pressure on the country's independent National Electoral Council during the signature-gathering and verification process. Eventually the head of the OAS mission had to be replaced by the OAS secretary general because of his unacceptable public statements.

The Carter Center's team was headed by Jennifer McCoy, whose book, *The Unraveling of Representative Democracy in Venezuela* (2004), leans heavily against the government. One of its contributors is José Antonio Gil Yepes, of the Datanálisis polling firm, most often cited for US media analysis. The *Los Angeles Times* quoted Gil on what to do: "And he can see only one way out of the political crisis surrounding President Hugo Chávez. 'He has to be killed,' he said, using his finger to stab the table in his office far above this capital's filthy streets. 'He has to be killed.'"

Media manipulation is an essential part of the script, and, right on cue, here comes Bill Clinton's erstwhile pollster, Stan Greenberg, still a leading Democratic Party strategist. Greenberg was under contract to RCTV, one of the right-wing media companies leading the Venezuelan opposition and recall effort. It's a pollster's dream job. Not only does he have enormous resources against an old-fashioned, politically unsophisticated poor people's movement, but his firm has something comrades back home can only fantasize about: control over the Venezuelan media. Imagine if the right wing controlled almost the entire media during Clinton's impeachment.

That was the situation in Venezuela. Just think what Greenberg's associate, Mark Feierstein—a veteran of similar NED efforts in ousting the Sandinistas in the 1990 elections—could have done with this kind of totalitarian media control. NED? That's the National Endowment for Democracy, praised not so long ago by John Kerry, who, like Bush, publicly craved the ouster of Chávez.

The NED was coming over the hill arm in arm with the CIA and CIA-backed institutions in the AFL-CIO, where John Sweeney's team has dismally failed to clean house. The NED has helped fund the opposition to Chávez to the tune of more than $1 million a year. Among the recipients are organizations whose leaders actually supported the April 2002 coup: they signed the decree that overthrew the elected president and vice president and abolished the country's democratic institutions, including the Constitution, Supreme Court and National Assembly. The coup was thwarted only because millions of Venezuelans rallied for Chávez.

Left out of the coup government, despite his support for it, was Carlos Ortega, head of the CTV (Central Labor Federation). The AFL's Solidarity Center, successor to the CIA-linked AIFLD, gets more than 80 percent of its funding from the NED and USAID and has funneled NED money to Ortega and his collaborators. The Solidarity Center has been up to its ears in opposition plotting, a reprise of the Allende years when the AFL helped destroy Chilean democracy. The AFL has denied any role, but Rob Collier, an excellent *San Francisco Chronicle* reporter, recently gave a detailed refutation of AFL apologetics in an exchange in the current New Labor Forum. "In Venezuela," he writes, "the AFL-CIO has blindly supported a reactionary union establishment as it tried repeatedly to overthrow President Hugo Chávez—and, in the process, wrecked the country's economy."

The CTV worked in lockstep with FEDECAMARAS, the nation's business association, to carry out the three "general strikes/lockouts" of 2001, 2002 and 2003. The CTV, Collier says, was directly involved in coup organizing, and its leader was scheduled to be part of the new junta.

The left here in the United States could have helped make a difference if it had got off its haunches and threw itself into the fray.

Julian Assange: Wanted by the Empire, Dead or Alive

JONAH GOLDBERG, CONTRIBUTOR to the *National Review,* asks in his syndicated column, "Why wasn't Assange garroted in his hotel room years ago?" Sarah Palin wants him hunted down and brought to justice, saying: "He is an anti-American operative with blood on his hands."

Assange can survive these theatrical blusters. A tougher question is how he will fare at the hands of the US government, which is hopping mad. Hillary Clinton howled that the WikiLeaks disclosures represented "an attack on the international community" that puts the lives of innocent people at risk, which is the kind of language she uses before ordering up a humanitarian drone strike.

The US attorney general, Eric Holder, has announced that the Justice Department and Pentagon are conducting "an active, ongoing criminal investigation" into the latest Assange-facilitated leak under Washington's Espionage Act.

Asked how the US could prosecute Assange, a non-US citizen, Holder said, "Let me be clear. This is not saber-rattling," and vowed "to swiftly close the gaps in current US legislation…"

In other words, the espionage statute is being rewritten to target Assange. In short order, President Obama—who as a candidate pledged "transparency" in government—will sign an order Okaying the seizing of Assange and his transport into US jurisdiction. Render first, fight the habeas corpus lawsuits later.

Interpol, the investigative arm of the International Criminal Court at The Hague, has issued a fugitive notice for Assange. He's wanted in Sweden for questioning in two alleged sexual assaults, one of which seems to boil down to a charge of unsafe sex and failure to phone his date the following day.

The prime accuser, Anna Ardin, has ties to US-financed anti-Castro and anti-communist groups and was herself deported from Cuba for subversive activities.

It's certainly not conspiracism to suspect that the CIA has been at work in fomenting these Swedish accusations.

The CIA has no doubt also pondered the possibility of pushing Assange off a bridge or through a high window (a mode of assassination favored by the Agency from the earliest days) and has sadly concluded that it's too late for this sort of executive solution.

The irony is that the thousands of diplomatic communications released by WikiLeaks contain no earth-shaking disclosures that undermine the security of the American empire. The bulk of them merely illustrate the well-known fact that in every capital city around the world, there is a building known as the US Embassy. It is inhabited by people whose prime function is to vanquish informed assessment of local conditions with the swaddling clothes of ignorance and prejudice instilled in them by what passes for higher education in the United States. America's governing elites are now more ignorant of what is really happening in the outside world than at any time in the nation's history.

The reports in the official press invite us to be stunned by the news that the King of Saudi Arabia wishes Iran was wiped off the map, that the US uses diplomats as spies, that Afghanistan is corrupt and also that corruption is not unknown in Russia! These press reports foster the illusion that US embassies are inhabited by intelligent observers zealously remitting useful information to their superiors in Washington, DC. To the contrary, diplomats—assuming they have the slightest capacity for intelligent observation and analysis — soon learn to advance their careers by sending reports to Foggy Bottom carefully tuned to the prejudices of the top State Department and White House brass, powerful members of Congress and major players throughout the bureaucracies. Remember that as the Soviet Union slid towards extinction, the US Embassy in Moscow was doggedly supplying quavering reports of a puissant Empire of Evil still meditating whether to invade Western Europe!

This is not to downplay the great importance of the latest batch of WikiLeaks. Millions in America and around the world have been given a quick introductory course in international relations and the true arts of diplomacy—not least by the third-rate, gossipy prose with which the diplomats rehearse the arch romans à clef they will write when they head into retirement.

Years ago, Rebecca West wrote in her novel, *The Thinking Reed,* of a British diplomat who, "even when he was peering down a woman's dress at her breasts managed to look as though he was thinking about India." In the updated version, given Hillary Clinton's orders to the State Department, the US envoy, pretending to admire the figure of the charming French cultural attaché, would actually be thinking how to steal her credit card information, obtain a retinal scan, her email passwords and her frequent flier number.

There are also genuine disclosures of great interest, some of them far from creditable to the establishment US press. Writing for *CounterPunch,* Gareth Porter identified a diplomatic cable from last February released by WikiLeaks which provides a detailed account of how Russian specialists on the Iranian ballistic missile program refuted the US suggestion that Iran has missiles that could target European capitals or that Iran intends to develop such a capability. Porter points out that: "Readers of the two leading US newspapers never learned those key facts about the document. The *New York Times* and *Washington Post* reported only that the United States believed Iran had acquired such missiles—supposedly called the BM-25—from North Korea. Neither newspaper reported the detailed Russian refutation of the US view on the issue or the lack of hard evidence for the BM-25 from the US side.

> The *Times*, which had obtained the diplomatic cables not from WikiLeaks but from the *Guardian,* according to a *Washington Post* story Monday, did not publish the text of the cable. The *Times* story said the newspaper had made the decision not to publish 'at the request of the Obama administration'. That meant that its readers could not compare the highly distorted account of the document in the *Times* story against the original document without searching the Wikileaks website.

Distaste among the "official" US press for WikiLeaks has been abundantly apparent from the first of the two big releases of documents pertaining to the wars in Iraq and Afghanistan. The *New York Times* managed the ungainly feat of publishing some of the leaks while simultaneously affecting to hold its nose, and also publishing a mean-spirited hatchet job on Assange by its reporter John F. Burns, a man with a well burnished record in touting the various agendas of the US government.

There have been cheers for Assange and WikiLeaks from such famed leakers as Daniel Ellsberg, but to turn on one's television is to eavesdrop on the sort of fury that Lord Haw-Haw—a.k.a. the Irishman William Joyce, who did Nazi propaganda broadcasts from Berlin—used to provoke in Britain in World War II. As Glenn Greenwald wrote in his column on the *Salon* site:

> On CNN, Wolf Blitzer was beside himself with rage over the fact that the US government had failed to keep all these things secret from him… Then—like the Good Journalist he is—Blitzer demanded assurances that the Government has taken the necessary steps to prevent him, the media generally and the citizenry from finding out any more secrets: 'Do we know yet if they've [done] that fix? In other words, somebody right now who has top secret or secret security clearance can no longer download information onto a CD or a thumb drive? Has that been fixed already?' The central concern of Blitzer—one of our nation's most honored 'journalists'—is making sure that nobody learns what the US Government is up to.

These latest WikiLeaks files contain some 261,000,000 words—about 3,000 books. They display the entrails of the American Empire. As Israel Shamir wrote in *CounterPunch* in November, 2010: "The files show US political infiltration of nearly every country, even supposedly neutral states such as Sweden and Switzerland. US embassies keep a close watch on their hosts. They have penetrated the media, the arms business, oil, intelligence, and they lobby to put US companies at the head of the line."

Will this vivid record of imperial outreach in the early 21st century soon be forgotten? Not if some competent writer offers a readable and politically vivacious redaction. But a warning: in November 1979 Iranian students seized an entire archive of the State Department, the CIA and the Defense Intelligence Agency (DIA) at the American embassy in Tehran. Many papers that were shredded were laboriously reassembled.

These secrets concerned far more than Iran. The Tehran embassy, which served as a regional base for the CIA, held records involving secret operations in many countries, notably Israel, the Soviet Union, Turkey, Pakistan, Saudi Arabia, Kuwait, Iraq and Afghanistan.

Beginning in 1982, the Iranians published some 60 volumes of these CIA reports and other US government documents from the Tehran archive, collectively entitled *Documents from the US Espionage Den*. As Edward Jay Epstein, a historian of US intelligence agencies, wrote years ago, "Without a doubt, these captured records represent the most extensive loss of secret data that any superpower has suffered since the end of the Second World War."

In fact the Tehran archive truly was a devastating blow to US national security. It contained vivid portraits of intelligence operations and techniques, the complicity of US journalists with US government agencies, the intricacies of oil diplomacy. The volumes are in some university libraries here. Are they read? Only by a handful of specialists. The inconvenient truths were swiftly buried—and perhaps the WikiLeaks files will also soon fade from memory, to join the inspiring historical archive of intelligence coups of the left.

We should honor here the "Spies for Peace"—the group of direct-action British anarchists and kindred radicals associated with the Campaign for Nuclear Disarmament and Bertrand Russell's Committee of 100. In 1963, they broke into a secret government bunker, Regional Seat of Government Number 6 (RSG-6) at Warren Row, near Reading, where they photographed and copied documents which showed secret government preparations for rule after a nuclear war. They distributed a pamphlet along with copies of relevant documents to the press, stigmatizing the "small group of people who have accepted thermonuclear war as a probability, and are consciously and carefully planning for it. ... They are quietly waiting for the day the bomb drops, for that will be the day they take over." There was a big uproar, and then the Conservative government of the day issued a D-notice forbidding any further coverage in the press. The cops and intelligence services hunted long and hard for the Spies for Peace, and caught nary a one.

And Assange? Hopefully he will have a long reprieve from premature burial. Ecuador had offered him sanctuary until the US Embassy in Quito gave the president a swift command and the invitation was rescinded. Switzerland? Istanbul? Hmmm... As noted above, he should, at the least, view with caution women eagerly inviting his embraces and he should certainly stay away from overpasses, bridges, and open windows.

In 1953 the CIA distributed to its agents and operatives a killer's training manual (made public in 1997) full of hands-on advice:

"The most efficient accident, in simple assassination, is a fall of 75 feet or more onto a hard surface. Elevator shafts, stair wells, unscreened windows and bridges will serve... The act may be executed by sudden, vigorous [excised] of the ankles, tipping the subject over the edge. If the assassin immediately sets up an outcry, playing the 'horrified witness', no alibi or surreptitious withdrawal is necessary."

The Libyan Enterprise: Hillary's Imperial Massacre

Good my lord, she came from Libya.
— The Winter's Tale, William Shakespeare.

THE WAR ON Libya must surely rank as one of the stupidest martial enterprises since Napoleon took it into his head to invade Russia in 1812.

Let's start with the fierce hand-to-hand combat between members of the coalition (Britain, France and the US), arguing about the basic aims of the killing operation. How does "take all necessary measures" square with the ban on any "foreign occupation force of any form on any part of Libyan territory." Could the coalition simply kill Gaddafi and recognize a provisional government in Benghazi? Who exactly are the revolutionaries and national liberators in eastern Libya?

In the United States, this debacle was instigated by liberal interventionists: notably three women, starting with Samantha Power, who runs the Office of Multilateral Affairs and Human Rights in Obama's National Security Council. She's an Irish American, 41 years old, who made her name back in the Bush years with her book *A Problem from Hell*, a study of the U.S. foreign-policy response to genocide and the failure of the Clinton administration to react forcefully to the Rwandan massacres. She had to resign from her advisory position on the Obama campaign in April of 2008, after calling Hillary Clinton a "monster" in an interview with the *Scotsman*, but was restored to good grace after Obama's election, and the new monster in her sights became Gaddafi.

America's UN ambassador is Susan Rice, the first African American woman to be named to that post. She's long been an ardent interventionist. In 1996, as part of the Clinton administration, she supported the multinational force that invaded Zaire from Rwanda in 1996 and overthrew dictator Mobutu Sese Seko, saying privately that "Anything's better than Mobutu." But on February 23 she came under fierce attack in the *Huffington Post* at the hands of Richard Grenell, who'd served on the US delegation to the UN in the Bush years. Grenell dwelt harshly on instances where in his judgment, Rice and her ultimate boss Obama were dropping the ball and displaying lack of leadership amid the tumults engulfing the middle east, and specifically in failing to support the uprising against Gaddafi.

Both Rice and Clinton took Grenell's salvo to heart. Prodded by the fiery Power they abruptly stiffened their postures. Clinton lobbed her furious salvoes at Gaddafi, "the crazy colonel". For Clinton it was a precise re-run of her efforts to portray Obama as a peace wimp back in 2008, liable to snooze all too peacefully when the red phone rang at 3am.

For his part, Obama wasn't keen on intervention, seeing it as a costly swamp, yet another war, one also opposed by his Defense Secretary, Robert Gates, as well as the Joint Chiefs of Staff. But the liberal interventionists and the neo-cons were in full cry and Obama, perennially fearful of being outflanked, succumbed and hastened to one of the least convincing statements of war aims in the nation's history. He earned a threat of impeachment from leftist congressman Dennis Kucinich for arrogating war-making powers constitutionally reserved for the US Congress, though it has to be said that protest from the left proved pretty feeble. As always, many on the left yearn for an intervention they can finally support and many of them murmured ecstatically, "This is the one." Of course, the sensible position simply states that nothing good ever came out of a Western intervention by the major powers, whether humanitarian in proclaimed purpose or not.

So much for the instigators of the mad intervention in the US. In France the intellectual author was the salon dandy and "new philosopher", Bernard-Henri Lévy, familiarly known to his admirers and detractors alike as BHL. As described by Larry Portis in *CounterPunch* magazine, BHL arrived in Benghazi on March 3, 2011.

> Two days later BHL was interviewed on various television networks. He appeared before the camera in his habitual uniform—immaculate white shirt with upturned collar, black suit coat, and disheveled hair.
> His message was urgent but reassuring. "No," he said, Gaddafi is not capable of launching an offensive against the opposition. He does not have the means to do so. However, he does have planes. This is the real danger." BHL called for the scrambling of radio communications, the destruction of landing strips in all regions of Libya, and the

bombardment of Gaddafi's personal bunker. In brief, this would be a humanitarian intervention, the modalities of which he did not specify.
Next step, as BHL explained: "I called him [Sarkozy] from Benghazi. And when I returned, I went to the Elysée Palace to see him and tell him that the people on the National Transition Council are good guys." Indeed, on March 6, BHL returned to France and met with Sarkozy. Four days later, on March 10, he saw Sarkozy again, this time with three Libyans whom he had encouraged to visit France, along with Sarkozy's top advisors. On March 11, Sarkozy declared the Libyan National Transition Council the only legitimate representative of the Libyan people. Back in Benghazi, people screamed in relief and cheered Sarkozy's name, popularity at last for Sarko, whose approval ratings in France have been hovering around the 20 per cent mark.

So much for the circumstances in which the intervention was conceived. It had nothing to do with oil; everything to do with ego and political self-promotion. But to whom exactly did the interveners lend imperial succor? There was great vagueness here, beyond enthusiastic references to the romantic revolutionaries of Benghazi, and much ridicule for Gaddafi's identification of his opponents in eastern Libya as Al Qaida.

In fact two documents strongly backed Gaddafi on this issue. The first was a secret cable to the State Department from the US embassy in Tripoli in 2008, part of the WikiLeaks trove, entitled "Extremism in Eastern Libya," which revealed that this area was rife with anti-American, pro-jihad sentiment.

According to the cable, the most troubling aspect

> ... is the pride that many eastern Libyans, particularly those in and around Darnah, appear to take in the role their native sons have played in the insurgency in Iraq ... [and the] ability of radical imams to propagate messages urging support for and participation in jihad.

The second document, or rather set of documents, are the so-called Sinjar Records, captured Al-Qaeda files that fell into American hands in 2007. They were duly analyzed by the Combating Terrorism Center at the U.S. Military Academy at West Point. Al-Qaeda is a bureaucratic outfit and the Records contain precise details on personnel, including those who came to Iraq to fight and when called for, to commit suicide, fighting American and Coalition forces.

The West Point analysts' statistical study of the al-Qaeda personnel records concludes that one country provided "far more" foreign fighters in per capita terms than any other: namely, Libya. The Records show that the "vast majority of Libyan fighters that included their hometown in the Sinjar Records resided in the country's Northeast." Benghazi provided many volunteers. So did Darnah, about 200 kms east of Benghazi, where an Islamic emirate was declared when the rebellion against Gaddafi started. *New York Times* reporter Anthony Shadid even spoke with Abdul-Hakim al-Hasadi who promulgated the Islamic emirate. Al-Hasadi "praises Osama bin Laden's 'good points,'" Shadid reported, though he prudently denounced the 9/11 attacks on the United States. Other sources have said that this keen admirer of Osama would prove most influential in the formation of any provisional government.

The West Point study of the Iraqi Sinjar Records calculates that of the 440 foreign al-Qaeda recruits whose hometowns are known, 21 came from Benghazi, thereby making it the fourth most common hometown listed in the records. Fifty-three of the al-Qaeda recruits came from Darnah, the highest total of any of the hometowns listed in the records. The second highest number, 51, came from Riyadh, Saudi Arabia. Darnah (80,000) has less than 2 per cent the population of Riyadh. Darnah contributed "far and away the largest per capita number of fighters."

As former CIA operations officer Brian Fairchild observed: "Amid the apparent absence of any plan for post-Gaddafi governance, an ignorance of Libya's tribal nature and our poor record of dealing with tribes, American government documents conclusively establish that the epicenter of the revolt is rife with anti-American and pro-jihad sentiment, and with al-Qaeda's explicit support for the revolt, it is appropriate to ask our policymakers how American military intervention in support of this revolt in any way serves vital U.S. strategic interests." (See Diana Johnstone's *Queen of Chaos* for a detailed account of the Libyan operation.)

+++

By October of that year, Muammar Gaddafi was dead and stuffed in a meat locker. Denied post mortem imagery of Osama bin Laden and Anwar al-Awlaki, the world was presented with photographs of Gaddafi, dispatched with a bullet to the head after being wounded by NATO's ground troops outside Sirte.

Did the terminal command, Finish Him Off, come via cell phone from the US State Department, whose Secretary, Hillary Clinton, had earlier called for his death, or by dint of local initiative, under winking eyes in Washington?

In any event, since Gaddafi was a prisoner at the time of his execution, it was a war crime and we trust that in the years of her retirement, Mrs. Clinton will be detained amid some foreign vacation and handed a subpoena.

We suppose the first triumphalist imperial post-mortem photo of such an execution in our lifetimes is that of Che Guevara, killed on the CIA's orders at La Higuera in Bolivia on October 9, 1967. Perhaps Che's finest hour came with his leadership of the Cuban anti-imperial forces deployed in Africa, defeating South African and white mercenary forces in one of the greatest acts of revolutionary solidarity the world has ever seen.

Gaddafi, even in his latter day accomodationist phase, was always a bitter affront to Empire, a "devil" figure in a tradition stretching back to the Mahdi, whose men killed General Gordon in the Sudan in 1885. We remember fondly the leftists and Irish Republicans who trekked to Tripoli in the 1960s to appeal to Gaddafi for funds for their causes, some of them returning amply supplied with money and detailed counsel.

Dollar for dollar, we doubt Gaddafi had a rival in any assessment of the amount of oil revenues in his domain actually distributed for benign social purposes. Derision is heaped on his Green Book, but in intention it can surely stand favorable comparison with kindred Western texts. Anyone labeled by Ronald Reagan as "This mad dog of the Middle East" has an honored place in our personal pantheon.

Camus in the Time of Drones

LUCIEN RISES FROM bed in the early morning. He dresses quietly, careful not to awaken his wife and infant son. He walks briskly across the city of Algiers in the pre-dawn light to a square that is already thick with people, their gaze fixed on a wooden platform and rising from it the stark outline of a guillotine.

The man has come to watch the execution of a notorious killer of an Algerian farm family. The man is curious and wants to see justice done. The prisoner is brought to the scaffold, blindfolded, then trussed to a plank and slid beneath the grim killing machine. The blade drops, severing the head and unleashing a surge of blood from the quivering torso.

The man rushes back across town. He runs all the way to his house, brushes past his wife to the bathroom. He locks the door and vomits, again and again. He will not go to work this day or the next. Instead he lies in bed, tormented by what he has witnessed. He tells his wife what he has seen and refuses to speak of it again for the remainder of his short life.

The man is Lucien Camus, father of Albert. The story was told to Albert by his mother years later and it haunted the writer all his life. The gruesome scene appears in his novels *The Stranger* and *The First Man* and became the centerpiece of his masterful essay "Reflections on the Guillotine," perhaps the most forceful denunciation of the death penalty ever written.

Camus' essay on the barbarity of the death penalty was written in 1956, against the backdrop of the executions of hundreds of dissidents during the Soviet crackdown in Hungary, as well as the execution of Algerian revolutionaries condemned to death by French tribunals. He notes that by 1940 all executions in France and England were shielded from the public. If capital punishment was meant to deter crime, why hold the killings in secret? Why not make them a public spectacle?

Because, Camus argues, deterrence isn't the purpose of state murder. The real objective is vengeance through the exercise of extreme state power. "Let us recognize it for what it is essentially: a revenge. A punishment that penalizes without forestalling is indeed called revenge. It is a quasi-arithmetical replay made by society to whoever breaks its primordial law."

Public executions became a threat to the state, because the dreadful act tends to provoke revulsion in ordinary citizens, like Camus' father, who see it clearly for what it is: a new form of murder "no less repulsive than the crime." A form of murder that is performed, in theory, in the name of the citizens and for which they are complicit.

This kind of state-sanctioned killing, Camus reasoned, leads only to more murder, a vast panorama of murder. "Without the death penalty," Camus writes, "Europe would not be infected by the corpses accumulated for the last twenty years on its soil."

So what would Albert Camus, the great moralist of the 20th century, think about the latest innovation in administrative murder, Obama's drone program, a kind of remote-control gallows, where the killers never see their victims, never hear their screams, smell their burning bodies, touch their mutilated flesh?

The conscience of the killer has been sterilized, the drone operator, fully alienated from the act he is committing, can walk out the door after his shift is over and calmly order an IPA at the local microbrew or play a round of golf under the desert sky. He is left with no blood on his hands, no savagery weighing on his conscience, no degrading images to stalk his dreams.

Drone strikes, Camus would argue, are not just meant to kill. They are programmed to terrorize. In this regard, whether the missile strikes its intended target or incinerates a goat-herder and his flock is incidental. In fact, the occasional killing of civilians may well be a desired outcome since collateral deaths intensify the fear. This is punishment by example, not for any particular crime or impending threat, but merely because of who you are, where you live, what you might believe. These new circuitries of death are meant to humiliate, subdue and dehumanize.

As more and more evidence of Obama's secret killing operations in Pakistan and Yemen began to leak out, public squeamishness over the deaths, especially of civilians and targeted American citizens, began to mount. Uncomfortable questions were raised, even on the political right. To salvage his program, Obama announced that new guidelines would soon be imposed on his high-tech assassinations.

But Camus would be the first to warn us that such regulations should be viewed with grave suspicion, since they will likely only serve to legitimize and normalize state murder, by making lawless killing legal.

Camus stresses that in the long run such killing regimes can only sustain themselves if they are indulged by a nation's elites: its press, its intellectuals, its political movements. And here we must confront the torpid moral character of the American left, which has been flaccid in the face of the drone killings, insensate to the mangled bodies, suffering and fragmented lives on the far side of the world.

Our task is to shatter this indifference, to condemn and resist the killing done in our names, to reassert the primacy of individual life over state authority. Otherwise, we become accomplices of the long-distance executioners.

Jeffrey St. Clair

The Origins of America's Vicious War on Its Own Kids

OURS IS NOT the first era in which adults have persecuted the young and criminalized them. But in this country it's not been done before with such methodical zeal, ever since that salesman of the virtues, Bill Bennett, co-chaired the Council on Crime in America and issued a 1996 report titled *The State of Violent Crime in America* containing these ominous words and utterly inaccurate predictions: "America is a ticking violent crime bomb. Rates of violent juvenile crime and weapons offenses have been increasing dramatically and by the year 2000 could spiral out of control."

These were the years when headline-seeking criminologists like John DiIulio of Princeton and Northeastern's James Alan Fox painted lurid scenarios of "superpredators", meaning urban youth of color, swelling Generation Y by as much as 24 per cent. In 1997, Congressmen William McCollum of Florida stated during a floor debate that today's youths are "... the most dangerous criminals on the face of the Earth."

A slice of the crude, unlovely obvious: It's not the criminalization of youth, it's the criminalization of youth from certain neighborhoods, of certain ethnic origins. Did you know that what neighborhood you live in is now an element of probable cause? Yes, indeed, if you live in a "high crime" neighborhood, they can search you with less evidence you've done anything wrong. Hence, people in bad (read: poor) neighborhoods have less of a 4th Amendment than the rest of us. Three-quarters of the youth who are incarcerated are black or Hispanic kids of color. A black teenager is 6 times more likely to be incarcerated for a first-time violent offense than a white kid. A black teenager is 48 times (yes, you read that right, 48) more likely to do time for a drug offense than a white kid.

"The law has taken many terrible turns in the last few years, and the pit of the law is the juvenile justice system." This is Catherine Campbell, a civil rights attorney in Fresno. "It stinks. It's rotten to the core. It should be wiped away and started over. A lot of it begins with putting the kids of poor parents into foster care. That's how authorities inspire hatred, anger, frustration and feelings of worthlessness. It's the 'I don't give a fuck zone', and with only a few months of that, most kids are pretty much destroyed. They are 'criminalized' when their behavior crosses over the almost unavoidable line of criminal behavior."

We've made criminal behavior that wasn't criminal ten years ago. Statutory rape is the latest craze—they had a little trouble figuring out what was wrong with an 18-year-old having sex with a 16-year-old, but then they decided it was too many teenage pregnancies, (Bill and Hillary Clinton's prime obsession) and bammo, they were out looking for boys to bring in for statutory rape.

All kids commit crimes. Most adults commit crimes. We smoke joints, we have stolen if we don't steal now, we walked the streets in groups (now called gangs, and just being in one is illegal), we lie on our tax returns, we commit crimes all the time. The point is not that youth is criminalized, but that only certain kids are criminalized, and these are kids from "bad" neighborhoods.

Campbell again:

> The laws have changed, and they are so awful. Take civil commitment. Used to be the wisdom was you can't predict criminal behavior. Now the wisdom is that a criminal is someone who committed a crime. He's a criminal now, and will be forever. Nowhere is this theory more controlling than as to sex crimes. I had a client who at age 15 had sex with a 7-year-old. Both boys. In the bathroom, at church. He was charged and convicted of lewd and lascivious behavior. He went to California Youth Authority. There he was diagnosed by diabolical, incompetent shrinks as a sexual psychopath, and they kept him in two years longer than his sentence based on our state's new civil commitment laws that allow that to happen. He finally got out when some shrink (he won't last) said the kid's gay, let him go. They extended this kid's term every time he had sex (he lived with other gay boys) or masturbated! Can you imagine? Six more months in the slammer for jacking off?
>
> They get them, and then if they're the right kind, if they're poor, of color, angry, and unsuccessful in school, they keep them. Through all means available, they keep them in the system. They search them, harass them, follow them, watch who they talk with, what they wear. The most minor infraction, they are back in jail, then they are sent away, or placed on probation, and then they are watched more.

+++

Do people realize how many "crimes" are committed in jails, juvenile facilities and prisons. A kid can go to California Youth Authority (CYA) for a burglary when he's 16, and 4 years later he gets his third strike and he's never even seen the streets. His entire adult life will be prison. There are no middle-class gangs, there are only lower-class gangs. And it's a crime to be in a gang, and it's more time in jail or prison if a crime is gang-related. You can't really survive on the streets in those bad neighborhoods without being in a gang (if you're male) so you're criminal just because you're alive and leave the house. Walk out the door, commit a crime. And of course the age at which you are considered an adult for jail and prison eligibility gets lower every year. That's part of that ugly companion to California's Three-Strikes, Proposition 21, the anti-youth crime bill.

The drug laws are of course key to criminalizing youth. The trick is to take something almost everybody does, and then make it a crime. That way you can pick and choose who you want to mess with. Kids from all backgrounds use drugs, but again only kids from bad neighborhoods get criminalized for it. It gets a kid into the system, and once in he won't get out unless he's exempt, and an exemption is given to the kids with aggressive, middle-class parents, who have good or passable grades.

The hysteria and lies about youthful criminals go virtually unchallenged. There are some worthy souls, like UC Irvine's Mike Males who published the excellent *Scapegoat Generation: America's War on Adolescents*, back in 1996 and who has run a one-man truth squad on the actual stats ever since.

"Now," Males writes, "the latest panacea for society seems to be restricting youths' access to media and entertainment. One leading authority, former West Point psychologist David Grossman, argues that violent video games, movies and music make today's teens more violent, even murderous. Certainly violent games (or Beatles music or even the Bible) might incite a disturbed individual, but Grossman and other media critics claim they're warping an entire generation. Yet, the evidence cited is peculiar: Grossman blames violent media for the increase in aggravated assaults over the last 35 years, but he fails to note that assault rates peaked in 1992 and have since fallen sharply.

"A curfew can create vacant neighborhoods, which offer better opportunities for crime, while occupying police with removing law-abiding teenagers from public. In Vernon, Conn., among 400 curfew citations, police reported virtually no criminal activity, intoxication or other misbehavior by youths they cited and sent home."

+++

Back in 1997 California's Office of Traffic Safety, warned that an "alarming population trend"—meaning more teenagers—would increase highway deaths and drunk-driving accidents. But teenage traffic deaths had been falling for two decades.

In fact, violent juvenile crime rates have plunged during the 1990s. Today's teenagers, Males points out "are not more criminally prone than past generations. Youth felony arrest rates declined by 40% in the last 20 years while felony arrest rates for over age 30 adults increased. In addition, California's general population aged by three years from 1978 to 1998, but its violent and felony arrestee population aged by six years. In 1978, the average violent crime arrestee was 21.5 while in 1998 the average violent crime arrestee was 27.7. Juveniles comprised 30% of California's felony arrestees in 1978 but comprised less than 15% in 1998."

Elsewhere Males notes that "older white adults display drug overdose death rates five to seven times higher than younger people of color, including for the major illicit drugs such as heroin, cocaine (including crack), methamphetamine, and hallucinogens. However, young people of color are three times more likely to be arrested for drugs and sent to prison for drug offenses than older white adults. The result is that at all ages, a Californian of color is four to five times more likely to be imprisoned for a drug offense than a white compared to their rates of drug abuse. In fact, young people of color display the largest declines and lowest rates of drug abuse of any group."

+++

You've heard about the race to the bottom. Well, how about the race to the cradle? Ohio legislators recently passed a bill authorizing the jailing of children as young as 10 years old. California's legislators had better look to their laurels.

The Bi-Partisan Origins of the War on Drugs

IN 1930 A new department of the federal government, the Bureau of Narcotics and Dangerous Drugs, was created under the leadership of Harry Anslinger to carry out the war against drug users. Anslinger, an avowed racist, was an adroit publicist and became the prime shaper of American attitudes about drug addiction, hammering home his view that this was not a treatable addiction but a deviant urge that could only be suppressed by harsh criminal sanctions.

Anslinger's first major campaign was to criminalize the drug commonly known at the time as hemp. But Anslinger renamed it "marijuana" to associate it with Mexican laborers who, like the Chinese before them, were unwelcome competitors for scarce jobs in the Depression. Anslinger claimed that marijuana "can arouse in blacks and Hispanics a state of menacing fury or homicidal attack. During this period, addicts have perpetrated some of the most bizarre and fantastic offenses and sex crimes know to police annals."

Anslinger linked marijuana with jazz and persecuted many black musicians, including Thelonious Monk, Dizzy Gillespie and Duke Ellington. Louis Armstrong was also arrested on drug charges, and Anslinger made sure his name was smeared in the press. In Congress, the drug czar testified that "coloreds with big lips lure white women with jazz and marijuana".

By the 1950s, amid the full blast of the Cold War, Anslinger was working with the CIA to charge that the new-born People's Republic of China was attempting to undermine America by selling opium to US crime syndicates. (This took a great deal of chutzpah on the part of the CIA, whose planes were then flying opium from Chiang Kai-Shek's bases in Burma to Thailand and the Philippines for processing and export to the US.) Anslinger convinced the US Senate to approve a resolution stating that "subversion through drug addiction is an established aim of Communist China".

In 1951, Anslinger teamed with Democrat Hale Boggs to marshal through Congress the first minimum mandatory sentences for drug possession: two years for the first conviction for possession of a Schedule 1 drug (marijuana, cocaine), five to ten years for a second offense, and ten to twenty for a third conviction. In 1956 Anslinger once again enlisted the aid of Boggs to pass a law calling for the death penalty to be imposed on anyone selling heroin to a minor, the first linking of drugs with Death Row.

This was Anslinger's last hurrah. Along with John Kennedy's New Frontier cantered sociologists attacking Anslinger's punitive philosophy. The tempo of the times changed, and federal money began to target treatment and prevention as much as enforcement and prison. But the interim didn't last long. With the waning of the war in Southeast Asia millions of addicted GIs came home to be ambushed by Richard Nixon's War on Drugs program. Nixon resurrected Anslinger's techniques of threat inflation, declaring in Los Angeles that "as I look over the problems of this country I see that one stands out particularly: the problems of narcotics."

Nixon pledged to launch a war on drugs, to return to the punitive approach and not let any quaint notions of civil liberties and constitutional rights stand in the way. After a Nixon briefing in 1969, his top aide, H.R. Haldeman noted in his diary: "Nixon emphasized that you have to face the fact that the whole problem is really the blacks. The key is to devise a system that recognizes this while not appearing to." And the Democratic congress played along.

But for all of his bluster, Nixon was a mere prelude to the full fury of the Reagan-Bush-Clinton years, when the War on Drugs became explicitly a war on blacks. The first move of the Reagan administration was to expand the drug forfeiture laws, first passed in the Carter administration. In 1981 Reagan's drug policy advisors outlined a plan they thought would be little more than a good PR sound bite, a public display of the required toughness. They proposed allowing the Justice Department to seize real property and so-called "substitute property"—that is, legally acquired assets equal in value to illegal monetary gains. They also proposed that the federal government be permitted to seize attorney's fees that they suspected might have been paid for through drug proceeds. The Reagan plan was to permit forfeitures on the basis of a "probable cause showing" before a federal judge. This meant that seizures could be made against people neither charged nor convicted, but only suspected, of drug offenses.

Contrary to the administration's expectations, this plan sailed through Congress, eagerly supported by two Democratic Party liberals, Senators Hubert Humphrey and Joe Biden, the latter being the artificer in the Carter era of a revision of the RICO statutes, a huge extension of the federal conspiracy laws. Over the next few years the press would occasionally report on some exceptionally bizarre application of the new forfeiture provisions, such as the confiscation of a $25 million yacht in a drug bust that netted only a handful of marijuana stems and seeds. But typically, the press ignored the essential pattern of humdrum seizures, which more often focused on such ordinary assets as houses and cars. For example, in Orange County, California, fifty-seven cars were seized in drug-related cases in 1989 alone. "Even if only a small amount of drugs is found inside," an Orange County narcotics detective explained, "the law permits seized vehicles to be sold by law enforcement agencies to finance anti-drug law enforcement programs."

In fact, the forfeiture program became a tremendous revenue stream for the police. From 1982 to 1991, the US Department of Justice seized more than $2.5 billion in assets. The feds confiscated $500 million in property in 1991 alone, and 80 percent of these seizures came from people who were never charged with a crime.

On June 17, 1986 University of Maryland basketball star Len Bias died, reportedly from an overdose of cocaine. As Dan Baum put it in his excellent book *Smoke and Mirrors: the War on Drugs and the Politics of Failure*, "In life, Len Bias was a terrific basketball player. In death he became the Archduke Ferdinand of the Total War on Drugs." It was falsely reported that Bias had smoked crack cocaine the night before his death. (He had, in fact, sniffed powder cocaine and, according to the coroner, there was no clear link between this usage and the failure of his heart.)

Bias had just signed to play with the Boston Celtics and amid Boston's rage and grief Speaker of the House Tip O'Neill, a representative from Massachusetts, rushed into action. In early July of that year he convened a special meeting of the Democratic Party leadership on the Hill: "Write me up some goddamn legislation," O'Neill ordered. "All anybody in Boston is talking about is Len Bias. They want blood. If we move fast enough we can get out in front of the White House."

The Reagan White House was moving fast itself. Among other things the Drug Enforcement Agency had been instructed to allow ABC News to accompany it on raids against crack houses. "Crack is the hottest combat-reporting story to come along since the end of the Vietnam War", the head of the New York office of the DEA exulted.

All this fed the congressional frenzy to write tougher laws. House Majority leader Jim Wright, the Texas Democrat, called drug abuse "a menace draining away our economy of some $230 billion this year, slowly rotting away the fabric of our society and seducing and killing our young". Not to be outdone, South Carolina Republican Thomas Arnett proclaimed that "drugs are a threat worse than nuclear warfare or any chemical warfare waged on any battlefield".

So the 1986 Anti-Drug Abuse Act was duly passed. It boasted 29 new minimum mandatory sentences. Up until that time in the entire history of the Republic there had been only 56 minimum mandatory sentences. The new law enacted a death penalty provision for drug "king pins" and prohibited parole for even minor possession offenses. But the chief target of the bill was crack cocaine. Congress established a 100-to-1 sentencing ratio between the possession of crack and powder cocaine. Under this provision, possession of five grams of crack carries a minimum sentence five years in federal prison. The same mandatory minimum is not reached for any amount of powder cocaine under 500 grams. John Kerry voted for the measure.

The sentencing disparity in the 1986 law was based on faulty testimony that crack was fifty times as addictive as powder cocaine. Congress then doubled this ratio as a so-called "violence penalty". Yet there is no inherent difference between the drugs, as Clinton drug czar Barry McCaffrey was forced to admit. The federal Sentencing Commission, established by Congress to review sentencing guidelines, found that so-called "crack violence" was largely attributable to the drug trade itself and has more to do with the setting in which crack is sold than the drug itself: crack is sold on the street, while powder cocaine is often vended by house calls.

As Nixon and H.R. Haldeman would have approvingly noted, Tip O'Neill's new drug law was aimed squared at blacks, reminiscent of the early targeting of Chinese smoking opium rather than post-bellum ladies sipping their laudanum-laced tonics.

In 1995 the US Sentencing Commission reviewed eight years of application of this provision and found it to be undeniably racist in practice: 84 percent of those arrested for crack possession where black, while only 10 percent were white and 5 percent Hispanic. The disparity for trafficking arrests was even wider: 88 percent blacks, 7 percent Hispanics and 4 percent whites. By comparison, defendants arrested for powder cocaine possession were 58 percent white, 26 percent black and 15 percent Hispanic.

In Los Angeles all twenty-four federal defendants in crack cases in 1991 were black. The Sentencing Commission recommended to Congress that the ratio should be one-to-one between sentences for offenses involving crack and powder cocaine, arguing that federal law allows for other factors to be considered by judges in lengthening sentences (such as whether guns or violence was associated with the offense). But for the first time in its history the Congress rejected the recommendations of the Sentencing Commission and retained the 100-to-1 ratio. Clinton likewise declined the advise of his drug czar and his attorney general and signed the bill.

One need only look at the racial make-up of federal prisons to appreciate the consequences of the 1986 drug law. In 1983 the total number of prisoners in federal, state and local prisons and jails was 600,800. Of those, 57,975 (8.8 percent) were incarcerated for drug-related offenses. In 1993 the total prison population stood at 1.4 million, of whom 353,564—25.1 percent—were inside for drug offenses. The Sentencing Project, a DC-based watchdog group, found that the increase was far from racially balanced. Between 1986 and 1991 the incarceration rate for white males convicted on drug crimes increased by 106 percent. But the number of black males in prison for kindred offenses soared by a factor of 429 percent, and the rate for black women went up by an incredible 828 percent.

The queen of the drug war, Nancy Reagan, said amid one of her innumerable sermons on the issue: "If you're a casual drug user, you're an accomplice to murder." In tune with this line of thinking, the Democratic-controlled Congress moved in 1988 to expand the crimes for which the federal death penalty could be imposed. These included drug-related murders, and murders committed by drug gangs, which would allow any gang member to face the death penalty if one member of the gang was linked to a drug killing. The new penalties were inscribed in an update of the Continuing Criminal Enterprises Act.

Convictions under the new law between 1989 and 1996 were 70 percent white and 24 percent black. But 90 percent of the times the federal prosecutors sought the death penalty it was against non-whites: of these, 78 percent were black and the rest Hispanic. From 1930 to 1972 (when the Supreme Court found the death penalty unconstitutional), 85 percent of those given death sentences were white. When the federal death penalty was reapplied in 1984, with the Anti-Drug Abuse Act, the numbers for black death penalty convictions soared. Of those on Death Row, both federal and state, 50 percent are black, although blacks constitute only 16 percent of the US population.

The Real Purpose of the Drug War

A HEART IN love will decipher every squiggle in a letter as a kiss. In the final days of the 2008 campaign and in the opening ones of his administration, Obama and his top legal aides seemed to the eager ears of marijuana legalizers on the West Coast to be opening the door to a new, sensible era.

Here was the basic line as dispensed by Attorney General Eric Holder on March 18, 2009:

> The policy is to go after those people who violate both federal and state law. To the extent that people do that and try to use medical marijuana laws [such as California's Prop 215] as a shield for activity that is not designed to comport with what the intention was of the state law, those are the organizations, the people, that we will target. And that is consistent with what the president said during the campaign.

The next day drug activists exulted in a big win. "Today's comments clearly represent a change in policy out of Washington," Ethan Nadelmann of the Drug Policy Alliance told the *LA Times*. Holder, Nadelmann added in the *New York Times*, had sent a clear message to the DEA that the feds now recognize state medical marijuana laws as "kosher."

Striking a different sort of exultant note, the US Attorney's spokesman in Los Angeles, Thom Mrozek, told the *LA Times*: "In every single case we have prosecuted, the defendants violated state as well as federal law." On January 22 (two days after Obama's inauguration) DEA agents conducted a raid on a South Lake Tahoe cannabis dispensary run by a wheelchair-bound entrepreneur named Ken Estes. They seized about five pounds of herbal medicine and a few thousand dollars. No arrests were made. "It was a typical rip-and-run," Estes said. On February 3, the DEA raided four cannabis dispensaries in the LA area. Eight days later

DEA agents busted the MendoHealing Co-operative farm in Fort Bragg, California.

The love-flushed Obamaists had forgotten how to read political declarations with a close and realistic eye, and to bear in mind the eternal power struggles between federal prosecutors and enforcers—e.g., the DEA and equivalent state bodies. The feds wanted to make it completely clear that, whatever Obama might hint at, they weren't going to be hog-tied by wussy state laws. Bust a guy in a wheelchair, bust a dispensary, make your point: I'm the man.

Meanwhile, what has been happening out in the fields, dells, plastic greenhouses, indoor grows in the counties of Mendocino and Humboldt? The timeless rhythms of agriculture: overproduction, plummeting prices, the remorseless toll of costly inputs like soil and fertilizers.

Back in the early 1990s the price to grower per pound was around $5,000. A couple of years ago, the average had dropped to about $2,000, more for really skilled growers, who "black box" their greenhouses, darkening them earlier each day to trick the plants into putting out an early crop. Right now, it's down to maybe $1,000 a pound in the fall, dropping to $600 in the Christmas rush. Do these prices bear any relation to the prices in the fancy dispensaries in southern California? Guess.

Bruce Anderson, editor of the Boonville-based *Anderson Valley Advertiser*, describes the realities:

> Do a Google Earth on your Mendo neighborhood. Now knowing what to expect, we did one on Boonville. As the satellite camera zeroes in, the grows look like lemon groves, neatly arrayed in the backyards on both sides of Highway 128 from one end of Boonville to the other. Of course the in-door grows can't be googled, but they are just as numerous throughout the Anderson Valley and every other area of vast Mendocino County. When you hear statements like 'Everyone in this county is in the pot business' it's not that far short of the reality. In an imploding economy does anyone seriously expect an enterprise that pays lots of off-the-books, tax-free cash can be stopped short of full-on legalization? In just the last week, raids were conducted on two homes, one in Eureka, one in Redwood Valley, where better than $400,000 cash was confiscated by the forces of law and order. Every time the cops make big cash hauls more people are convinced that they, too, should get into the pot business. A smaller number of people, of course, are convinced to try to find dope houses to rip off, hence X-number of annual home invasions, most of them

unreported. Looked at objectively, and all things considered, the nebulous legal status of marijuana is perfect for Mendocino County's financial well-being: Every year the cops take off just enough dope to keep pot prices to at least a thousand a pound, with prices falling around Christmas to five or six hundred a pound as surpluses are unloaded for spending cash. Legalization would further depress the Mendocino County economy, and depress it big time.

But legalization is not a realistic prospect and so the status of the herb will inevitably remain cloudy. For its part the DEA is announcing big impending raids in Mendocino county, some targeting the vast stretches of the (federally) controlled Mendocino National Forest, and the growers drawing on the waters of the middle Eel. There are serious environmental and criminal issues here. Obama said at the start of his administration, 'I can't ask the Justice Department to ignore completely a federal law that's on the books. What I can say is, use your prosecutorial discretion and properly prioritize your resources to go after things that are really doing folks damage.'

As Mark Scaramella, also of the *AVA*, ticks off the list, "there are growers, many of them violent, using public lands. Who wants to go hiking and run into a criminal operation? These same growers are responsible for associated illegal water diversions and serious environmental degradation. In one recent raid they took a mile of black plastic irrigation pipe out of the Mendocino National Forest."

Fine for the Feds to go into action here. What's not fine is a far-reaching national campaign against medical growers right across the US. All the usual arsenal of harassments has been brought into play by multiple agencies, starting with the IRS, bankrupting dispensaries by simply denying elementary business expenses.

Has the drug war—as a war on the poor—slowed down? In 2010 some 850,000 Americans were arrested for marijuana related offenses of which the vast majority was for possession. That means since Obama took office it is likely well over 2.5 million Americans have been arrested for marijuana. This under the aegis of a President who cozily discloses his marijuana habit as a young man. One bust, Mr. Obama, and you'd be still on the South Side. But then, your sense of self-righteousness is too distended to be deflated by any sense of hypocrisy.

Take a look at New York City.

In the Bloomberg years in New York City "stop and frisks" have gone through the roof. In 2002, when Bloomberg had only just stepped into the Mayor's office, 97,296 New Yorkers were stopped by the police under Stop and Frisk. 80,176 were totally innocent (82 percent).

By 2009, 581,168 New Yorkers were stopped by the police. 510,742 were totally innocent (88 percent). 310,611 were black (55 percent). 180,055 were Latino (32 percent). 53,601 were white (10 percent). 289,602 were aged 14–24 (50 percent). (For reference, according to the Census Bureau, there were about only 300,000 black men between the ages of 13 and 34 living in the city that year.)

In 2011, 685,724 New Yorkers were stopped by the police. 605,328 were totally innocent (88 percent). 350,743 were black (53 percent). 223,740 were Latino (34 percent). 61,805 were white (9 percent). 341,581 were aged 14–24 (51 percent).

What happens *after* the initiation of Stop and Frisk when the person "complies" with an NYPD officer's directive to "empty their pockets"? If up to 25 grams of marijuana stays out of view, that constitutes only a violation. If the cop forces the weed into public view we're looking at a misdemeanor, with potentially devastating career consequences for the target. Low level arrests for possession of marijuana in New York have gone up from about 2,000 in 1990 to 50,684 arrests in 2011 for possession of a small amount of marijuana, more than for any other offense, according to an analysis of state data by Harry G. Levine, a sociologist at Queens College.

From 2002 to 2011, New York City recorded 400,000 low-level marijuana arrests, according to Levine's analysis. That represented more arrests than under Bloomberg's three predecessors put together—a period of 24 years. Most of those arrested have been young black and Hispanic men, and most had no prior criminal convictions.

Don't forget: Drug policy in the US is about social control.

That's the name of the game.

Options in America: Kill Yourself or Have a Baby

TIME MADE VLADIMIR Putin its Man of the Year. Chalk it up as nostalgia for the cold war, when America was great, and a working man in a state like Michigan had two cars, a nice house, a country cabin, a health plan, a pension and a wife who stayed at home, canning fruit and batting her eyes at the postman. These days he has two lousy jobs, she has three and they have negative equity in their home, no health plan and no pension.

A couple of indices of how down many Americans are feeling about the future: The suicide rate among middle-aged Americans has reached its highest point in at least 25 years, the U.S. Centers for Disease Control and Prevention recently reported.

The rate rose by about 20 percent between 1999 and 2004 for U.S. residents ages 45 through 54 far more than among younger adults, whose own suicide stats are also on the rise.

In 2004, there were 16.6 completed suicides per 100,000 people in the 45–54 cohort, the highest it's been since the CDC started tracking such rates, around 1980. The previous high was 16.5, in 1982, a year when there was a terrible farm crisis in the Mid-West.

These days it's the health care crisis. People can't even afford to get finished off respectably by a doctor or a hospital, so they have to do it themselves.

The second index of desperation is a sudden spike in teen pregnancies, particularly among young black women. As R.F. Blader wrote in *CounterPunch*, "When we believe in our opportunities, we safeguard our futures. Conversely, we behave self-destructively when we have no hope. For many teenagers in America, the options aren't heartening. In a society where opportunities are scarce and life is getting harder, getting pregnant puts a positive spin on a vote of no-confidence." Indeed some argue that having babies early is a very rational choice for a young black teen, since her support network of kin are still alive, and her own body not wasted by the toxins associated with low-income neighborhoods.

America will soon start trudging through the endless months of Campaign 2008. Worthy Iowans, their quadrennial season in the limelight at its apex, will cram into the caucuses and kick off the horse races. In all the torrents of rhetorical hot air thus far expended, it's hard to find a single sentence from any politician that could give any comfort to that suicidal 50-year-old or the teen with a toddler as her only solace. There are gestures to populism by the Democrat John Edwards, but I've not met anyone who believes that there is the slightest chance of substantive reform of health care or a reversal of soaring trends in inequality. The bad guys have a lock on the system.

The default option these days is fantasy a trend in American politics kicked off in this epoch by Ronald Reagan. Reagan knew how to keep things simple. When Reagan died a Pentagon official told me that when Ron became president in 1981, and thus "commander in chief" the Joint Chiefs of Staffs mounted their traditional show-and-tell briefings for him, replete with simple charts and a senior general explicating them in simple terms. Reagan found these briefings way too complicated and dozed off. The Joint Chiefs then set up a secret unit, staffed by cartoonists. The balance of forces was set forth in easily accessible caricature, with Soviet missiles the size of upended Zeppelins, pulsing on their launchpads, with the miniscule US ICBMs shriveled in their bunkers. Little cartoon bubbles would contain the points the joint chiefs wanted to hammer into Reagan's brain, most of them to the effect that "we need more money". Reagan really enjoyed the shows and sometimes even asked for repeats.

Reagan set the bar for the level of national political debate. They called him the Great Communicator and no one has moved the bar since. So who cares if his great contribution to the national fantasy "missile defense", aka, "the strategic defense initiative" aka "Star Wars, is now scheduled to consume 19 per cent of the defense budget even though it's well-nigh universally admitted the system is useless. The system is impregnable to reform and everyone knows it.

Alexander Cockburn

The Whack 'Em and Stack 'Em Mentality of American Cops

POLICE WORK CONTINUES to be a relatively safe occupation. In the 1970s, an average of 220 officers died each year. In the 1980s, 185 officers were killed on average, with the average number dropping to 155 in the 1990s. The number of police deaths continues to decline, year by year. According to the publication Officer Down, there were only 95 "duty related" officer deaths in 2013. Forty-two of these fatalities were vehicle related. Another 14 deaths resulted from heart attacks while on the clock. Only 27 cops died from gunfire last year and several of those were shot by other cops.

Craig Floyd, chairman of the National Law Enforcement Officers Memorial Fund, contends that "law enforcement remains the most dangerous occupation in America today, and those who serve and make the ultimate sacrifice are true portraits in courage."

This is nonsense. Compared to the daily perils of being a retail clerk in a 7-Eleven or toiling on a construction site, let alone working on a trawler in the Gulf of Alaska, logging in the Pacific Northwest or working in a deep mine, policing is a fairly invulnerable trade.

But as vividly recounted by James Bovard in a piece for *CounterPunch* this week, it has probably never been riskier to be pulled over by a cop on one of America's roads. Bovard writes:

> Killings by police are not a negligible proportion of the nation's firearms death toll. Shootings by police accounted for almost 10 percent of the homicides in Los Angeles County in 2010, according to the *Los Angeles Times*.
>
> Jim Fisher, a former FBI agent and criminal law professor, compiled a database of police shootings and estimated that in the United States in 2011 police shot more than 1,100 people, killing 607.

The public apprehension that cops are often borderline psychotic, hair-trigger-ready to open fire on the slightest pretext, virtually immune from serious sanction, is growing apace, fueled by such incidents as the dog slaughter on an interstate in Tennessee. CNN featured grainy film of the episode taken from one of the police cruisers.

James Smoak plus wife Pamela and son Brandon were traveling from Nashville along Interstate 40 to their Saluda, NC, home on New Year's Day when they noticed a trooper following them. In Cookeville, about 90 miles east of Nashville, the Smoaks were pulled over by the trooper and three local police cars. The cops ordered them out of the car, made them kneel and then handcuffed them.

At this point the Smoaks family implored the police to shut the doors of their car so the two family dogs couldn't jump out. The cops did nothing. Out hopped Patton the bulldog. A cop promptly raised his shotgun and blew its head off, amid the horrified screams of the Smoaks family.

Of course, the cops later said Patton was acting in a threatening manner and that the uniformed shot-gunner "took the only action he could to protect himself and gain control of the situation," but the film seems to show Patton wagging his tail the moment before he was blown away.

Why were the Smoaks stopped by the four-car posse? Mr. Smoaks had left his wallet on the roof of his car at the filling station, and someone phoned in a report that he'd seen the wallet fly off of a car and fall onto the highway with money spilling out. Well, Mr. Smoaks won't make that silly mistake again.

Scroll through some Middle America websites and you'll find much fury about what happened to Patton, as an episode ripely indicative of how cops carry on these days. Here's "Police State in Progress," by Dorothy Anne Seese writing in the sparky *Sierra Times*. The *Times* bills itself as "An Internet Publication for Real Americans."

After relating the death of Patton, Seese brought up other recent police rampages:

> A couple of months ago, a woman was shot to death in her car at a drive-through Walgreens pharmacy for trying to get Soma by a forged prescription. The officer who shot the woman—who had a 14-month-old baby with her in the car—claimed self-defense because the woman was trying to run over him. However, the medical examiner found she had been shot from an angle to the left and rear

of her position in the driver's seat. Self-defense? The officer is under investigation for second-degree murder and has been fired from the Chandler police department. However, a child is motherless, a man has been deprived of his wife and companion, the mother of his child, because his wife tried to get a drug with a phony prescription. Florida Governor Jeb Bush's daughter did the same thing and got a slap on the wrist. It seems the law now considers everyone guilty until proven innocent, with people in high places excepted. The number of horror stories increases daily in Amerika.

There was a time when "Amerika" was a word solely in left currency. Not anymore, if the conservative, populist *Sierra Times* is any guide. Check out its Whack'em & Stack'em feature about killings by cops and you'll sense the temperature of outrage.

Hate Versus Death

ALMOST EVERY WEEK, it seems, we get to read about some state execution, performed or imminent, wreathed in the usual toxic fog of various prejudices, or incompetency of counsel, or prosecutorial misconduct.

Take the recent execution in Ashcroft country, February 7, of Stanley Lingar, done in the Potosi Correctional Center in Missouri, for killing 16-year-old Thomas Allen back in 1985. In the penalty phase of Lingar's trial, prosecutor Richard Callahan, who may now be headed for a seat on the Missouri State Supreme Court recently vacated by his mother-in-law, argued for death, citing Lingar's homosexuality to the jury as the crucial factor that should tilt poison into the guilty man's veins. Despite the on-the-record anti-gay bias, Governor Bob Holden, a Democrat, turned down a clemency appeal and told the press he'd "lost no sleep" over signing off on Lingar's fate.

Is there any hope that the ample list of innocent people either lost to the executioners or saved at the eleventh hour will prompt a federal moratorium such as is being sought by Senator Russell Feingold of Wisconsin? Or that states will suspend or, better still, end the death penalty? Or that judges will decline to impose this cruel and unusual punishment?

A year ago it seemed possible. On January 31, 2000, Illinois Governor George Ryan, a Republican, suspended imposition of the death penalty in his state on the grounds that he could not support a system "which, in its administration, has proven so fraught with error." In the months that followed Ryan's commendable decision abolitionists took comfort from a number of polls that the tide of public opinion was beginning to turn.

By June a Field Poll reported the sensational finding that in the state with the most crowded death row in the nation, Californians by nearly 4 to 1 favored stopping state executions to study how the death penalty was being applied. The Field poll respondents were told about wrong convictions, also about appeals to Governor Gray Davis by religious leaders for a moratorium. Polling in California at the end of last year, without the background used by Field, put support for a moratorium at 42 percent, just behind those opposed to any such move. A national poll last fall found 53 per cent for a moratorium.

The discrepancy in the California polls actually affords comfort to abolitionists, since it shows that when respondents are told about innocent people saved from lethal injection, often at the last moment, support for a moratorium soars. It's a matter of public education.

But where are the educators? Many eligible political leaders have fled the field of battle, convinced that opposition to the death penalty is a surefire vote loser. In the second presidential debate last fall Al Gore wagged his head in bipartisan agreement when George W. Bush declared his faith in state executions as a deterrent.

A few years ago Hillary Clinton spoke of her private colloquies with the shade of Eleanor Roosevelt. Mrs. Roosevelt's passionate opposition to the death penalty either did not come up in their conversations or left her unpersuaded, since now-Senator Clinton stands square for death, as does her husband, as does New York's senior senator, Charles Schumer.

Indeed the death penalty is no longer a gut issue, or even a necessary stand, for those, like Schumer, who are associated with the Democratic Party's liberal wing. On February 12 the *New York Post* quoted Kerry Kennedy Cuomo, long known as a leading death-penalty opponent, as saying that "it would be futile" to try to repeal capital punishment in New York.

Mrs. Cuomo, daughter of Robert F. Kennedy, told the *Post* that she believes her husband, Andrew, a contender for the Democratic nomination for governor, shares her views. "To tell you the truth, on the death penalty, it's not as big an issue in the state as it was a few years ago." In the *Post* account, Mrs. Cuomo didn't mention her father-in-law, Mario, who repeatedly vetoed death-penalty measures during his 12 years as governor.

In line with Kerry Kennedy Cuomo's spineless stance, many liberal or what are now cautiously called "human rights" groups have also found it politic to sideline capital punishment as an issue. No better illustration is available than the recent tussle over John Ashcroft's nomination as Attorney General. Scores of groups flailed at him on choice, homophobia, racism and hate crimes, but not on the most extraordinary application of hate in the arsenal of state power: the death penalty.

Return for a moment to the fight to save Lingar's life. Privacy Rights Education Project, the state-wide Missouri gay lobby group, endorsed

Holden in his gubernatorial race. PREP, however, was quite muted on Lingar's fate, taking little action except sending a one-paragraph letter to the governor the day before the execution. Another gay organization, the Gay and Lesbian Alliance Against Defamation, the folks who want to shut down Dr. Laura, is a national group but happens to have an office in Kansas City, MO. Surely what prosecutor Callahan did to Stanley Lingar is well beyond defamation. Where was GLAAD on this case? Not a peep from them. Noisy about hate crimes but similarly silent on the death penalty is the inaptly named Human Rights Campaign, the nation's largest gay advocacy group. To their credit, Amnesty International, ACLU, Missourians to Abolish the Death Penalty and Queer Watch were there in the Missouri trenches, trying to save Lingar's life.

The issue of capital punishment is drawing much more attention these days. Just when help could really make a difference, where are all these (ostensibly) liberal and progressive groups? The Anti-Defamation League (okay, strike "ostensibly"), whose national director, Abraham Foxman, pulled down $389,000 in 1999, was busy writing letters for Marc Rich. Why? Its position on capital punishment? The ADL backed Bill Clinton's appalling Antiterrorism and Effective Death Penalty Act of 1996 which eviscerates habeas corpus review for prisoners on death rows across the country. People for the American Way? Not a bleat about the death penalty, though now launching an 18-state campaign for hate crimes legislation.

The impetus given by Ryan last year could fall apart. Governor Ryan himself faces very difficult reelection prospects in 2002, and a successor could rescind the moratorium. Liberals should abandon their absurd and dangerous obsession with hate crime laws and muster against this most hateful excrescence on the justice system—capital punishment.

Let them take encouragement from the District Attorney of San Francisco, Terrence Hallinan, who told a San Francisco Court on February 6 that he would not participate in the capital sentencing of one Robert Massey since "the death penalty does not constitute any more of a deterrent than life without parole" and, among other evils, "discriminates racially and financially, being visited mainly on racial minorities and the poor.… It forfeits the stature and respect to which our state is entitled by reducing us to a primitive code of retribution."

Alexander Cockburn

The Death Penalty and the American Mind

SHORTLY AFTER FIVE o'clock in the morning on April 29th, a prison SWAT team arrives at Clayton Lockett's cell on death row in the Oklahoma State Penitentiary in McAlester, the very prison from which Tom Joad was released in the opening pages of Steinbeck's *The Grapes of Wrath*. The burly guards unlock Lockett's door and order him to the ground to be cuffed and shackled for a trip to the prison infirmary, where the prisoner is to be x-rayed prior to his execution by lethal injection. Lockett, who has been incarcerated for fourteen years, largely in solitary confinement, refuses to comply.

As the SWAT team prepares to forcibly enter Lockett's cell, the prisoner jabs his wrist with a crudely-fashioned tool. The guards storm the cell and repeatedly taser Lockett as his body spasms on the floor. Incapacitated by the jolts of electricity, Lockett is restrained and hauled to the prison medical unit, where he is left in a cell, bleeding and semi-conscious for an hour and 15 minutes, before his wounds are examined by a physician's assistant.

The raid on Lockett's cell is witnessed by Charles Warner. Warner is locked in the adjacent cell, awaiting his own execution, scheduled for two hours after Lockett has been put to death. That April night was meant to be a macabre double-header, staged by the state's Governor Mary Fallin, whose neck is usually adorned by a necklace with a dangling golden cross. Fallin, who had brazenly defied two court injunctions halting the executions, was eager to show the nation the cheerless efficiency of Oklahoma's death machine in the face of lingering questions over the efficacy of its experimental cocktail of lethal drugs.

For the next 10 hours, Clayton Lockett is kept shackled in an observation cell. Still dazed and bleeding, Lockett refuses food and an opportunity to visit with his attorneys.

At 4:10 pm, armed guards once again enter his cell and march him to the shower in the prison's H-Unit. Showing a perverse sense of historical irony, Oklahoma officials use the prison showers as the holding cell for the execution chamber. Thirty minutes later, "mental health personnel" enter the room and talk with Lockett for 10 minutes. No mention is made in the post-execution documents of what these prison shrinks concluded about the mental state of a man who is only minutes away from being put to death.

Ten minutes later, the prison's new warden Anita Trammell enters the shower cell and, surrounded by prison guards, leads Lockett into the execution chamber. At 5:22 PM, guards strap Clayton Lockett to the death table. Five minutes later a phlebotomist appears and begins probing Lockett's veins for the best place to insert an IV. The phlebotomist is not a doctor, but a technician specializing in the drawing of blood. In Oklahoma, as in most states, phlebotomists do not need to be licensed and their training, such as it is, is often done in online courses.

The prison's blood man pokes at the veins in Lockett's arms and legs, without finding a "viable insertion point." Next he pricks both of the condemned man's feet and then his neck, without locating a willing vein. Finally, the technician "went to the groin area" and at 6:18, after 50 minutes of repeated poking and prodding, an IV is jabbed into a vein in Lockett's groin. A sheet is draped over the needle and tubes to "prevent witnesses" from viewing Lockett's genitals and the phlebotomist leaves the killing chamber.

At 6:23, Warden Tramell is ordered to begin the execution by Robert Patton, director of Oklahoma's Department of Corrections. The shades to the execution chamber are raised. In front of a gallery of witnesses, Trammell asks Lockett if he wants to make a final statement. Lockett declines. Then Midazolam, a sedative meant to knock Lockett out, begins to flow through the tube and into his bloodstream. Ten minutes later a doctor determines that Lockett is unconscious and two killing drugs are pumped into his system: vecuronium bromide, a suffocating agent, and potassium chloride, which is meant to paralyze the heart

Within seconds, Lockett, who is supposed to be unconscious, begins to shake and gasp. In agonizing pain, he attempts to rise up and screams out: "Oh, man!" The shades are suddenly lowered and over the next crucial 12 minutes the attending physician examines Lockett and determines that his vein had ruptured and the "line had blown."

At 6:56, the prison director Patton calls off the execution. Lockett is now unconscious and has a faint pulse. No attempt is made to revive him. At 7:06, the death room doctor pronounces Lockett dead. The cause of death is recorded as heart failure.

These gruesome events prompted a national uproar for a few days and a rare scolding from the President, who, naturally, called for a review. But why? Yes, Lockett's execution was badly botched. But it was not all that different than the 1348 executions that had preceded it since the reinstitution of the death penalty in 1976. The outrage was focused on the incompetence of the execution, rather than the corrupt and morally repugnant system itself.

Gov. Fallin's mistake, as she might have learned had she fully absorbed her Aeschylus, was her hubris. Her fanatical grandstanding at the chemical gallows only drew unwelcome attention to a deed most Americans support (60 percent in a post-Lockett poll), but don't really care to know too much about.

As Obama the drone warrior could have advised her, the death industry feeds on silence and secrecy. When Clayton Lockett resisted those guards in his cell, the veil began to lift on the hideous machinery of death. Given a view to a kill, many Americans seemed momentarily unnerved by the casual savagery being done in their name. Americans want their killing done quick and clean—so that they can call it humane.

Jeffrey St. Clair

Constitutional Entropy

IT IS A somber measure of the accelerating pace of constitutional entropy in America that Alan Dershowitz, that avid advocate of torture, strutted forth as one of the few voices of restraint following the capture of young Dzhokhar Tsarnaev. When most commentators were making carnivorous howls for the bullet-ridden teenager to be stripped of his constitutional rights and declared an enemy combatant, Dershowitz, who has previously endorsed waterboarding suspected terrorists under the outlandish "ticking time-bomb" theory, urged the Obama administration to treat Tsarnaev as an ordinary criminal suspect, read him his Miranda rights and provide him access to an attorney.

This sensible legal advice, which is regularly used in cases involving mass murderers, serial killers and abortion clinic bombers, was promptly steamrolled by Eric Holder's Justice Department as it rushed to invoke an "emergency exception" to abrogate Tsarnaev's rights under the Fifth Amendment.

Citing only the most tenuous thread of legal authority, federal prosecutors and military interrogators subjected Dzhokhar Tsarnaev to sixteen hours of questioning, while he was cuffed to his hospital bed in the Intensive Care Unit. This sordid treatment was rationalized through the so-called Quarles Exemption, which derives from a 1984 Supreme Court case where New York police questioned an unarmed suspect in a rape case about a missing gun without advising him of his rights. Quarles soon pointed the police toward the weapon. Ironically, prosecutors chose not to charge Quarles with rape, but did try and convict him on gun charges, which he had essentially confessed to while in police custody. The cops later lamely cited an immediate risk to public safety as the reason for not issuing Quarles a Miranda warning. That case was the subject of a scorching dissent by Justice Thurgood Marshall, who wrote that the ruling "endorsed the introduction of coerced self-incriminating statements in criminal prosecutions."

Since 2010, the Obama administration has mounted an assiduous assault on the Fifth Amendment by boring even larger holes in Miranda protections. The first major blow was struck in the interrogation of the Times Square bombing suspect Faisul Shahzad. Like Tsarnaev, Shahzad was an American citizen. Like Tsarnaev, Shahzad was detained and grilled for hours before being read his rights and offered an attorney. After softening up Shahzad through the initial interrogation, the Times Square bomber eventually waived his rights and continued to blab away to the FBI about the logistics of his failed plot.

Sensing the keen prosecutorial advantages of this strategy, Holder sent a memo to the FBI in March of 2011 urging federal criminal interrogators to invoke the Quarles Exception in domestic terrorism cases, using the rule to aggressively probe for information well beyond looming threats to public safety: "There may be exceptional cases in which, although all relevant public safety questions have been asked, agents nonetheless conclude that continued unwarned interrogation is necessary to collect valuable and timely intelligence not related to any immediate threat, and that the government's interest in obtaining this intelligence outweighs the disadvantages of proceeding with unwarned interrogation."

So the stage was set for the wide-ranging Tsarnaev interrogation. Over the course of more than two days, federal agents from the High Value Detainee Interrogation Group queried Tsarnaev, who was suffering from bullet wounds to his head, neck and legs, about every aspect of the bomb plot, about his family, his friends, his finances and his political and religious beliefs. Ignoring Tsarnaev's repeated requests to consult with a lawyer, the inquisitors duly extracted a full confession from the young man and selectively leaked some of his most incriminating statements to the press, so that even if a court eventually rules his pre-Miranda confession inadmissible at trial, the contents will already have been seared indelibly on the minds of potential jurors.

Even this sinister suspension of bedrock legal rights that reach back to the Magna Carta wasn't enough to satiate the terror-hawks. The congressional warlords, odious figures like Lindsay Graham and Peter King, launched a frantic scramble to exploit the bombing by calling for expanded police and surveillance powers. Of course, this means fresh financial opportunities for the Homeland Security Complex, that ravening claque of consultants and contractors who are feasting at the trough of America's last growth industry. Their loathsome lobbyists, many of them former Pentagon officials and CIA operatives, swirl like wraiths around the still smoldering ruins scenting out fresh opportunities to cash in. It is a morbid form of legalized looting.

In the wake of the bombings, Boston itself became a vast panorama of paranoia. Police entered homes without warrants, detained citizens without probable cause, shut down sprawling neighborhoods in a spastic search for a lone seriously wounded teen. Over a single night, the cradle of our revolution became fully pacified, docile, willing to offer up the most cherished liberties of the Republic without even being asked.

We've reached the end of something vital in America. The instruments of social control have become deeply internalized. The psychological conditioning no longer requires siege sirens or color-coded alerts. Now entire cities reflexively obey the dictates of authority and are snugly sequestered behind cordons of the mind.

Jeffrey St. Clair

Agency of Fear

It's nearing dusk on November 26, 2010. More than 25,000 people have gathered in a light rain at Pioneer Square in downtown Portland, Oregon to watch the annual lighting of the holiday tree, a 100-foot-tall Douglas-fir logged from the Willamette National Forest.

Three men in a nearby hotel room have just finished eating a take-out pizza. The TV turned to a local news channel, which is covering holiday celebration. The men spread towels on the floor and say an Islamic prayer, asking that Allah bless their operation. The men pat each other on the back, leave the room and walk to their vehicle, a white van.

One of the men is a teenager named Mohamed. The other two men are older. One is called Youssef. The leader of the group is a man in his fifties who is known only as Hussein. Hussein is a bomb-maker for al-Qaeda. He's been making explosives for three decades. Their operation to set off a massive bomb in the heart of Portland has been in the works for more than three months.

Hussein unlocks the doors to the van and takes the driver's seat. The young Mohamed, who is wearing a hard-hat, slides into the passenger seat. In the cargo hold of the van sit six 55-gallon blue drums filled with nearly 2,000 pounds of fertilizer-based explosives. Each drum has an explosive cap. They are linked together by a detonation cord, which runs up to a toggle switch.

As Hussein pulls the van, which reeks of diesel fuel, out into traffic, the bomb-maker begins to chant loudly in Arabic. Hussein parks the van on Yamhill Street, directly across from Pioneer Square. He orders Mohamed to flip the toggle switch, arming the bombs.

The two men get out of the van and scurry down Broadway Street and then up to 10th avenue, where Youssef is waiting for them in an SUV. They drive to the Portland train station, where they drop Youssef off, and then park the vehicle in a lot a couple of blocks away.

Hussein mutters "Allahu Akbar." Then turns to his teenage sidekick and asks, "You ready?" Mohamed nods his head, "Ready."

The bomb-maker hands Mohamed a cell phone. The phone is meant to activate the bomb. He reads out a number. Mohamed nervously enters the digits on the phone. There is no explosion.

Hussein suggests that the signal may be poor and that they should step out of the van. The two men get out of the van and Mohamed reenters the numbers. The phone begins to ring. Then dozens of voices shatter the tense scene, screaming "FBI! FBI!" The two men are ordered to the ground. As Hussein is being handcuffed, he struggles with the federal agents and continues to chant "Allahu Akbar! Allahu Akbar!" When Mohamed spits at an officer, Hussein says, "I love that."

The federal agents have arrived, it seems, just in the nick of time. Their felicitous intervention has disrupted a sophisticated terrorist operation and saved thousands of innocent lives. The bomb plotters had been caught and trundled off to prison: another triumphant day in the battle to protect the homeland from al-Qaeda's terror cells.

But wait a minute. Almost nothing about this scenario was true. The cell phone wasn't connected to the toggle switch. The detonation cords weren't wired to an explosive device. The blue drums weren't filled with diesel-saturated fertilizer, but harmless grass seed. Mohamed wasn't a member of al Qaeda. Of Somali origin, he was a troubled college dropout from Beaverton, Oregon, home of Nike. Youssef wasn't a member of al Qaeda. Hussein was not one of al Qaeda's top bomb makers. Youssef and Hussein were not really arrested and neither was charged with being part of a terrorist plot. Youssef and Hussein were both federal agents.

The bomb plot itself was not an al Qaeda idea. It was hatched by the FBI. Young Mohamed Mohamud did not seek out the bomb plotters; they found him and seduced the young man into joining their conspiracy. The teenager did not build the bomb. The fake bomb was actually constructed by John Hallock, who later testified that he designed the device for "maximum effect." Mohamed did not select the target. The order to activate the device came from a federal agent. The order to detonate the bomb also came from a federal agent. From conception to execution, the infamous Portland Christmas Tree Bomb Plot was scripted by the FBI.

Yet it was Mohamed Mohamud who was arrested, slapped with federal terrorism and conspiracy changes, subjected to a bruising trial in January and convicted on all counts by a jury that deliberated less than six hours.

After the verdict was read, the gleeful FBI agents and federal prosecutors hailed their victorious sting operation, braying that they had rid the streets of a dangerous jihadist. But this was not a government sting. It was a textbook case of entrapment, where federal agents recruited a disaffected kid, whose only previous legal entanglement had been an unproven allegation of date rape during his freshman year at college, into a fake bomb plot that they had concocted.

Mohamed Mohamud was not a terrorist when the FBI began spying on him while he was still in high school. In the two years he was under FBI surveillance, he did not commit a terrorist act or join a terrorist group. It took the FBI to recruit him into a terrorist cell, indoctrinate him into terrorist ideology and lure him into participating in its bomb plot.

Our government increasingly fantasizes about blowing things up here at home. This is the sixth case where the FBI has invented a bomb plot aimed at snagging hapless, often alienated, individuals who were not terrorists until they were enticed into joining the agency's own conspiracy. So what is the point of these operations? To scoop up a handful of estranged, young Muslim men? To make suburban Americans feel safer?

Hardly. The point is fear. The government needs to keep the public in a state of terror anxiety in order to justify its own ever-encroaching powers.

So, Mohamed sits in prison. The Constitution lies in tatters. Fear rules the land.

Jeffrey St. Clair

America Enters a New Time

I WENT TO get my hair cut the other day in the town of Fortuna and waited ten minutes when the elderly barber finished buzz-cutting a young Mexican American. After the young man had exited under his thin skullcap of black stubble, Don the barber sighed and said, "That's the third boy I've cut today who's headed into the Marines. They all say the same thing: 'There's no work around here and I've got a family to support.'" When I tell them to hold off, they say the same thing: "Too late. I've signed up."

This is Humboldt county, northern California, where the marijuana boom is in its final paroxysms, with people flocking from around the world to get a piece of the action, just like they did in the Gold Rush. One of the many places selling bags of good soil to marijuana growers ($10 a bag, 8 bags to each marijuana plant, grown in a 100-foot x 30-foot plastic greenhouse, $25,000 or so) had a $300,000 day lately. So there's more money here than most places across America, where the situation is truly desperate.

Profits are up 41 percent since Obama's election; yet half of American workers have suffered a job loss or a cut in hours or wages over the past 30 months. They're saying around 28 million people either have no job or one that doesn't yield them enough money to get through the week. On Friday, August 13, the Bureau of Labor Statistic noted on its home page that "Employers initiated 1,851 mass layoff events in the second quarter of 2010 that resulted in the separation of 338,064 workers from their jobs for at least 31 days."

Millions are plummeting into total destitution, having reached the end of their 99-weeks of unemployment benefits. Their only option then is the soup line at a church and getting on the waiting list for a shelter. The nearest big city north of me is Portland, Oregon, adjacent to the *CounterPunch* co-editor bunker in Oregon City of Jeffrey St Clair. The downtown area in Portland is filled with homeless people, napping on steps, bedding down on cardboard in doorways. Jeffrey kayaks frequently down the Willamette and can see colonies of the destitute all along the river bank, from North Portland to Willamette Falls, sleeping under thin plastic and grey skies.

    California agriculture and much of the construction industry depends on undocumented workers coming across the border from Mexico—minimum cost $1000—for an 8-day walk through the Arizona desert. Since building is in a terminal slump, many Mexicans would like to head back home till times improve, but nowadays it's so tough to come back across, that they daren't risk it. Hence the paradox: trying to lock "illegals" out means locking them in. Frank Bardacke who lives in the farm town of Watsonville, a couple of hours south of San Francisco, recently described in *CounterPunch* a bank robbery by one young, desperate immigrant. Frank writes:

> Several months ago, Jario took his father's pickup truck, drove 20 miles to the upscale tourist playpen Carmel-By-the-Sea, and walked into the local branch of the Bank of America. He waited in line to see a teller, and, when his turn came, he pretended to have a gun under his shirt and quietly demanded that the teller give him her cash. As she was passing out the money, he apologized for frightening her; meanwhile, she was hiding a GPS device among the bills.
>
> He left the bank, his crime apparently unnoticed, and returned to the truck for the drive home. On the way, he got confused and took a wrong turn through Monterey before he got back on the right road home. Twenty police cars from four different police jurisdictions followed the GPS signal and stopped him 45 minutes after he left the bank. He immediately confessed, explaining that he needed the money to help his dad pay the family mortgage. When his case came to trial, the DA pressed for two years in State Prison. The judge decided that six months in the county jail and five years' probation would be enough.

    In Texas or anywhere in the South, the fellow would probably have got 25 years. But in desperate times one can expect people to do desperate, stupid things, and this decent judge showed compassion and understanding. One can't say the same for many Americans, starting with the Republicans in Congress who've been happily voting for a cut-off in benefits for the jobless, while simultaneously engaging in the politically insane enterprise of repealing the 14th Amendment, no longer making it a constitutional provision that those "born or naturalized in the United

States and subject to the jurisdiction thereof, are citizens of the United States." Do the Republicans want to cede Texas and Florida permanently to the Democrats?

Conspicuous good works are always a feature of Depression, the rich zealous to purchase moral insurance. Some billionaires, led by Warren Buffett and Bill Gates, have been pledging that they will earmark not less than 50 per cent of their personal wealth for charity. But since whatever they give away is tax deductible, revenues to Uncle Sam will drop.

The rich don't get to be rich by being the nicest guys in the shark tank. As Carl Ginsburg recently remarked in *CounterPunch*, "In its fledgling years, profits on Bill Gates' software were reportedly 70 per cent annually. Another way to gauge Gates's billions is by catching a glimpse of the multitudes of students priced out of the computer market—thanks in part to that Great Giver's expensive software—lined up daily at community college libraries for some free access to computers, each machine an expression of Gates' creative commitment to profit in the +40 percent range—a gift Gates gave himself that keeps on giving. As Gates told *Fortune*: 'The diversity of American giving is part of its beauty.'"

We can probably expect more laid-off workers going postal, as David Rosen wrote in another *CounterPunch* essay.

On August 3, at seven am, Omar Thornton showed up for a disciplinary hearing at the Hartford Distributors, a Budweiser distribution warehouse in Manchester, Connecticut. Thornton had been caught on video pinching some beer. They asked him whether he wanted to be fired, or just quit. Thornton pulled out a handgun and killed seven fellow employees before shooting himself dead. Before he loosed off his last shot into his head, Thornton, a black man, called a friend on his cellphone and said he's taken care of some racists who'd been giving him a hard time. Unemployment means fear and fear nourishes racism, all the more because we have a black president. Racism is drifting across America like mustard gas in the trenches in World War One.

And, a final token of hard times, we have Bonnie and Clyde on the run. In their latest guise the duo consists of John McCluskey and his cousin and fiancée, Casslyn Welch, who's no Faye Dunaway. She threw some wire cutters over the fence of her man's Arizona prison. Cops suspect them of killing a couple of retirees, then stealing their truck and heading north up to the Canadian line through Glacier National Park. That's the last sanctuary in America of *Ursus horribilis*, the American grizzly. Behind them the cops, ahead the bears. It could be the first movie of a new time.

Alexander Cockburn

The Myth of Microloans

THE COMMITTEE THAT gave Henry Kissinger the Nobel peace prize has given it this year to Mohammad Yunus, the economist who put the word "microloan" on the map with the Grameen Bank in his native land of Bangladesh. That's progress of a sort. But in terms of hot air, any sentences linking "peace" with "Henry Kissinger" aren't immeasurably more vacuous than the notion that microloans can help—to use the language of the Nobel Committee's citation—"large population groups find ways in which to break out of poverty."

Throughout the late Eighties and Nineties, in the verbal currency of first-world do-gooders, "microloans" became one of those magically fungible words (like "sustainable"), embedded in a thousand Foundation and NGO annual reports. What could be more virtuous in terms of prudent philanthropy than giving very small loans to very poor women? Microloans breath healthful uplift, as divorced from the sordid world of mega-loans (though not, it turns out, mega interest rates), as are micro-brews from Budweiser.

The trouble is that microloans don't make any sort of a macro-difference. They have helped some poor women, no doubt about it. But in their own way they're a register of defeat. Back in the early 1970s there were huge plans afoot to change the entire relationship of the Third to the First World, to speed Third World economies towards decent living standards for the many, not just the few. At the United Nations radical economists were hard at work drafting plans for a New World Economic Order. All that went out the window and here are the caring classes thirty years later, hailing microloans.

Microloans are micro-band aids in a scale of things today where—to take the example of India—well over 100,000 farmers, including a large number of women, have killed themselves because their federal and state governments, plus large international institutions, have promoted the savage priorities of neoliberalism.

As the economist Robert Pollin put it pithily when I asked him what he thought of the award to Yunus, "Bangladesh and Bolivia are two countries widely recognized for having the most successful micro credit programs in the world. They also remain two of the poorest countries in the world."

In the statistical tables of human development Bangladesh ranks 139th, worse than India, with 49.8 per cent of its population of 150 million below the official poverty line. In the homeland of the Grameen Bank, about 80 per cent of the people live on less than $2 a day. A UN Development Program study in the early 1990s showed that the total microcredits in Bangladesh constituted 0.6 per cent of total credit in the country. Hardly a transformation.

Against this backdrop, what have microloans achieved? I put the question to P. Sainath, author of *Everybody Loves a Good Drought* and India's most outstanding journalist on rural destitution and the consequences of economic policy. Yes, he said, microloans can be a legitimate tool in certain conditions, as long as you don't elevate the tool into a gigantic weapon. No one was ever liberated by being placed in debt. That said, a lot of poor women have eased their lives by using microloans, bypassing bank bureaucracies and money lenders.

But today the World Bank and the IMF, along with state-owned and commercial banks, are diving into microfinance. The microloan business is fast becoming a gigantic empire, bringing back into control the very banks and bureaucracies women have been trying to bypass. Microcredit is becoming a macro-racket.

Sainath points out that the interest rates micro-indebted women are paying in India are far higher than commercial bank lending rates. "They are paying between 24 and 36 per cent on loans for productive expenditures while an upper-class person can finance the purchase of a Mercedes at 6 to 8 per cent from the banking system."

The average loan of the Grameen bank is $130 in Bangladesh, lower in India. Now, the basic problem of the poor in both countries is landlessness, lack of assets. In the Indian province of Andhra Pradesh, where there are thousands of microloan groups, land costs 100,000 rupees an acre, poor land maybe 60,000 rupees—over $2000. $130 doesn't buy you the ranch, not even a good cow or buffalo. So how many poor women have escaped the poverty trap in AP, Sainath asks. "Try getting an answer."

"With that $130 the most basic assets do not come to you," Sainath says. "The amount is tiny. Interest rates are high and the default sanctions savage. During recent floods in AP, freelance journalists came to a village where everything had been washed away. The first people back in were the micro creditors threatening women, demanding monthly installments from women who had lost everything."

Governments like microloans because they allow them to abdicate their most basic responsibilities to poor citizens. Microloans make the market a god.

Let's suppose USAID or some kindred agency decides to put $10 million into microloans. What used to be an initiative of a group of women at the village level, has become a high-profile, international funding activity. Long before the first rupee is seen by women in a village, NGOs, consultants, bank managers and their relatives have all taken their cut. By the time the loan gets to the women in the village the cost is prohibitive, with the very poor and women of low caste often excluded. On top of this, some revolving-fund models require each women to put in a rupee a day. But often women don't have a rupee a day, so they go to the local moneylender to be able to repay the microloan.

As Sainath says, microlending can be a useful tool but it should not be romanticized as some sort of transformational activity. On that plane it's useless. By contrast, as Bob Pollin stresses, "the East Asian Tigers, like South Korea and Taiwan, relied for a generation on massive publicly-subsidized credit programs to support manufacturing and exports. They are now approaching West European living standards. Poor countries now need to adapt the East Asian macro-credit model to promote not simply exports, but land reform, marketing cooperatives, a functioning infrastructure, and most of all, decent jobs."

The trouble with publicly-subsidized credit programs is that they're public and they're large and run contrary to the neoliberal creed. That's why Yunus got his Nobel prize, whereas radical land reformers get a bullet in the back of the head.

Alexander Cockburn

Creatures of Capital

> When the waters poured into Atlantis, the rich men
> still screamed for their slaves.
> — Bertolt Brecht, "Questions from a Worker Who Reads"

THE BRIEF MUTINY is over. The Democrats, who control Congress, have pushed through the outrageous Paulson swindle, giving an initial $700 billion or so to Wall Street. The Democratic presidential nominee, Barack Obama, lobbied hard for the bankers' bailout, according to reps and senators receiving his phone calls. Obama voted for the package of course, and so did the vice-presidential Democratic nominee, Joe Biden.

With McCain one could at least speculate that he might have opposed the bailout in one last desperate throw to rescue his flagging campaign. In the event he disdained that lifebelt, clicked his heels and saluted the big money, just like Obama and Biden.

I never heard anyone speculate that Obama might, against all the odds, rally to the "No to Bailout" cause. His "Yes" was pure. He told reporters in Clearwater, Florida that "issues like bankruptcy reform, which are very important to Democrats, is probably something that we shouldn't try to do in this piece of legislation." In addition, he said that his own proposed economic stimulus program "is not necessarily something that we should have in this package."

In the crunch, almost invariably, Obama does the wrong thing and in my opinion he always will. Just count out the moments of surrender: reauthorize the Patriot Act? Aye, from Obama. The "class action fairness act", sought by Big Business for years. Aye from Obama. Capping credit card interest rates? No-o-o from Obama. FISA? Aye from Obama. With Robert Rubin at his side, his bailout vote was as sure as that of the harlot of the credit card companies, the six-term senator from Delaware, Joe Biden.

Normally, in these elections, one tries to peer forward into the future, to alert people to impending villainies, still dim in contour. Rare is it to have corrupt servility to the Money Power so brazenly displayed by the Democratic ticket merely a month before the ballot. We have just witnessed a class struggle where, for once, we had a huge popular coalition stretching all the way across the political spectrum. The coalition was there; the anger was there; the timing was perfect. " The great appear great to us," James Connolly wrote, "only because we are on our knees. Let us rise." This time it was Paulson who was on his knees. Could not Obama, at this moment of extraordinary power, have extorted extraordinary concessions from these frantic bankers? He could, but he fled the task. Could not Bernie Sanders have filibustered the bill? Of course not. That would have taken the Vermont blowhard "independent" far beyond his ritual bluster.

Obama's designated role in these fraught times is to de-fuse, not inspire; to urge the angered crowd to remain calm, and disperse quietly, not to march upon the citadel, pitchforks upraised.

But somehow Obama is not the focus of the liberals' fury. From many of the pieces pouring into my inbox, I can scarcely deduce that he was even at the scene of the crime. Sparing Obama, the left and the progressives reserve their venom for the Republican vice-presidential candidate, Sarah Palin.

We read more than one piece from these gallant leftists hailing Biden for his fine performance. Biden! This is a man with six full terms of infamy in the US senate. Find a Palestinian kid maimed from a cluster bomb, and you'll likely read "Greetings from Joe Biden" scrawled on the casing. Find someone crippled from 25 per cent interest charges on credit card debt, and you'll espy "Best wishes, Joe Biden" scrawled across the front of the bill. He's a poster boy for all that is foul about the Democratic Party.

Alexander Cockburn

The Economics of Contempt

IF IT'S SPRING, it must be time for Barack Obama's annual drive-by of black America, where he piously lectures African-Americans on the state of their lives. Though the tinsel adorning his rhetorical flourishes is getting somewhat frayed, the president didn't disappoint this year. Indeed, he treated the nation to two speeches on civil rights in a single week—a rare double-header for the commander of drones.

On April 10, Obama could be found in Texas, delivering an arid speech at the LBJ Presidential Library, studded with pompous non-sequiturs ("history not only travels forwards, it travels backwards") and awkward allusions to civil rights leaders, such as Martin Luther King, for whom Obama has little natural affinity.

The main takeaway from the Austin speech was that the legislative landmarks of the mid-1960s were about as good as it's ever going to get. "Half a century later, the laws LBJ passed are now as fundamental to our conception of ourselves and our democracy as the Constitution and the Bill of Rights," Obama said. There was no mention of new legislation or programs to address unemployment, job discrimination, malnutrition, decaying public schools or poverty. At best Obama made a rather timid call for the defense of the old Johnson era laws, which, in his tendentious narrative, are being gnawed away by the reactionary right.

As usual, Obama confessed no regrets, offered no apologies, copped to no transgressions against any of the battered ideals of the Great Society, even as that very week his administration quietly surpassed the mark of deporting two million undocumented immigrants. (Predictably, Michelle tweeted a few days later that she and Barack just loved the new Cesar Chavez movie.) What Obama doesn't say outright, but surely believes, is that the brawny liberalism of LBJ is passé, a relic of a bygone political tradition, the legislative ruins of a former age. The president is, of course, the grinning face of neo-liberalism, an ideology that rejects legislative cures for the magical elixir of financial incentives and market-driven remedies. How's that working out for you, Detroit?

Obama is a master of casual condescension. His true gift as an orator is in making you feel as if your misfortunes in life—losing your job, being evicted from your house, going bankrupt—are the products of your own lack of initiative or moral failing. And then, remarkably, he entices the victims into applauding their own humiliation. That's a kind of political prestidigitation even Reagan, with his strange power of seduction, couldn't quite pull off.

This bag of ineluctable parlor tricks was on full-display a few days later in New York, when Obama spoke at the National Action Network conference. NAN is run by Rev. Al Sharpton, who had, only days earlier, been outed as a former FBI snitch, having deployed a bugged briefcase in attempts to gather damaging information on both mobsters and, more pungently, black radicals. No wonder Sharpton has a running gig on MSNBC.

Obama gave a jauntier talk at the NAN convention, tuning his banal homilies to the rhythms of a Jay-Z rap. You know: Uptown and sanctimonious. His mission that day was to skewer Republicans (easy enough) and offer up some rationale for Sharpton's troops to remain loyal retainers of the Democratic Party (a more vexing challenge). In the end, he chose to present himself as a vigorous champion of the Voting Rights Act and proclaimed the election of Democrats in the midterms as the last line of defense for the franchise. The audience lapped it up, naturally. After all, he'd made a special visit just to see them.

But in the context of his presidency (or any president since LBJ, for that matter), what does the right to vote mean, if there's no one to vote for? No one who represents your interests? No one who will speak for you? If each pull of the ballot lever simply rings up the same merciless policies?

The returns are in on the Obama economy. He saved Wall Street, bailed out the banks, declined to prosecute felonious executives and redistributed billions upward into the off-shore accounts of the mega-rich. Pretty much everyone else got the shaft. But no community has fared worse under Obama, than urban blacks. The plight of black Americans is more extreme today than when Obama assumed command. Fresh evidence of this travesty rolls in every day. On April 1, a report by the Ann Casey Foundation described the conditions of black children as being "dire," significantly worse, in terms of health, nutrition, education and housing, than even Native American children. This bleak assessment received scant attention in the national press.

The new Jim Crow extends far beyond the savage politics of mass incarceration, documented in such striking detail by Michelle Alexander. The American economy is more and more segregated and hostile to the aspirations of minorities. The black unemployment rate remains twice that of whites, a disparity that has not narrowed over the course of Obama's term. In fact, it's almost certainly widened since blacks are much more likely to be part of the long-term unemployed and thus uncounted. Even during the so-called recovery, black unemployment rates remained far above recession levels.

The income gap between blacks and whites is widening, with white workers earning nearly $20,000 more a year on average than blacks. The wealth disparity is even more extreme. A recent report by the Urban Institute reveals that family wealth for whites is more than six-times that of blacks, a gap of more than $450,000 per family. Meanwhile, public schools are more segregated than at any time since 1970.

The insidious economic violence of everyday life in America grinds on, all but unnoticed except by those on the receiving end. Welcome to the economics of contempt.

Jeffrey St. Clair

Making the Rich Happy

NICELY IN TIME for the end-of-year job ratings, President Obama has crawled from the political graveyard, where only a month ago wreaths were being heaped around his sepulcher. The Commentariat now gravely applauds his recent victories in the US Congress: repeal of the Don't Ask, Don't Tell inhibitions on gays in the military; Senate ratification of the new START treaty on nuclear weapons with the Russians; passage of a $4.3 billion bill—previously blocked by Republicans—providing health benefits for emergency rescue workers in the 9/11 attacks of 2001.

Something missing from my list? You noticed? Yes indeed: first and absolutely foremost, the successful deal with Republicans on taxes, better described as a $4 trillion gift to America's rich people, by extending the Bush tax cuts. With the all-important tax surrender under their belts the Republicans don't seem too upset in having allowing Obama's his mini-swath of victories. There aren't too many votes in insisting that 1500 nukes aren't enough for Uncle Sam, particularly since Obama did his usual trick a year ago of surrendering before the battle began, pledging vast new outlays to the nuclear-industrial-complex. Would it have been that smart to deny benefits to 9/11 responders or say that gays in the military have to stay in the closet. Presumably they'll fight all the more fiercely now they can stand Out and Proud. On things that really matter, once they reassemble after the break, the Republicans will probably stay awake, though with a President who surrenders with the alacrity of Obama, excessive vigilance probably isn't necessary.

You give $4 trillion to the rich and they express their thanks in measured terms. Their hired opinion formers laud the spirit of admirable compromise enabling responsible members of Congress to come together in bipartisanship to keep the hog wallow open for business.

True, there are the nay-sayers, the left-leaning tribunes of the people who say, accurately enough, that the great "compromise" was, in the economist Michael Hudson's words, "all for the rich—not to promote stability and recovery—creating new public debt to hand out to the bankers which future tax payers will spend generations paying off".

It was a deal of refined cynicism, containing the poison pill of what has been billed as a generous gesture to working people—a $120 billion reduction in Social Security contributions by labor—reducing the rate of contributions to the Social Security pension fund from 6.2 per cent of wages to 4.2 per cent. But in fact this is a tripwire, setting up an onslaught on Social Security a year down the road as underfunded and going swiftly bankrupt and ready to be auctioned off to Wall Street.

The prime constant factor in American politics across the past six decades has been a counter-attack by the rich against the social reforms of the 1930s.

Twenty years ago the supreme prize of the Social Security trust funds—the government pensions that changed the face of America in the mid-1930s—seemed far beyond Wall Street's grasp. No Republican president could possibly prevail in such an enterprise. It would have to be an inside job by a Democrat. Clinton tried it, but the Lewinsky sex scandal narrowly aborted his bid.

If Obama can be identified with one historic mission on behalf of capital it is this—and though success is by no means guaranteed, it is closer than it has ever been.

This brings us to the upcoming 112th Congress, reflecting Republican gains in November, which will spend the evening of February 2 listening to Obama's "bipartisan" agenda laid out in his State of the Union address.

The *Politico* website—reflecting informed political opinion in Washington DC—recently predicted that in this next address, "the teleprompter in chief is expected to announce cuts in Social Security." As Robert Kuttner of *Politico* speculates: Obama's rationale will be "to preempt an even more draconian set of budget cuts likely to be proposed by the incoming House Budget Committee chairman, Rep. Paul Ryan as a condition of extending the debt ceiling. This is expected to hit in April."

But surely for progressives, infuriated by the tax giveaway to the rich, and whose support Obama will be counting on for re-election in 2012, cuts in Social Security will be the last straw? Don't bet on it. As political beasts of burden, progressives have backs that can sustain a virtually infinite number of straws.

Against the tax betrayal these middle-class progressives will tout the end of Don't Ask, Don't Tell. Identity politics will trump class politics, as has been the case for middle-class progressives for the past quarter-century.

Nor will they make much of another major failure by Obama: a calculated "inability" to get the 'Development, Relief and Education for Alien Minors (DREAM) Act', through Congress. This would have enabled millions of undocumented immigrants who came to the US before they turned 16 to become conditional permanent residents and then citizens if they graduated from high school, completed military service or college, and kept their noses clean.

Republicans blocked the bill in the Senate, though it would have passed if Democrats had shown unity. But the White House was markedly disinclined to expend any political capital on this, just as it has failed to live up to any of its commitments to the blacks or to labor, whose money and organizers were the determining factor in getting Obama elected in 2008.

Right now Obama's job approval rating, as measured by Gallup, is running at about 46 per cent, as against the disapprovers who are around 48 per cent, having dropped back from an early autumn high of over 50 per cent. He's now fairly set upon the right-wing course Clinton embarked on after 1994: wars abroad (Yugoslavia for Clinton, Afghanistan for Obama); a war-on-terror policy worthy of Bush-Cheney, as exemplified in the abandonment of pledges to shut down Guantanamo and the swift drafting of new and repressive espionage laws in the wake of WikiLeaks. Bill Quigley and Vince Warren wrote an ominous piece for *CounterPunch* about Obama's liberty Problem:

> Advisors in the Obama administration have floated the idea of creating a special new legal system to indefinitely detain people by Executive Order.
> Why? To do something with the people wrongfully imprisoned in Guantanamo. Why not follow the law and try them? The government knows it will not be able to win prosecutions against them because they were tortured by the US.
> Guantanamo is coming up on its ninth anniversary—a horrifying stain on the character of the US commitment to justice. President Obama knows well that Guantanamo is the most powerful recruitment tool for those challenging the US. Unfortunately, this proposal for indefinite detention will prolong the corrosive effects of the illegal

and immoral detentions at Guantanamo rightly condemned worldwide.

The practical, logical, constitutional and human rights problems with the proposal are uncountable.

Clinton, the self-proclaimed 'Comeback Kid', took the same turn with his 1996 Counter-Terrorism and Effective Death Penalty Act, which was a prelude to the Patriot Act. Clinton launched his successful onslaught on welfare in his second term, also the attack on Social Security which Obama now aims to consummate.

As with Clinton, we have an opportunistic, neoliberal president without a shred of intellectual or moral principle. We have disconsolate liberals, and a press saying that Obama is showing admirable maturity in understanding what bipartisanship really means. Like Clinton, Obama is fortunate in having pwogs to his left only too happy to hail Don't Ask, Don't Tell as the rationale for continuing to support this spineless slimeball. The landscape doesn't change much, as evidenced by the fact that Jeb Bush, former governor of Florida and George W's brother, looks as though he's ready to make a bid for the Republican nomination.

Masters of Perfidy: The Crash of AIG

THE FIRST CLUE that something was terribly amiss with the insurance giant AIG should have been made manifest when the conglomerate began offering products—and financial products at that. What exactly does an insurance company produce? The short and nasty answer is that AIG manufactured precisely what it was meant to guard against. Namely, risk. Extreme risk.

Ultimately, AIG was cashiered on several trillion dollars of risky financial products, sewn together by Ivy League math whizzes and aces in the arcane art of arbitrage. These were fanciful consolidations of debt that no sane insurer would ever have indemnified. When the company crashed in the dismal autumn of 2008, it turned sheepishly to the insurer of last resort for rescue: the U.S. government. The disgraced executives made the case that the rot in AIG was spreading and was threatening to go systemic. Too big to fail became the mantra of the bailout. AIG, perhaps the most recklessly managed company in the world, was so thoroughly enmeshed in nearly every sector of the American—and even global—economy that to let it sunder would be to risk the crash of the nation. Or so they said.

Both the Bush and the Obama teams—themselves thoroughly marinated in the AIG mindset—quickly capitulated to financial extortion and infused the company with more than $182 billion in taxpayer cash—a sum that continued to rise each month with the inexorability of a lava dome inside an active volcano. Thus did the Obama administration in one of its first official acts endorse the remorseless logic of throwing good billions after bad.

The Treasury Department and AIG's management were so harmonious that Timothy Geithner allowed AIG's executives to continue to run the company even after the bailout. The top brass at AIG had successfully duped Geithner and his political puppet master Larry Summers into buying the far-fetched idea that the collapse of AIG had been perpetrated by a handful of rogue traders operating out of satellite offices in distant London and suburban Wilton, Connecticut.

Indeed, Geithner and Summers were so sympathetic to the plight of these corporate titans that they sanctioned more than $450 million in executive bonuses to managers at AIG, including its disgraced Financial Products Division.

Of course, AIG had, among other giants of Wall Street, insured Goldman Sachs, which had made its own dementedly bad investments in subprime loans to the tune of tens of billions of dollars. And there was no way in hell that Geithner, Summers or Hank Paulson was going to let Goldman Sachs eat those loans. And that bit of political sleight-of-hand seems to have paid off handsomely for Goldman Sachs, which just posted record quarterly profits of $700 million only a brief nine months after it seemed like the investment house was on the verge of an ignominious collapse. In other words, the $54 billion in direct payments the feds had lavished on Goldman, Merrill-Lynch and the other Wall Street firms was just the icing on a very rich cake.

In a sense, it's only fitting that the government ended up as the ultimate guarantor for those furious seasons of Wall Street greed. After all, by consciously dismantling the regulatory framework that tended to constrain the felonious instincts that come naturally to the Wall Street player (such as the Glass-Steagall Act), the government played a decisive role in fostering the rampant financial criminality and looting that reached its apogee in 2008, crashing the global economy, draining retirement funds and pension accounts and casting millions from their homes and millions more into the perdition of long-term unemployment. All of this coming down in an era of extreme government austerity, typified by over-burdened and underfunded social welfare programs. As with the defunct regulations to restrain corporate crimes, so too had the economic safety net been sheared away—its tethers sliced by Reagan, the Bushes and Clinton—long before the economy cratered. Now there is nothing to cushion the blow on the long fall to the bottom.

The architects of this economic deregulation achieved a truly fearful bi-partisan symmetry that persists to this day. Even now, amid the rubble of Wall Street's collapse, the neo-liberals and neo-conservatives remain as uniform as conjoined twins in their devotion to a broadly deregulated market. Any talk of bringing back forceful correctives such as a new and improved Glass-Steagall Act was immediately squelched by Obama, flanked by John McCain and Mitch McConnell, as well. If the crash of AIG—the largest in history—was in the sclerotic parlance of the times a "teachable moment" it is apparent that while much was ventured, nothing was learned.

The problem is that the government bailout, which some accounts now estimate will eventually top $24-cap T-for Trillion—flowed almost entirely in the wrong direction. Instead of helping to mend the lives of Wall Street's victims—the unemployed, the uninsured, the destitute and homeless—Bush and Obama rewarded the perpetrators. They even gave them bonuses.

+++

As the financial writer Michael Lewis explains in a fascinating article on the AIG FP division in *Vanity Fair*, the financial products offered by AIG were little more than complex iterations of the bizarre financial instruments designed in the 1980s by Drexel, Burnam, Lambert—the company that brought us the junk bond and other improvised explosive devices of high finance.

The young turks at AIG FP, led by Joseph Cassano, improved on the Drexel, Burnham model—or at least mutated it for their own purposes. The game was all about swallowing risk—hiding it, hedging it and repackaging it as, yes, a financial product and not a liability. In other words, something to swap, buy, sell and make money on. Lots and lots of money.

And it worked—for a while. Soon Cassano's division was piling up $300 million a year in profits and making the platoon of financial tricksters themselves hugely wealthy. Bonuses of more than $25 million a year were commonplace. The executives were making a killing in looting their own hedge funds by skimming 35 per cent of the profits, a self-asserted gratuity that would shame even the most rapacious personal injury lawyer.

All through the high-flying 90s, the AIG risk-swallowing business continued to defy gravity, posting amazing profits on ever more opaque financial confabulations. Then in 2002 came the first whiff of rot. AIG insiders told Michael Lewis that the decomposition began to gnaw away at the FP Division the very moment Cassano replaced his mentor Tom Savage as CEO of the subsidiary. Of course, this retrospective was almost certainly motivated in large measure by post-fall ass-covering. But there's no question that Cassano was an abrasive personality and not, like many of the traders, an Ivy Leaguer with a DNA profile shaped by generations of old money.

Like AIG's former CEO, Hank Greenberg, who had been chased out of the company by Eliot Spitzer, Cassano was viewed by his rivals and subordinates as a reckless bully, who ruled the company through the humiliation of nearly everyone he encountered from secretaries to junior executives. Cassano's father was a police office and the son brought the brute mentality and creepy paranoia of the street cop into the executive suites and the trading room floor. He ruled the London office by fear and did not countenance contrarian opinions, even as the trading instruments passing before the insurers became more fantastical and the economic perils ever more extreme.

Lewis' AIG confidents blamed the terminal descent of their company on Cassano's over-weening arrogance and his rather crude understanding of the very products his FP Division was manufacturing.

In other words, Cassano simply didn't have the head for the complex math at play in those deep derivatives. He didn't see the pitfalls, trapdoors and inevitable apocalypse at the end of the road. And his team of math geniuses—many with minds minted by MIT and Harvard—went along for the ride, swallowing his torrents of abuse, glossing over the hollow core of the hedge funds. Why? Because, naturally, they were making too much money to object and Cassano, despite his tyrannical fits, was dishing out eight-figure bonuses for Christmas. Indeed, many of the top AIG traders did worse than merely endure Cassano's abuse—bother personal and organizational. They coddled his worst financial impulses and sucked up to him. In other words, they did their damnedest to suppress their consciousness of guilt.

In the aftermath of the wreckage, Cassano's supervisors back at AIG HQ in Manhattan have worked sedulously to create the impression that they scarcely knew the man running their hottest division. From Hank Greenberg to Edward Libby, the top brass has sought to portray Cassano and his team as an out-of-control unit that had somehow fled the reservation.

This won't wash. Not for those in the know, anyway. The man who was running AIG's darkest appendage had been installed as boss of the division by Greenberg himself, who saw in Cassano a man who shared his own despotic management style in playing billion-dollar shell games with other people's money. When Eliot Spitzer brought down Greenberg in 2005 for the executive's accounting high-jinks, some inside AIG thought that Cassano might eventually end up taking his place. Others in the company believed that he should've been slapped in leg irons. Opinions on Cassano four years ago were divided, but there was no shortage of them. Now Cassano is suddenly the man no one knew about.

According to his colleagues in London, Cassano was ascetic in his total commitment to the company he was steadily destroying. So devoted, in fact, that Cassano recycled most of his $38.5 million salary right back into AIG and its toxic products. The remainder of his AIG trove—estimated at some $238 million—he cached in that most timid of financial parking lots, the U.S. Treasury Bill. Say this for Cassano, he was no preening financial playboy. He dressed casually, drove a modest car and lived to work—and terrorize his staff. "Without AIG FP, he had nothing," one trader quipped.

+++

With Greenberg and Savage by his side, Joseph Cassano turned AIG FP into a kind of recycling station for toxic financial properties held by corporations, equity firms, banks and institutional hybrids, those freaks and sports of the post-Glass-Steagall era. Cassano opened the gates of AIG FP to them, one and all, eventually absorbing $450 billion in corporate credit-default swaps and another $75 billion in the fatal subprime mortgages. He became Wall Street's one-stop waste manager, insuring and amalgamating bad debts of every stripe, from credit cards to student loans, corporate buyouts to commercial mortgages, transmuting this junk into big new packages with a glossy veneer that masked the entropic nature of the whole enterprise.

After the attacks of 9/11 and subsequent nosedive of the global economy, AIG's business began to pick up, as troubled executives desperately scrambled for someplace to dump their risky debts. Cassano and Co. were happy to provide the landfill services, charging a very healthy tipping fee.

But gradually, almost imperceptibly, the weight of the debt-load began to shift, tilting away from traditional corporate investments and decisively toward the necrotic subprime mortgages. By 2005, AIG FP's consumer loan insurance portfolio consisted of 95 per cent subprime mortgages.

The seeds of destruction had been sown. When housing prices began to plummet, AIG was doomed.

But was Cassano the arch villain of this particular chapter in the annals of American capitalism or was he, in the end, Wall Street's willing dupe?

To reach a plausible assessment it's vital to remember that AIG was digesting what the big Wall Street houses fed it. Often these packages were artful mixes of consumer and corporate debt. So artful, in fact, that AIG's brain trust wasn't entirely clear what they were bonding. The risks were blended, sliced and pressurized into indecipherable collages of debt, like mutual funds from Mars. One top analyst thought that AIG's credit-default packages consisted of no more than 10 per cent subprime loans. Another put the figure at 20 per cent tops. Cassano, it appears, had no clue about the real number and didn't care. In his mind, there was simply no way the housing market would go bust—not across the board, anyway. And his Wall Street clients at Goldman, Sachs and Merrill-Lynch backed him up in this delusion. After all, what did they have to lose?

In 2007, Cassano, as blissfully ignorant of the peril immediately before him as Wile E. Coyote ten feet off the cliff, boasted in a talk to a seraglio of investors that it was hard for him to even imagine a scenario "that would see us losing one dollar on any of these transactions."

Less than six months later, it was all over. Cassano had been evicted from AIG (though he continued to get paid $1 million a month as a consultant without portfolio) and Goldman, Sachs was knocking at the door of the company demanding that AIG compensate the investment firm for its own landslide of bad debts. AIG was in no position to pay up, naturally, but Goldman, Sach's man at Treasury, its former CEO Hank Paulson, did—dollar for dollar.

In for a dollar, in for a trillion.

It has been said by Wall Street apologists that the crash of AIG was an aberration, a singularity of greed run amok. No one could have predicted the fall, they say. Wall Street analysts were beguiled by the blizzard of prospectuses and portfolios on AIG operations that were, they claimed, as immune from explication as the most arcane passages in *Finnegans Wake*. So too with the business press, which was apparently so mesmerized by these chimerical reports that they completely missed the financial fun-and-games transpiring inside AIG FP.

The regulators at the SEC have also connived to claim ignorance about the true condition of AIG and it's more malign operations as it veered toward the cliff of no return, fooled, they claimed, by the company's diction of deceit. Somehow missing the daily bulletins of impending ruin, the regulators have tried to offload all the blame on Cassano and his traders for perverting the system.

This is all nonsense. AIG operated at the very heart of the system, a system enabled by the SEC and its political overlords. Indeed, AIG served as the system's great backstop, its failsafe. What happens when the failsafe fails?

So now the bills from this tableau of financial debauchery have come due. That $182 billion pay-out wasn't a final call, but merely an opening bid. Tens of trillions may yet follow.

No, AIG didn't pervert the system. It was a creature of a perverse system. One that is literally consuming itself from the inside out. A mighty leveling looms.

Jeffrey St. Clair

The Fall of the House of Stanford

On June 14th, 2012, R. Allen Stanford was sentenced by US District Judge David Wittner to 110 years in federal prison for his role in a $7 billion fraud scheme. On pronouncing the sentence, Judge Wittner said that Stanford treated his victims like "economic roadkill." Here is the story of his rise and fall.

THIS IS THE story of a deadbeat banker. His name is Allen Stanford and he was once known as the $7 billion man. Now, he faces federal indictments that charge him with running a vast Ponzi scheme that bilked depositors out of billions.

Born in Mexia, Texas, the mysterious arc of Stanford's career sees him rise from burger-flipping gym rat in Waco to globe-trotting banker, a lord of cricket, a friend (and travel agent) of politicians. His robust resume also includes strangely intimate histories with numerous female acquaintances (known in his circle as the "Outside Wives"), as well as the Drug Enforcement Agency.

Blinking stridently on the radar of federal investigators at various agencies for more than 20 years, Stanford's banking empire was finally shut down in February by the Securities Exchange Commission, which claims, in self-congratulatory language, that Stanford's fraudulent operations put the "integrity of the of the markets" at risk. Stanford and six of his partners now face an imposing list of charges, ranging from banking fraud to bribery of regulatory officials in Antigua to personal enrichment from the vaults of depositors.

Stanford, who was taken into federal custody by the FBI, denies all. He claims that the sudden insolvency of his banking operations stemmed not from embezzlement or fraud but from, in the words of his lawyer Dick DeGuerin, "the SEC's heavy-handed actions." Now there's a first.

Left to sort their way through the rubble of Stanford International are more than 30,000 angry depositors, many from Latin America, who bought certificates of deposit, and other glittering financial instruments from Stanford-owned banks, only to discover, according to federal investigators, that Stanford had diverted large chunks of those deposits into his own accounts to support the familiar playthings of today's high roller: personal jets, yachts, sports teams, restaurants, women and gaudy mansions, including a 57-room palazzo in Coral Gables that is ringed by a moat.

Still, connoisseurs of financial crimes—and perhaps even the principals, themselves—are scratching their heads as to why the Stanford case, with its rich veins of scandal, sex and villainy, has yet to generate the same kind of media and governmental outrage sparked by the crimes of that other master Ponzi-schemer, Bernie Madoff. Some speculate that Madoff picked the pockets of a finer class of clientele: movie stars, writers, socialites, charitable foundations Holocaust survivors. Stanford's victims, on the other hand, were either Latin American or obscure residents of the Sun Belt with more new money than they knew how to handle. Others hint at an even darker narrative involving the fruitful and symbiotic relationship many off-shore banks in the Caribbean have enjoyed over the decades with certain secretive federal agencies.

+++

R. Allen Stanford is a large man. Some might call him imposing. He stands six-foot four and is, in parlance of the meatlocker, pumped, whether by hours at the gym or through the targeted administration of certain muscle-enhancing elixirs is unknown. He wears his hair clipped and sports a moustache favored by street cops and certain stars of seventies porn flicks. He once claimed to be descended from Leland Stanford, the former governor of California after whom Stanford University is named—a claim urgently debunked by officials at the university. He has a voice like a leafblower. It tends to steamroll people. He is a Texan and proud of it—though unlike many Lone Star tycoons he doesn't affect the persona of a rancher or oil baron. In fact, he is something of an Anglophile. The England of the Empire, which became the world's biggest booster of cricket, the game that Britain imposed on its colonies and which the colonials learned to play better, with far greater elan.

Stanford likes the colonial style. His notorious bank in Antigua resembles a colonial plantation house out of a late Victorian photograph. He is so sensitive on the subject that he once sued a principal at a Catholic school in New York for calling him a "neo-colonialist." Touchy, in other words.

As a business man, Stanford got his start in the late 1970s in sun-scorched and wind-blasted Waco, Texas, where he set up a network of swank—for the high plains of Texas, anyway—fitness clubs, called Mr. & Mrs. Health. He later changed the name to Total Fitness Center. From these humble beginnings a first-rate hustler was born. This pedigree is scarcely unique in the ranks of global swindlers. Recall that the infamous arbitrageur Ivan Boesky got his start in high finance after bankrupting the family business: a chain of Detroit strip clubs.

A profligate loudmouth, Stanford would buzz around Waco in his Jaguar and make surprise landings at the local football stadium in his private helicopter. "If you looked up narcissist in the dictionary," former employee Tim Gardner told *Vanity Fair* writer Bryan Burrough, "you'd probably see a photo of Allen."

By 1982, it had all gone bust. Stanford's fitness empire crumbled during the Texas oil recession. The bruised bigwig filed for Chapter 11 bankruptcy protection, claiming $13.6 million in debts and only $200,000 in assets. The creditors and investors got shafted and Stanford, after a brief stint flipping meat pies at a place called Junior's Hamburgers, disappeared.

A year later, though, Stanford resurfaced, running his own bank on the tiny Caribbean island of Monserrat, the kind of indulgent locale favored as a financial safe-haven by swindlers, tax cheats, drug runners and intelligence agencies. Stanford has variously claimed that the six million in cash to start up the bank came from shrewd real estate swaps in recession-battered Houston and a heaven-sent investment by oil refinery workers in Aruba.

Why smoky Monserrat, the volcanic island with fewer than 12,000 inhabitants? Stanford supposedly fell in love with the island while he was there supporting himself by giving lessons to novice scuba divers. It's really anyone's guess.

But this sanctuary was not to be a mere postage-stamp operation, not one of the so-called Instabanks for which Monserrat had become famous in the twilit world of money circulation. Stanford, unlike the vast majority of Monserrat's 350 off-shore banking houses, actually put a sign on a two-story building and hired local women to work there, even giving them computers for their desks, but apparently never actually turning the power on. He dubbed his new operation the Guardian International Bank.

Stanford busied himself concocting a Dickensian fable about the origins of the bank—claiming that it had been opened during the depression in 1932 by his barber grandfather Lodis. Meanwhile, his associates in Houston and Miami begin marketing the bank, largely to Latin American clients and Cuban exiles in south Florida, by using sultry young women to hawk the bank's enticingly high interest rates on certificates of deposit, guaranteed by Stanford to levitate at least two percentage points above the rates of the best American banks. It was called the two-point-more promise, a come-on often paired in ads with a shot of the cleavage of one of the bank's models.

Silly as it sounds, the scheme worked. In 1989, the year the bank's tiny office was flattened by Hurricane Hugo, Stanford's Monserrat institution claimed $55 million in deposits. Ten months later, this figure had more than doubled.

Of course, who knows how closely those eye-popping numbers paralleled the reality in the vaults. The bank's annual reports were objects of mystification. These crudely designed documents were hastily written after hours at the bank, presenting streams of numbers as opaque as an Oregon fog.

The money was coming in fast and, by most accounts, going out even faster—much of it into Stanford's personal account and thence into sports cars, jets and a lawn-flamenco-pink hacienda near Houston.

In a mere six years, Allen Stanford had matriculated from the failed owner of a chain of Waco gyms to a global banker with hundreds of millions in assets, on paper at least.

So how did he did he do it? Stanford told friends that he was able to pay such gravity-defying interest rates because of shrewd investments and because of the delightful circumstance that his bank didn't have to pay taxes in the libertarian paradise of Monserrat. Few swallowed the facile explanation, but even fewer really cared, as long as the money kept rolling in and the authorities, wherever they were, didn't intrude on the festivities.

+++

As it happened, the FBI was at that very moment beginning to sniff around the periphery of Stanford's fishy enterprise, starting a game of approach-and-avoidance that lasted nearly twenty years. In 1989, while pursuing a wide-ranging, though typically shallow, probe into a panoply of financial crimes being committed by off-shore banks, the feds began to follow the rising tide of Colombian drug cartel money then washing through Caribbean banks. Some of that money led them right to the steps of Guardian International and the Stanford Financial Bank.

When word reached the governor of Monserrat in 1991 that both Scotland Yard and the FBI were probing Stanford and his bank for laundering cocaine money, the government precipitously yanked the bank's license to do business on the island.

Once again Stanford, expert scuba diver that he is, submerged from public view, only to resurface on the balmy, pink-sand shores of Antigua, another Caribbean island that was virgin ground in terms of nettlesome banking regulations. In the Antiguan capital of St. Johns, Stanford swiftly made an alliance with the fabulously corrupt Bird family, which had run the island as a kind of private holding company since Antigua gained its independence in 1991. The Birds soon unloaded the troubled Bank of Antigua on Stanford. In the steps of this initial foothold, Stanford opened a second version of the Stanford Financial Bank, in a white colonnaded plantation house-style building—a gleaming, Disneyfied caricature of colonial potency.

Not wanting a repeat of his ungracious eviction from Monserrat, Stanford set about showering Antigua with charitable contributions. The financier soon inveigled his way into admired status as the island's financial patron saint: he built a hospital, libraries, cricket fields, bought the island's leading newspaper and made multiple loans to the cash-strapped government. Those loans—eventually totaling nearly $90 million—tightly shackled the government of Antigua to Stanford's fortunes, even after the Bird dynasty's power came to an end in the elections of 2004.

The largesse paid off smashingly. By marketing the bank's atmospheric interest rates to Latin American millionaires and businesses, Stanford Financial's holdings began to soar, hitting $400 million by 1995. This windfall sparked an expansion of Stanford's operations, as he opened new banks in Venezuela, Mexico, Panama, Peru and Ecuador. To market his operations, Stanford recruited young greedheads fresh from American's finest business schools. These miscreants with MBAs, working in teams with nicknames like "Money Machine" and "Superstars," were lavishly rewarded with what some called "banker's crack," an unprecedented one percent commission for every dollar they brought into the bank and out-of-the-blue bonuses that included pricey sports cars. The message: sell the product and keep your mouth shut.

On the flip side, employees who asked too many troubling questions about the enigmatic ways the company claimed to be making money tended to get 86'd from the bank, and fast. Many of these hyper-curious former employees, including Gonzalo Tirado, head of Stanford's operations in Venezuela, conveyed their concerns to federal investigators—usually to no avail.

Meanwhile, back in Washington, a raft of federal agencies, including the SEC, US Customs, the FBI and the DEA, continued to regularly monitor Stanford's affairs. Curiously, however, these probes did not seem to pick up on the fact that Stanford was engaged in a high-finance hustle, a con which promised a kind of cold fusion of the banking world, offering bottomless aquifers of cash with little or no risk. Instead of busting up this transparent Ponzi scheme, the feds spent their time trying to determine if the bank was serving as a money-washing station for the drug cartels. Lots of trace evidence, no indictments.

For nearly twenty years, the only federal agency that caused Stanford any real irritation was the Internal Revenue Service, which pounced on some disagreeable irregularities in his tax returns. The IRS sued Stanford for failing to file income tax returns in 1990. The IRS alleged that Stanford and his wife Susan, a former dental hygienist, owed the government more than $420,000 in unpaid taxes. Two decades later, the IRS was still hounding Stanford, claiming that he owed more than $26 million in back taxes for the years 1999 to 2003 alone.

The staggering increase in taxes imposed by the IRS roughly charts the meteoric rise in income claimed by Stanford to have flowed into his Antiguan banks. By 2001, Stanford Financial boasted of having more than $1.2 billion in assets. By 2008, this figure had ballooned to $8.5 billion. Of course, when the vaults were opened, $7 billion of that figure ended up missing, filched, according to federal prosecutors, by Stanford and his inner circle.

+++

As billions began to multiply and the investigators circle closer to the heart of the scam, Stanford bought himself some protection. For one thing, he had deeply penetrated the very law enforcement agencies that were snooping into the seamier reaches of his business empire. As head of his corporate security division, Stanford hired the former chief of the Miami office of the FBI. He also retained Kroll Security Group, the global private investigations company that functions like Blackwater for the corporate world. Kroll's offices are thickly stocked with former spooks and FBI agents. These investments paid dividends for many years.

In the summer of 2006, the SEC appeared to be closing in on Stanford for running his bank as a Ponzi scheme. Then, in the winter of that year, the agency's investigation was suddenly ordered to a skidding halt by the Bush Justice Department, which told the SEC to back off because another, unidentified federal outfit was involved with Stanford.

Which agency would that be? Speculation has focused on the Drug Enforcement Agency, whose relationship with Stanford stretches back to the late 1990s. In that year, Stanford turned over a $3.1 million check to the DEA. The money had been originally deposited in Stanford's bank by a notorious Mexican drug kingpin Amado Carrillo Fuentes, known as the Lord of the Heavens.

The circumstances of this transaction remain murky, but the check served as evidence that Stanford's bank had been a resting place on the migratory path of Mexican drug money. According to an investigative report by the BBC news program Panorama, at the time he turned over the check, Stanford was already working as a paid informant for the DEA, snitching for the agency on the flow of narco-dollars by bank clients from Venezuela, Colombia and Mexico. Sources interviewed by the BBC assert that this cozy relationship bought Stanford a decade's worth of protection from criminal inquiries by other federal agencies, including the SEC. That was, of course, the same period of time which saw bank deposits and CD purchases soar from $1 billion to $8 billion. Thousands of depositors lost their savings, in part it seems, as a consequence of the federal government's strange bargain with the brash banker.

Around this same period, Stanford putting high-ranking politicians in his pocket, notably the two Toms: Daschle and DeLay. Stanford's prime concern at the time was an anti-money laundering bill introduced by Bill Clinton before he left office. Stanford sank $40,000 into Daschle's "527" senate leadership fund and Daschle promptly helped to kill the legislation in the senate. During the same period, Tom DeLay collected $20,100 from Stanford. The ever-pliant DeLay also racked up beaucoup frequent flier mileage from his eleven trips on Stanford jets. The toilet seats on those jets are emblazoned with Stanford's logo, a gold eagle.

Up in Miami, Stanford cultivated a relationship with Florida regulators almost as cordial as the ones he enjoyed down in Antigua. In a one-of-a-kind deal, Florida regulators granted Stanford the right to operate in the state as a foreign trust company. As detailed by Lucy Komisar in the *Miami Herald*, this unique arrangement allowed Stanford's operation to channel tens of millions of dollars from deals in Florida to accounts in Antigua without reporting any of it to Florida regulators.

In addition, Stanford's brokers in the resplendent office tower on Biscayne Bay were permitted to sell nearly a billion dollars in bank notes without opening their records to state inspectors cruising for fraudulent sales. Indeed, the transaction receipts from the sales of Stanford CDs were routinely shredded by the firm, loaded into 95-gallon barrels and trucked to the landfill. Florida regulators knew about the document destruction and did nothing to stop it. And those documents—so-called Single-Purpose Trust Agreements—were, of course, the hard evidence of a massive swindle.

Why the mad rush to transfer the money to Antigua? Because down on the island, as detailed in the federal indictment, government regulators were being lavishly bribed to turn a blind eye or two to the looting of deposits and the giant bank's supposedly independent auditors were a tiny firm of locals under the sway of the company. Pity the depositors. For down in Antigua, those CDs did not enjoy the protection of the FDIC insurance. Once the money was gone, there was no getting it back.

"Nobody was even asking questions about it," said Mark Raymond, a Miami lawyer. "All you had to do was examine those certificates; you would have known they were fraudulent. It was more like Monopoly money."

+++

As the clock began to tick on Stanford's scam, his behavior became more and more audacious. In 2008, Stanford landed his private helicopter at Lord's, the Valhalla of cricket in London. Stanford hauled out a glass case containing $20 million, the winner-take-all reward for a challenge match between his Caribbean "Superstar" team and the English all-stars. The Caribbeans routed the English in the match, but the real scandal played itself out up in Stanford's box seats, where he was caught on camera pawing the wives and girlfriends of the English players, including the pregnant wife of wicketkeeper Matt Prior.

"If that was my missus," one player told the *Daily Mail*, "I'd have punched him."

Stanford's marriage to Susan had broken up in 1999, though she delayed filing for divorce until 2007. Sir Allen (for by now he'd been knighted by Antiqua) had not been a faithful husband. Indeed since the mid-1990s Stanford had entered into long-term relationships with what bank insiders referred to as "the outside wives." These included another woman named Susan, who lives outside Dallas with Stanford's 17-year-old son; Beki Reeves-Stanford, who resides in Florida, with her two children by Stanford; and Louise Sage, an English woman who also gave birth to two of Stanford's six (known) children, Ross and R. Allena.

To this list we can add Stanford's current girlfriend, 31-year-old Andrea Stoekler, a former Stanford employee. When a federal order froze Stanford's assets this spring, Sir Allen went into hiding in Stoekler's mother's basement in Fredericksburg, Virginia, where he ultimately surrendered himself for arrest by the FBI on June 18 of this year.

For Stanford it ended not with a bang, but with a blogger. His name is Alex Dalmady, a financial analyst in south Florida, who had been asked to investigate the soundness of the bank by a friend who had sunk his life-savings into Stanford CDs. It took the inquisitive Dalmady only a few hours of digging through the bank's corporate filings posted on its own website to reach the conclusion that there were serious financial shenanigans going on inside the company. He picked up the phone, called his friend and told him to "take your money out as soon as possible."

What did Dalmady see that so many others had missed? "There were a number of things that struck me, from the lack of detail to the simplicity of the business model to the lack of sophistication in the language they used," Dalmady said.

Then he wrote up his suspicions in an article titled "Duck Tails" for the January edition of a Venezuelan financial paper called *Venecononmia*. Even with the Madoff scandal unfolding in New York, the exposé attracted scant attention until it was reposted on an economic blog called *The Devil's Excrement*, where the story went global. A few days later *Business Week's* Matthew Goldstein published a long piece on Stanford that followed up on many irregularities exposed by Dalmady.

By the end of February, Stanford's offices were aswarm with SEC investigators and FBI agents, showing up, as usual, about a decade too late for most investors and depositors.

Then suddenly Stanford disappeared from public view for months, into the basement of that house in Virginia, perhaps hoping that this storm too would blow over and he could resurface once again on some island paradise. But it wasn't to be.

During a perp walk to a pre-trial hearing in Houston, Stanford, with his hands shackled at his waist and dressed in an orange jumpsuit, mugged for the cameras one more time, flashing a louche grin that seemed to say: "Who? Me?"

Jeffrey St. Clair

The Myth of the Knowledge Economy

"IN THE 21ST century, the best anti-poverty program around is a first-class education," President Obama famously declared in his 2010 State of the Union Address, just as millions of high schoolers across the nation were embarking on the annual ritual of picking their preferred colleges and preparing the grand tour of the prospects, with parents in tow, gazing ashen faced at the prospective fees.

The image is of the toiling students springing from lecture room to well-paying jobs demanding advanced skills in all the arts that can make America great again—outthinking, outknowing the Chinese, Japanese, Indians, South Koreans and Germans in the cutting edge, cut-throat high-tech economies of tomorrow.

Start with the raw material in this epic knowledge battle. As a dose of cold water over all this high-minded talk it's worth looking at Josipa Roksa and Richard Arum's recently published "Academically Adrift: Limited Learning on College Campuses." The two profs followed more than 2,300 undergraduates at 29 universities, selected to represent the range of America's 2000-plus four-year college institutions. As resumed by Steven Kent in *Daily Finance*:

> Among the authors' findings: 32 per cent of the students whom they followed in an average semester did not take any courses that assigned more than 40 pages of reading per week. Half did not take any courses in which more than 20 pages of writing were assigned throughout the entire term. Furthermore, 35 per cent of the students sampled spent five hours or less a week studying alone.

Typical students spent about 16 per cent of their time on academic pursuits, and were "academically engaged," write the authors, less than 30 hours a week. After two years in college, 45 per cent of students showed no significant gains in learning; after four years, 36 per cent showed little change. And the students who did show improvement only logged very modest gains. Students spent 50 per cent less time studying compared with students a few decades ago.

Students who majored in traditional liberal arts fields like philosophy, history and English showed 'significantly higher gains in critical thinking, complex reasoning and writing skills over time than students in other fields of study.'" But of course these are the courses and instructors being ruthlessly pruned back.

One of the study's authors Richard Arum, says college governing boards, shoveling out colossal sums to their presidents, athletic coaches and senior administrative staff, demand that the focus be "student retention," also known as trying very hard not to kick anyone out for not doing any measurable work. As Arum put it to *Money College*, "Students are much more likely to drop out of school when they are not socially engaged, and colleges and universities increasingly view students as consumers and clients. Unfortunately, there is no guarantee that all students want to be exposed to a rigorous academic program."

Rick Santorum briefly struck out at ingrained snobbery about going to college: "President Obama once said he wants everybody in America to go to college. What a snob." Amid howls from Republican governors, this was a piece of derision it didn't take him long to retract. Actually, it turns out only about 30 per cent of Americans over the age of 25 have bachelor's degrees. Jack Metzgar, emeritus professor of humanities at Roosevelt University in Chicago, had a very useful piece in *Working Class Perspectives*, the blog of the Center for Working Class Studies site, with this and other useful facts and reflections.

The US government's Bureau of Labor Statistics (BLS) reports that in 2010 only 20 per cent of jobs required a bachelor's degree, whereas 26 per cent of jobs did not even require a high school diploma, and another 43 per cent required only a high school diploma or equivalent.

Please note that the latter 69 per cent were therefore free of the one debt in America that's even more certain than taxes—a student's loan. At least, if you're provably broke the IRS will countenance an "offer in compromise." In fact they recently made the process slightly easier. No such luck with student loans. The banks are in your pocket till the last dime of loan plus interest has been extorted.

Now for the next dose of cold water. The BLS reckons that by 2020 the overwhelming majority of jobs will still require only a high school diploma or less and that nearly 3/4ths of "job openings due to growth and replacement needs" over the next 10 years will pay a median wage of less than $35,000 a year, with nearly 30 per cent paying a median of about $20,000 a year (in 2010 dollars).

As Metzgar correctly remarks, "Put these two sets of numbers together, and it is hard to avoid the conclusion that Americans are over educated for the jobs that we have and are going to have. It's hard to imagine why anybody would call us 'a knowledge economy.'" In other words millions of Americans are over-educated, servicing endless debt to the banks and boosting the bottom lines of Red Bull and the breweries.

The snobbery, as Metzgar points out, stems from the fact that America's endless, mostly arid debates about education are conducted by the roughly one third who are college-educated and have okay jobs and a decent income.

The "knowledge economy" in the U.S., now needs more than 6 million people with master's or doctoral degrees, with another 1.3 million needed by 2020. But this will still be less than 5 per cent of the overall economy.

Even if we expand the definition to include jobs requiring any education beyond high school, the "knowledge economy"—now and a decade from now—will still represent less than one-third of all available jobs.

This is a lot of jobs, about 44 million now, and if you work and live in this one-third, especially in its upper reaches, more education can seem like the answer to everything.

Indeed, according to the BLS, having a bachelor's degree should yield a person nearly $30,000 a year more in wages than a high school graduate. But most of the American economy is not like this.

The BLS's three largest occupational categories by themselves accounted for more than one-third of the workforce in 2010 (49 million jobs), and they will make an outsized contribution to the new jobs projected for 2020. They are: Office and administrative support occupations (median wage of $30,710);- Sales and related occupations ($24,370); Food preparation and serving occupations($18,770). Other occupations projected to provide the largest number of new jobs in the next decade include child care workers ($19,300), personal care aides ($19,640), home health aides ($20,560), janitors and cleaners ($22,210), teacher assistants ($23,220), non-construction laborers ($23,460), security guards ($23,920), and construction laborers ($29,280).

As Metzgar writes, "As an individual, get a bachelor's degree or you are doomed to work hard for a wage that will not provide a decent standard of living for a family. You may not get such a wage even with a bachelor's degree, but without it your chances are slim and getting slimmer." Here's his kicker: But as a society, "the best anti-poverty program around" cannot possibly be "a first-class education" when more than 2/3rds of our jobs require nothing like that…we need to stop fostering illusions that good educations can ever substitute for the organized collective action — in politics, in the workplace, and in the streets—that will be required to reverse the increasingly miserable future."

So what is the best anti-poverty program? Higher wages for the jobs that are out there, currently yielding impossibly low annual incomes. The current American minimum wage ranges between $7.25 and $8.67 per hour. From time-to-time senior executives of Wal-Mart call for a rise in the minimum wage since, in the words of one former CEO, Lee Scott, "our customers simply don't have the money to buy basic necessities between pay checks." The minimum wage in Ontario, Canada, is currently well over $10 per hour, while in France it now stands at nearly $13. Australia recently raised its minimum wage to over $16 per hour, and nonetheless has an unemployment rate of just 5 percent.

Any Republican candidate seriously pledging to raise the minimum wage to $12 would gallop into the White House, unless—a solid chance—he wasn't shot dead by the Commentariat, or maybe by a Delta team acting on Obama's determination relayed to him by the bankers, that this constituted a terrorist assault on America.

Alexander Cockburn

Temple of Mammon, Planet of Doom

WHEN FRANK GEHRY gets around to designing America's answer to the Sistine Chapel, we trust this postmodern Temple of Mammon on Las Vegas Boulevard will have a ceiling fresco depicting Warren Buffett's consignment of $31 billion to Bill and Melinda Gates. As the older billionaire sits on his pillow of cloud, his outthrust hand with its bag of securities is grasped by Gates—the Adam of Software Commerce—while seraphs and cherubs muse delightedly over the IRS regulations governing the sheltering of Buffett's swag in tax-exempt nonprofit foundations.

Let us not waste too much time here advising Mr. and Mrs. Gates how to spend Buffett's money. At the moment it seems that the Gates couple's core focus is the war on AIDS and malaria, both ravaging Africa. How to improve the Dark Continent's overall well-being? America's senators and representatives can be bought for bargain-basement sums. A modest disbursement by the Gates Foundation—let us say $50,000 for each senator and $20,000 for each rep—would most certainly buy enough votes to end the current government subsidy, $4.5 billion for 2004, to cotton growers. The entire crop that year, the last for which figures are available, was worth $5.9 billion and the subsidy enables US growers to export three-quarters of their harvest and control about 40 percent of world trade, thus destroying the farm economies of countries like Mozambique, Benin and Mali. The WTO found the United States in violation this spring, but the ten largest cotton growers here—virtuous Jeffersonian toilers such as Kelley Enterprises (Tennessee) and JG Boswell (California)—have the necessary political clout to keep the subsidies coming. From 1995 to 2004, JG Boswell Co of California received $16,808,427 in cotton subsidies from the US government, while Kelley Enterprises received $8,694,643.

With overthrow of the cotton subsidy as a pilot program, Gates could launch a wider onslaught on the subsidies doled out to large wheat, rice and corn growers. Economists are slightly more costly than politicians, but generous Gates "scholarships" to prominent neoliberal economists would be contingent on these economists' swift revision of their foolish theories, currently ravaging rural India.

In Vidharbha, a cotton-growing area of the state of Maharashtra, journalist P. Sainath has reported in *The Hindu* that 540 suicides of ruined cotton farmers occurred between June 2005 and May 2006. As many as 325 farmers have killed themselves since January. May saw nearly eighty farmers taking their own lives, ten of them doing so on a single day. Some weeks, Sainath reports, there have been suicides every eight hours, usually by the ingestion of pesticide.

The reason for this catastrophe is the neoliberal onslaught on India's peasantry, which has been advancing without remit for more than the past decade, promoted by the World Bank and executed by India's federal and state governments. The traditional NGO approach-ecstatic boasts in grant applications and annual reports, zero benefits for the farmers-has been futile. It should be the job of the Gates Foundation to turn the tide inside the ivory towers generating the economic nonsense that has wrought such a dreadful toll.

One particularly delightful aspect of Buffett's $31 billion transfer was its stately mime of the Great American Pageant. Here was no twitchy trader but Buffett the wise investor, cherishing his favored stocks over decades, ambling around his headquarters in homely Omaha. And here was the younger entrepreneur, no longer the ruthless Master of Microsoft but the Third World's Santa Claus.

Could America desire any more potent evocation of virtuous capitalism at work? Surely not. And is this not a good time to evoke such virtues? It surely is, because it's clear, that the world capitalist system is out of control. Literally so. In the older order of things, international bodies such as the International Monetary Fund, the central banks and kindred bodies could claim to have some purchase on the overall situation. Not anymore. The major players these days are thousands of managers of private equity funds-traders in shares, bonds, derivatives and other instruments of a complexity that would require the genius of the late Stanislaw Lem to evoke, as he did the planet of Solaris.

It's virtually impossible now to penetrate, let alone oversee, this vast Solaris of speculative recycling of financial instruments such as credit derivatives. As the historian Gabriel Kolko recently remarked in a *CounterPunch* essay on the looming crisis, "The credit derivative market was almost nonexistent in 2001, grew fairly slowly until 2004 and then went into the stratosphere, reaching $17.3 trillion by the end of 2005. Banks simply do not understand the chain of exposure and who owns what. Senior financial regulators and bankers now admit as much. The Long-Term Capital Management hedge fund meltdown in 1998, which involved only about $5 billion in equity, revealed this. The financial structure is now infinitely more complex and far larger. The top 10 hedge funds alone in March 2006 had $157 billion in assets."

The Bank for International Settlements is no circus-tent Cassandra shrieking about the onrush of Doom. Bankers don't shriek. But here's the BIS, trembling before its crystal ball and talking, in its most recent annual report, about "planning for the worst. Consider first a discrete event which, if it occurred, would disrupt financial markets. What might be done in advance to prepare for such an eventuality? One important step would be to ensure the integrity of domestic lines of communication among core financial firms, their supervisors, the central bank and the operators of systemically critical parts of the financial infrastructure. Another would be to ensure similar openness at the international level. Stress testing is now almost universal in financial firms, which is highly desirable. Yet stress tests are based on simplifying assumptions that necessarily fail to match the complexity of real-world events." That's a banker's way of saying, "The show could blow up tomorrow, and there may not be any way to stop it." Steve Wynn should get Gehry to work on the Temple of Mammon sooner rather than later.

The Strategists of Urban Destruction

THERE ARE SOME sure things in the gamble called Life. Among them the following:

> Unless they're so down on their luck that the barman is playing solitaire, nightclubs are by definition unsafe. You want to play by the odds, stay home and read Tolstoy.

In the event of panic or fire, your chances are going to be less than 50/50. Drunken revelers don't tend to stand at attention singing "Nearer, My God, to Thee" while the women proceed at an orderly pace to the exits.

There are other certainties: that the club's promoters will have secured their liquor license, immunity from complaints by the neighbors, etc., by dint of bribery and political clout. Duane Kyles, owner of E2, the Chicago club where 21 died last week, had the Jackson family—Jesse and Jesse Jr.—going to bat for him.

It was a busy week for the Reverend since he also assigned himself the task of comforting the survivors and the bereaved. Jesse's shuttle was too much for one Chicago city council member, Madeline Haithcock, who called him a hypocrite: "He's with the victims one minute holding prayer vigils…and with his friends the next. That's him. That's the role he plays. He likes to get in the papers."

True. All politicians do. Back in the fall of 1991, there was a fire in the Imperial chicken processing plant in Hamlet, NC, that killed 25 workers, mostly women on minimum wage. Jackson rushed to Hamlet, bible in hand. This being North Carolina and not the South Side of Chicago, there was no likelihood of Imperial being owned by a Brother. There was an authentic villain in the form of plant owner Emmett Roe, who had suspected the workers of stealing chicken and therefore locked or blocked doors. Roe was sentenced to 19 years, 11 months, but was let out after serving four.

Crowds and fire. Darkness and panic. These are the currency of these weird times as the Pentagon divulges its plan to "shock and awe" the people of Baghdad with a 48-hour barrage of missiles. Two weekends ago, we had the unity of vast crowds asserting life; and then, a few days later, we saw the crowd in the guise of panic-stricken throngs, in Chicago and Rhode Island, crushing each other to death and being burned.

At the start of the 1960s, another high decade for crowds, fire and war, Elias Canetti published his eerie, eccentric book, *Crowds and Power*. It has a brilliant opening passage describing how a man feels amid the panic of a burning theater:

> The people he pushes away are like burning objects to him... Fire, as a symbol for the crowd, has entered the whole economy of man's feelings and become an immutable part of it. That emphatic trampling on people, so often observed in panics and apparently so senseless, is nothing but the stamping out of fire.

Amid newscasts switching between reports from the charred club in Rhode Island and George W. Bush calling on Saddam to lay down his arms, pending attack, can any decently sensitive person not imagine Baghdad or Basra once the missiles start to fall and anticipate dreadful episodes like the careful targeting of the Al-Amariya shelter, targeted because, as one Pentagon man told the press, they wanted to alert Saddam's elite that their wives and children weren't safe?

Actually, the elites had left Baghdad and the poor women and children were in the shelter when the U.S. missile penetrated the reinforced concrete roof and killed them.

This brings us to the consoling topic of luck: the mother who missed her chance to get to the shelter; the fellow who left the nightclub five minutes earlier. At some level, we pay hopeful respect to the whims of Providence.

But in the bigger picture, accidents turn into certainties. Back in 1998, Deborah and Rodrick Wallace published *A Plague on Your Houses* (Verso), a carefully researched book about how, in the 1970s era of "planned shrinkage," social engineers, some of them mustered in the Rand Corporation Fire Project, supervised the deliberate degradation of fire control resources in areas the engineers of shrinkage had slated for clearance.

About 10 percent of New York's fire companies were eliminated, manpower cut back, emergency response systems whittled down. After the inevitable fire epidemic, there was an equally inevitable epidemic of housing abandonment by landlords. Poor neighborhoods collapsed. When the dust settled, the Wallaces calculated that about two million poor people had been uprooted.

Those strategists of urban destruction were never rushed into the pillory the way Kyles or Roe were. True, they were exposed by the Wallaces, but that was many years later.

Maybe, many years later, there'll be a definitive account of why the Twin Towers fell as rapidly as they did. As things stand, one can find accounts that it was design incompetence and cost-cutting married to the desire to maximize rentable space. See, for example, my colleague Jeffrey St. Clair's excellent account of the architectural flaws of the WTC or go to scieneering.com, and you'll find a compelling account of the extreme vulnerability of the panels and square tubes.

Here's how the scieneering.com essay concludes:

> Weak floor-to-wall connections and missing connections between segments of the exterior wall columns contributed significantly to the collapse of the World Trade towers. If these defects were not present, the collapse of the towers might have been prevented or delayed. However, the aircraft would still have penetrated into the core, and the ensuing fire would have trapped the occupants above the crash zone.

In other words, the odds were bad from the very start.

Alexander Cockburn

An Architecture of Doom and Dread

ON NOVEMBER 3, 2014, the first tenants moved into the new Freedom Tower, the 1776-foot-tall glass-and-steel structure built on the site of 6 World Trade Center. Those employees of the Condé Nast publishing company probably entered the monstrous building with some trepidation. You can understand their anxiety. The old World Trade Center had been targeted by terrorists at least four times and ultimately completely destroyed in the 9/11 attacks. The new building, rising from the tip of Manhattan, dominates the skyline which such audacity that it seems to flash a "I dare you to hit me again" sign from its imposing spire. The structure has the ungainly heft and bulk of a skyscraper on steroids, but, in reality, is no more secure than its notorious predecessors, which used to sway tremulously in winter winds.

Over the course of 12 years, the cost of the Freedom Tower rose much faster than the building itself. By the end of the summer, when the finishing touches were being applied to the interior, the price tag had escalated to nearly $4 billion, with about a quarter of the cost coming from the killing that real estate mogul Larry Silverstein had made from insurers and reinsurers following the destruction of the WTC complex. Nowhere along the line did anyone in power seem to consider that those billions might be more efficaciously spent aiding the thousands of people still suffering cancers and lung diseases from the airborne toxins that shrouded the city following the collapse of the Twin Towers or assisting the tens of thousands of working-class New Yorkers displaced from lower Manhattan by the takeover of the one-percenters and their political hacks.

Initially designed by Daniel Libeskind, a pop architect who has been described as the "Jeff Koons of building blocks," the shape of the Freedom Tower suggests a brutal monument to the inviolate power of finance capitalism, a mirrored spike thrusting into the empty sky. Strangely, it is the kind arrogant tower that one expects to encounter rising from the desert in some oil sheikdom on-the-make like Dubai. There is an irony here that will, perhaps, bite deeper in the decades to come.

If there was even the slightest consolation to be mined from the collapse of the Twin Towers, it was that the Manhattan skyline had been purged of two of the ugliest buildings ever constructed. I had hoped that those haunted grounds would remain sacrosanct. A few days after the attacks, I wrote the following essay calling for the site to be set aside as a memorial, a public commons in the heart of a city that has too often chosen to pave over and bury its history. Naturally those calls for a space of contemplation went unheeded. Instead, the WTC site has been impaled with a lurid building that rivals the Twin Towers for the banality of its design and the oppressiveness of its structure. You weren't expecting a measure of humility from the new masters of capital, were you?

September 16, 2001

These are days of lamentation: for the horrifying toll of the innocent dead, for the near certain prospect of thousands more—American and Middle Eastern—slated to die in the impending retaliatory strikes, and even for a weird kind of innocence and naivete that seemed uniquely American, a naivete that persisted in the heart of the nation's most cynical city.

But one loss that mustn't be mourned are the Twin Towers themselves, those blinding prongs that rose up like a tuning fork above the Battery. Under other circumstances, thousands would have gathered to cheer the planned demolition of these oppressive structures as lustily as they have the implosions of the Kingdome in Seattle and other misbegotten monstrosities of the 1970s. You could say the World Trade Center was a singular atrocity—except there were two of them. As architectural historian Francis Morrone wrote in his 1998 *Architectural Guidebook to New York*: "The best thing about the view from the indoor and out observation decks of Two World Trade Centers that they are the only high vantage points in New York city from which the World Trade Center itself is not visible."

But now there's talk, serious talk from people like Hillary Clinton, Rudy Giuliani and the building's new owner Larry Silverstein, of rebuilding both skyscrapers. This impulse must be resisted. Those buildings terrorized the skyline of Manhattan for too long. They combined ostentation and austerity with all the chilling precision of an economic package devised by the IMF.

The architect of the World Trade Center complex, Minuro Yamasaki, was morbidly afraid of heights. It shows in his work. Like the tycoon in Akira Kurosawa's wonderful film *High and Low*, Yamasaki has projected his own nightmares on all of us. His towers are more than blunt symbols of corporate power. They are erections of dominion that inject a feeling of powerlessness in those who must encounter their airy permanence. His architecture does violence to the psyche as surely as those planes did violence to the human body. Yamasaki said he wanted enough space around the base of the towers so onlookers could be "overwhelmed by their greatness."

Yamasaki, who died in 1986, saw himself as a field marshal of space, a kind of Japanese-American version of Philip Johnson, the avatar of the glass curtain skyscraper. Johnson's neo-fascist erections made him the favorite architect of Fed chairman Alan Greenspan, with whom he once debated the finer points of Martin Heidegger in the salon of Ayn Rand. Yamasaki is like Johnson only duller. He was more ruthless in his desire to shave all aesthetic pleasure out of his cubes and tubes, to make them monuments to functionality.

The towers were meant to be impervious to the elements, as if they could not only defy space, wind, and the colors of nature, but time as well. That was Yamasaki's biggest lie, a conceit as big as the ever-expanding bull market or the prospect of an impenetrable missile defense shield. But the lie was shattered in a matter of minutes, as first the load-bearing exo-skeleton quivered and buckled, then the joints melted in the inferno of the burning jet fuel, and finally one floor after another collapsed with all the finality of an Old Testament prophecy fulfilled.

Compare Yamasaki's structure to the great old spire just down the avenue and you can almost read the arc of corporate America. The Woolworth Building, Cass Gilbert's gothic confection, offers the city a kind of airy whimsy. Illusory, yes, but self-consciously fun. It doesn't demand your attention so much as it seduces it.

Yamasaki was a favorite of the new corporate order because, unlike Frank Lloyd Wright or the spendy Johnson, he built on the cheap. The WTC towers cost only $350 million. The early price tag on rebuilding the structures is put at $2.5 billion. Also recall that the towers were for most of their life public buildings, owned by the city of New York. But there was little truly civic about them: they were cold, sterile, forbidding symbols of a government that had turned inward, that had begun to co-inhabit with the very corporations and financial houses it was charged with regulating.

Jeffrey St. Clair

The Parable of the Shopping Mall

IN TOWN AFTER town across America these days one can physically see the economic mantras of an entire generation turning to boarded-up wasteland before one's eyes. Shopping malls, which changed the American landscape within the course of a generation, are dying week by week.

Take the Bayshore Mall in my own town of Eureka, northern California—a covered, pedestrian arcade opened in the 1980s, owned by the Utah-based General Growth company. Located on the edge of Humboldt Bay, though facing the opposite direction towards Highway 101, our mall was an optimistic place in the early days. People dressed up to go there. A friend of mine who opened a coffee stall, wore a tie—purchasing it from Ralph Lauren which opened an outlet. Every pretty girl in Humboldt county wanted to work there, to see and to be seen. People drove for three hours through the Yolly Bolly Wilderness all the way from Redding in the Central Valley to savor its glories. There were stylish concerts in its ample Food Court.

Today the Bayshore Mall moulders, embodying the misfortunes of General Growth—the second largest mall owner in the U.S.—whose stock trades now for 55 cents, down from $44 last May. General Growth has now ousted its CEO, John Bucksbaum, (who is related to Ann Bucksbaum, wife of the *New York Times'* Thomas Friedman, world's wealthiest pundit. In 2006, the value of General Growth Properties was estimated at about $2.7 billion. Last October 8, *Business Week* headlined an article "General Growth Properties Staggers Under Debt Load" (of $27 billion).

Some major retailers, like Ralph Lauren's Polo, have long since fled from Bayshore Mall. Walk east along one of the arcades and you come to a wall of plywood, behind which lies the desolation that was Mervyn's, a clothing chain which has now filed for bankruptcy. The little stores nearby have a somber mien, like people compelled to live in the chill shadow of a funeral home. The food court, serviced by six or seven fast food businesses, is becoming a sanctuary for the poor who sit in the warmth with modest snacks and while away the hours.

Across the past 40 years some 200 cities built pedestrian malls. Today, only 30 remain. Drive around any town and one can see strip malls in similar decline, their parking lots nearly empty, boarded stores in the retail frontage like a mouth losing its teeth, as the lights of Circuit City go out and Linen 'n Things, Zales, Ann Taylor and Sharper Image retrench or collapse entirely.

Out of crisis comes opportunity, one that's been discussed for some years by movements such as the New Urbanists and crusaders for the refashioning of the American urban landscape such as James Howard Kunstler, author of *The Geography of Nowhere*. A mall can be razed to the ground, like the Belle Promenade, on the west bank of the Mississippi in New Orleans. Eureka's too poor a town to do that. But a mall can be refashioned into a more congenial quartier, one blessed with easier parking.

In the same way that coastal cities like Boston finally realized the asset of nineteenth-century quaysides with their warehouses and customs depots, today's failed or failing malls can be reconfigured, converted to mixed use, with residential housing, public spaces and constructive social uses. In the Bayshore even now I see groups of the mentally ill being brought along for an outing in a place that's sheltered, still physically safe, and equipped with bathrooms, and plenty of space with chairs or benches where they can relax.

In many towns one can imagine that energetic councils and resourceful financing could offer the reeling mall operators terms and take the properties off their hands, reconfiguring the malls as social assets.

On the larger economic front, similar reconstructive engineering for the public good is vital, however adamantly Wall Street, Timothy Geithner, Larry Summers and President Obama may proclaim earnestly that the architecture of "free enterprise" capitalism must be preserved. We're at that stage that Thurman Arnold captured so wittily in his 1937 book, *The Folklore of Capitalism*. Arnold, from Laramie, Wyoming, was installed as head of the Justice Department's Anti-Trust Division when FDR swerved to the left amid the slump of 1937. No greater foe of the corporate cartel than Arnold ever worked in government service in Washington.

In an early chapter, "The Folklore of 1937", Arnold describes with vivid humor the tenacity with which supporters of untrammeled "private enterprise" held to beliefs whose operating principles had engendered the Great Depression. He likened it to the University of Paris insisting in the seventeenth century that bleeding was still the cure for malaria, even though quinine, promoted by the Jesuits in Peru, seemed to offer a more effective remedy.

But, Arnold wrote, "The medieval physician could see no profit in saving a man's body if thereby he lost his soul. Nor did he think that any temporary physical relief could ever be worth the violation of the fundamental principles of medicine. The remedy for fever was the art of bleeding to rid the body of those noxious vapors and humors in the blood which were the root of illness. Of course, patients sickened and died in the process, but they were dying for a medical principle…"

Is there a better description for the Republicans opposing the stimulus plan on principle, or Geithner stoutly proclaiming his zeal to preserve the banking system as presently constituted?

Opportunity is there, to be seized from the jaws of capitalism's shattering reverses. This is a chance richer than the opportunity offered and annulled in the mid-70s. Circumstances will in all likelihood push Obama's government to the left, just as they did FDR when orthodoxy failed. The left should not be shy about pressing the challenge out of some misguided notion of preserving a polite progressive consensus.

From the malls to the commanding heights of the economy, let the Reconquest begin.

Alexander Cockburn

The Dollar General Theory of Money and Employment

I'm so tired
Tired of waiting
Tired of waiting for you
— The Kinks

FOR THE LAST month and a half I've driven the backroads of southern Indiana, crisscrossing the unglaciated hill country 40 miles south of Indianapolis and 40 miles north of Louisville. It's mostly forested here, large remarkably unbroken stretches of deciduous woodlands, thick with red oak and shagbark hickory, tulip poplar and black walnut, white ash and wild cherry, American beech and sugar maple. The soil is mainly red clay, not productive for farming (or septic systems), but quite satisfactory for morel mushrooms, homegrown weed, and copperheads. The towns are small, little more than villages, clustered near the railroads and old blue highways.

I spent my summers here for 20 years and lived here for a decade. We raised both of our kids here. And since moving to Oregon in 1990, we've come back every year or so. For most of that time nothing much about the landscape, the people or the towns changed. They were much as they were in 1982 or 1972. To the north, the suburbs of Indianapolis gnawed up more and more farmland and woodlots, including the 40-acre farm of my mother's family, which dated back to the 1820s. The fields are now covered by a super-drugstore, a Kroger, a Chick-Fil-A, a furniture store, and a church with a vast parking lot, where carloads come in search of salvation. The place is Jesus mad, though few could tell you more than a couple garbled lines of his teachings. I can't bear to go back without wanting to blow something up.

For years, the hill country seemed immune to this kind of cultural entropy billed as progress. But in the last five years, the economic decay has accelerated. Familiar stores are boarded up. Houses have been abandoned. Cars left to rust in fields and yards where they stopped running months ago. Handmade for sale signs are tacked to telephone poles. It's a yard sale economy. Even churches have padlocks on their doors, especially the denominational churches of my youth—Lutheran, Presbyterian, Methodist and Catholic—replaced by evangelical and Four Square churches in trailers, barns and pre-fab buildings, their devotional services announced on yard signs like advertisements for the Second Coming.

The old family-owned grocery, which served people in a 20-mile radius for 50 years, is gone, replaced by a Dollar General store, whose aisles haven't been washed in weeks, where the air smells of body odor and spilled dairy products. I took it as a sign. When Dollar General shows up in your town, it's like a death notice for your community and don't expect it to offer you a chance to win your life in a game of chess or quick-mart Keno.

These stores are replicating across rural America. There are now more dollar stores (50,000 of them by one count) than there are McDonalds and Walmarts combined. They rang up $34 billion sales during the first year of the pandemic, selling crap for a dollar, more or less. As they drive out the local groceries, fresh food is replaced with the kind of high-calorie, sugar-rich processed junk that is fueling the health crisis in low-income America. The owner of an IGA in a town 10 miles to the north, where a Dollar General store sprouted up, told me that his store lost 35% of its sales the first year after Dollar General moved in and the sales have kept declining each year since. "We can't keep up," he told me. "We're hanging on by our fingernails and not long for this world."

The average hourly wage for Dollar General workers—sales associates, they call them—is $9 an hour. An assistant store manager makes, on average, $11 an hour. That's hardly enough to shop for essentials at Dollar General, if you can find any essentials on those forbidding shelves.

The rot is metastasizing. Dollar General and Dollar Tree want to add another 30,000 stores in the next few years. Their corporate executives are attuned to the scent of decay. They are retail carrion feeders. Their stores are as austere and bland as any state-run outlet in Ceaușescu's Bucharest. Step inside one and you couldn't tell whether you were standing in Bean Blossom, Indiana or Hinton, West Virginia.

There have been three suicides in this sparsely populated county in the past two weeks, all of them men younger than 30. One was an acquaintance who shot himself in his mother's house, while his younger brother slept in the adjacent room. No one saw it coming. Some hoped it had been an accident, that he had been cleaning his gun when it went off. Those hopes, slim as they were, were dashed when they found his note. But there was no why. Yet deep down, everybody seemed to know that he'd looked into the future and saw none.

He had come to believe that his life was a failure, that he was a burden on those he loved, a burden they were struggling to afford, a burden that weighed on his conscience, a burden he just couldn't think about anymore and had to silence with a bullet to the head.

But it was this increasingly perverse society that failed him, failed his family, failed his dying community. A society that failed to listen, that failed to care, that failed to act, until his funeral when the trustees donated some money for his funeral and burial.

I didn't know the young man well, but I knew the contours of his life. He was bright, honest, good with his hands. He could fix a broken engine or rewire an exterior outlet. He could hang drywall and shoe a horse. He could lay a septic system and trim trees. These are valuable skills in a functional economy. But this isn't a functional economy—it doesn't function for people, anyway. It grinds them down and doesn't look back.

He should have been able to make it. Life shouldn't have been as hard as it was for him. But opportunities kept shutting down, options for escape kept closing. Abandoned by his father, protective of his mother and brother, he was stuck, as the community around him, the few stable anchors in his life, began to crumble. There was nowhere to go, nowhere left to turn.

Of course, I'm not attributing his death to the coming of Dollar General…directly…but to an economic model that favors, in nearly every aspect of our lives, that kind of predation on the vulnerable and the marginalized.

Just down the block from the funeral home, there was a big sign advertising jobs in the county. The local high school can't find a head custodian. Little wonder. The starting salary pay is $13.50 an hour. The McDonalds in another nearby town, a regional tourist spot, put up a sign announcing they were closing at 8PM on Friday and Saturday nights because they were short of staff. They too are advertising jobs at less than $14 an hour for dull, thankless work. Corporate America thinks rural America has no choice but to take these jobs at shit pay. The unions have been beaten down. The politicians blame extended unemployment benefits. The churches are obsessed with gun rights and the tyranny of Covid masks.

Still people are starting to refuse the slops that are offered them. The Covid lockdowns—hated here in the hollows and hills as intensely as anywhere—have taught people there are other ways to get by, modes of life that don't require you to submit to the least that's offered, to work crap jobs for crap wages in dangerous conditions with no health care. It may be a silent resistance, but its building.

People don't trust their bosses, their banks, or their government. They don't trust that the insurance they pay out the ass for will really cover them if they have a stroke or get cancer or contract Covid on the job. Yet, the people most in need of national health care are among the least likely to support it. If you don't trust the government—if it's never done much of anything for you, except demean your existence, humiliate you for asking for help, and make life harder than it already is—why would you want them tending to your failing body or injecting a vaccine (no matter its efficacy) into your bloodstream? The fear isn't irrational. It's been learned over generations.

The Dollar General Theory is as cruel as it is simple. They want you to work cheap, live cheap and die cheap. They don't want to pay you what you're worth or pay for you when you're ill, even if they caused your sickness. Where are you going to go? Who are you going to turn to? The town you've known all your life is boarded up. The grocery store and hardware store are gone. The coffee shop is closed. The gas stations no longer have mechanics. Most don't even have attendants. Just insert a card and go. You need a credit card for everything now, even if your credit is in the toilet.

It's not just the supply chains that are broken. The threads that have bound these small communities together since the Great Depression are fraying. No one knows their banker any more. Many of the local banks have been replaced by ATM machines, racking up hidden fees for every impersonal service rendered. There hasn't been a town doctor here in five years. People have to drive 20 miles west to Bloomington or 30 miles east to Columbus and then they are often treated by a nurse or physician's assistant for the diseases that are ravaging these small towns: diabetes, congestive heart failure, emphysema, opioid addiction. The diseases of the passed over and forgotten. The diseases that don't pay.

For some reason, I was struck by the recent proliferation of MIA flags, which I'd rarely, if ever, noticed down here before. There are now more of them than Trump flags, of which there are still many. These black flags fly from houses and schools, Post Offices and fire stations, city parks and some of the few remaining local businesses. It's been nearly fifty years since the fall of Saigon and the end of that savage war seems more immediate than ever. I asked a few people if they knew any MIAs. None could name a single one. No surprise, there were hardly any. Few people even knew anyone that served in Vietnam. It seemed clear that what had really gone missing was an idea of America itself, a void in the national identity, that remains dark and inexplicable, and, as the scenes of planes ferrying desperate people out of Afghanistan play endlessly on cable TV, it's a hole that continues to grow, consuming what we thought we knew about ourselves.

A couple of nights ago, I met up with some old friends in a bar we used to frequent near Lake Lemon. It's seen better days and is now kept afloat largely by the throngs of bikers who pass through on most weekends. As a group, we didn't have much in common except our youth. Those differences in background and education never stood in the way before. But tonight the room crackled with tension. You could feel it in the air. It was palpable. I grew up with many of these people. Played baseball with them. Got lost in the woods looking for chanterelles with them. Fished for small-mouthed bass with them. Got drunk on the porch with them. Now every conversation seemed hard, strained, freighted with suspicion and latent anger. Everyone seemed wary of each other. The camaraderie of youth had been broken, like so much else. The mood was as sour as the beer. I rarely talk about politics. I usually find it the most boring topic on earth, aside from NFL football. But now everything seems intensely political, which is, perhaps, as it must be. Each phrase, no matter how inconsequential, was spoken with caution, as if the wrong inflection might set off some chain reaction. All patience has been lost. People are tired of waiting, though waiting for what no one would, or perhaps even could, say. Yet, we all agreed and then almost immediately questioned our agreement: Politics has failed. But what comes next?

Something's gotta give. Something's gotta break wide open.

Jeffrey St. Clair

Gratis

To: Tiffany Wardle for the precision and clarity of her design (and the wine-stain); Becky Grant for navigating *CounterPunch* through hidden shoals and tempestuous waters; Joshua Frank and Nathaniel St. Clair for their tireless editorial labors; Deva Wheeler and Nichole Stephens for managing the control room; the three Cockburns in my life: Daisy, Andrew and Patrick; a tight circle of friends who have been on-call through thin and thinner, notably: Joe and Karen Paff, JoAnn Wypijewski, Ken Silverstein, Susan Davis, Steve Perry, Dick and Ester Cogswell, Karen Rudolph, Michael Yates, Julie Wark, David Price, Martin Billheimer, Melissa Beattie, Kevin Alexander Gray, Susie Day, Michael Donnelly, Laura Carlsen, Daniel Wolff, Roz Wolen, Ishmael Reed and Ralph Nader. Naturally, none of this would have been possible without the love and support across four decades of Kimberly Willson-St. Clair–partner, editor, librarian, and fearless defender of free speech.

In addition to the immeasurable loss of Cockburn, the last decade has inflicted a horrible toll on the ranks of my closest friends, collaborators and co-conspirators, including my father, T.H. St. Clair, my brother-in-law Gil Willson, James Ridgeway, Saul and Rebecca Landau, Larry Tuttle, Andy Levine, Margot Kidder, Chuck Larson, Lou Proyect, Barbara Yaley, Tom Cannon and Julie Taylor, Paul Krassner, Pierre Sprey, Dean Frank, Uri Avnery, Robert Fisk, Franklin Lamb, John Trudell, Dave Foreman, Marshall Sahlins and Boomer the Indomitable. From them, for the future. *Ar scáth a chéile a mhaireann na daoin! (In the shelter of others, the people survive.)*

Index

3M Corp., 42
60 Minutes (CBS), 27-28, 107
Abenaki tribe, 108
Abzug, Bella, 47
Association of Community Organizations for Reform Now (ACORN), 20-21
Adams, John, 42
Aeschylus, 150
Affirmative Action, 49-50
Afghanistan, 100-101, 113-114, 171
AFL-CIO, 38, 111
Africa, 64, 84, 118, 194
Agency for International Development, US (AID), 33
Agricultural policy, 77-80, 158-159, 194-195
Agricultural Research Service, USDA, 78-79
Agriculture Department, 78-79
Ahmad, Muhammad (Madhi), 122
AIG, Inc., 12, 173-179
Airline industry, 14-15
Al Qaeda, 31, 97-98, 120-121, 154-156
Al-Awlaki, Anwar, 121-122
Alabama, 86
Alaska, 95
Albright, Madeleine, 97-103, 106-107
Alexander, Michelle, 168
Aluminum industry, 67
Alvarez, Robert, 91
Amazonia, 84-85
American Bar Association (ABA), 25
American Cattle Trust, 44-45

American Chemical Society, 96
American Civil Liberties Union (ACLU), 56-57
Amin, Hafizullah, 101
Amnesty International, 147
Anderson Valley Advertiser, 137-138
Anderson, Bruce, 137-138
Ann Casey Foundation, 167-168
Anslinger, Harry, 130-131
Anti-Defamation League (ADL), 70-71
Anti-Drug Abuse Act, 132-133
Anti-nuclear movement, 92-93, 116
Antigua, 180-189
Architectural Guide to New York (Marrone), 201
Ardin, Anna, 113-114
Arizona, 158
Arkadelphia, AR, 26-27
Arkansas, 20-25, 26-29, 34, 75-76
Armstrong, Louis, 130
Arnold & Porter, LLP, 69-70
Arnold, Thurman, 205-206
Arthur Anderson Co., 7
Arum, Richard, 190-191
Ashcroft, John, 146
Assange, Julian 112-117
Assassination, 121-22
Asset forfeiture, 132
Atlantic-Richfield Oil Co. (ARCO), 95
Austerity, 7-13, 48-49
Azulay, Avner, 67-68
Babcock & Wilcox Co., 92
Bacillus thuringiensis (Bt), 77-80
Baghdad, Iraq, 98-100, 101
Bailouts, Wall Street, 164-165, 173-179
Baker, James, 60
Baker, Susan, 60-61
Balkans, 104-106
Balzac, Honoré de, 8
Bane, Mary Jo, 54

Bangladesh, 161-163
Bank for International Settlements, 196
Bank of America, 12
Barak, Ehud, 67, 69, 72
Bardacke, Frank, 158
Bardot, Brigitte, 1
Barrick Gold, Corp., 45
Baum, Dan, 132-133
Bayh, Evan, 55
Bayshore Mall, 204-206
Bean Blossom, IN, 208
Beatles, The, 60
Bechtel Corp., 92
Belgrade, Serbia, 30-31, 101-103
Belle Promenade, 205
Benghazi, Libya, 121-122
Benin, 194
Bennett, William (Bill), 8, 126
Berger, Samuel (Sandy), 73
Bernanke, Ben, 8
Bhutto, Benazir, 30
Biafra, Jello, 61
Bias, Len, 132-133
Biden, Joseph R., 132, 164-165
Bill and Melinda Gates Foundation, 194-195
Bin Laden, Osama, 97-98, 121
Biotech industry, 77-80
Bison, American, 84
Blackwater Security Co., 186
Blader, R.F., 140-41
Blair, James, 22-23
Bleifuss, Joel, 82
Blood Sport (Stewart), 23
Bloomberg, Michael, 138-139
Boggs, Hale, 131
Bolivia, 122, 162
Bonaparte, Napoleon, 118
Bone, Robert (Red), 22-23
Bonnie and Clyde (Penn), 159
Borbón y Borbón, Juan Carlos (King of Spain), 73

213

Bosnia, 104–105
Boston Celtics, 132–133
Boston Marathon bombing, 151–153
Boston, MA, 132–133, 151–153
Bovard, James, 142–143
Bovine Growth Hormone (BGH), 81–82
Brecht, Bertolt, 164
Breyer, Stephen, 14–16
British Broadcasting Company (BBC), 186
British Museum, 13
Broder, David, 2
Broderick, Douglas, 98–99
Bronx, NY, 59
Brooke, Edward, 18–19
Brookhaven Labs, 90
Brower, David, 88–89
Brower, Lincoln, 78–79
Brown, Edmund G. (Jerry), 95
Brown, James, 4
Bucksbaum, John, 204
Budget deficit, 48–49
Budweiser, 159, 161
Buffalo Commons, 84
Buffett, Warren, 159, 194–195
Bureau of Labor Statistics (BLS), 157, 191–192
Bureau of Land Management (BLM), 43–44
Bureau of Narcotics and Dangerous Drugs (BNDD), 130–131
Burg, Abraham, 72
Burke, Melvin, 40
Burnett, Chester (Howlin' Wolf), 1
Burns, John F., 114–115
Burson-Marsteller, PLC., 78–79
Bush, George H.W., 32–33, 40, 54, 60, 62, 75, 110–111, 174
Bush, George W., 7, 57, 119, 146, 172, 173, 174–175, 186, 198

Bush, Jeb, 144, 172
Business Leaders for Clinton, 34
Business Roundtable, 15
BusinessWeek, 8, 189, 204
Cable News Network (CNN), 115, 143
Califano, Joseph, 21
California Youth Authority, 128
California, xiii, 3–4, 7–8, 35, 39, 44–45, 83, 89–90, 95–6, 127–128, 134, 157–158
Callahan, Richard, 145, 147
CalPERS, 7
Campaign finance, 48–49
Campaign for Nuclear Disarmament (CND), 116
Campbell, Catherine, 126–128
Camus, Albert, 123–125
Canada, 32–39, 40–42, 45–6, 85, 95
Cancer bonds, 15–16
Cancer, 15–16, 81–82
Canetti, Elias, 198
Canon USA, 42
Cape Thornton, AK, 95
Carey, Ron, 8
Cargill, Inc., 42
Carter Center, 110
Carter, Jimmy, 7, 39, 131–132
Carville, James, 28
Cascadian Subduction Zone, 89–90
Cassano, Joseph, 175–179
Castle Grande, real estate deal, 24–25
Catholic Relief Services, 98–99
Cattle futures, HRC trading in, 22–23, 27
Cattle industry, 22–23, 27, 82–84
CBS News, 27–28, 98–99
Censorship, 60–61
Center for Disease Control (CDC) 140
Center for Working Class Studies, 191

Central America Labor Federation, 111
Central Intelligence Agency (CIA), 3–4, 31, 67–68, 86, 100–101, 106–107, 113–114, 130–131, 153
Champion International, 46
Chapel Hill, NC, 58–59
Chavez, Cesar, 166
Chavez, Hugo, 109–111
Cheney, Richard (Dick), 7, 31
Chernobyl nuclear disaster, 90–92
Chester, WV, 75–76
Chevron Corp., 44
Chiapas, Mexico, 46
Chicago School of Economics, 9
Chicago, 9, 54, 197–198
Chick-Fil-A, 207
Children's Defense Fund, 19–20, 21
Chile, 111
China, 102, 130–131
Chinese Embassy in Belgrade, bombing of, 102
Christian Right, 60–61
Christianity, 60–61, 97
Christmas Tree bomb plot, 154–156
Cisneros, Henry, 51
Citigroup, 12, 62
Civil Rights Movement, 17–19, 86
Clark, Gen. Wesley, 103
Clean Air Act, 15
Climate change, 86–87, 94–96
Clinton Foundation, 71–72
Clinton Presidential Library, 64, 72
Clinton, Hillary Rodham (HRC), 9, 17–31, 146, 201–202, and Assange 112–113, and criminal justice 50–51, 126–128, and Libya 118–122, and Rich pardon 64–73, and Serbia 107–108, and

INDEX

Whitewater scandal 22–25, 75–76
Clinton, William J. (Bill), 1–2, 9, 19–31, 47–50, 62–63, 74–76, 77–80, 110, 147, 174 and criminal justice 49–51, 126–128, and environment 77–80, and gay rights, 49–50, 169–170, and immigration 50, and NAFTA 32–39, and Marc Rich pardon 64–73, and Serbia 104–108, and social security 170–171, and welfare 50–60, Whitewater scandal 22–25, 75–76
Clipper Chip, 57
Coca-Cola Company, 21, 42
Cocaine, 56–57, 130–135
Cockburn, Patrick, 4
Collier, Rob, 111
Colombia, 184
Colorado, 43, 83
Colossal Wreck (Cockburn), xiii
Combatting Terrorism Center, 120–121
Committee of 100, 116
Commodities Futures Modernization Act, 10
Communism, 9
Community policing, 58–59
Condé Nast Co., 200
Congressional Budget Office (CBO), 54
Connecticut, 174
Connolly, James, 165
Conservative Party, of Canada, 36
Contours of Descent (Pollin), 11, 162–163
Contras, 3–4
Coral Gables, Florida, 181
Cornell University, 77–80
Corruptions of Empire (Cockburn), 2
Costa Rica, 34–35
Council on Crime in America, 126–127

Counter-Terrorism and Effective Death Penalty Act, 56–57, 147, 172
Coups, by CIA, 86, 100
Covid-19, 210
Crack cocaine, 56–57, 133–135
Creutzfeldt-Jakob disease, 82
Criminal justice policy, 29–30, 49–51, 56–57, 126–129, 142–144, 145–147, 148–150, 151–153
Croatia, 105
Croatian Army, 105
Croatian Police, 105
Crow, John, 36
Crowds & Power (Canetti), 198
Cuba, 122
Cullman, Joseph, 42
Cuomo, Kerry Kennedy, 146
Customs Office, US, 185
Dahl, Robert, 8
Daily Finance, 190
Daily Mail, 188
Daimler-Chrysler Corp., 69
Dairy industry, 81–82
Daley, Richard J., 17
Dalmady, Alex, 188–189
Daoud, Mahammed, 100
Daschle, Thomas (Tom), 186–187
Davis, Gray, 145–146
Dayton Accords, 104
Dead Kennedys, 61
Death penalty, 56–57, 123–124, 130–131, 134–135, 145–147, 148–150
Debt, international, 161–163
Defenders of Wildlife, 41–42
Defense Department, 198
Defense Intelligence Agency (DIA), 115
Defense of Marriage Act, 49–50
DeLay, Thomas (Tom), 186–187
Democratic Convention, of 1968, 18–19

Democratic Leadership Council (DLC), 20, 62–63
Democratic National Committee (DNC), 52, 71
Democratic Party, 18–19, 20, 52, 62–63, 71
Democratic Socialists of America (DSA), 105
Deportations, of immigrants, 166–167
Deregulation, 8–10, 14–16, 33–34, 48–50
Dershowitz, Alan, 151–153
Deschutes River, 1
Detroit, MI, 37, 166
Devil's Excrement, The, 188–189
Diablo Canyon nuclear plant, 88–89
Diallo, Amadou, 57, 59
Dickens, Charles, 183
DiIulio, John, 126–127
Doar, John, 20
Dobson, James, 60–61
Dodd, Christopher, 52
Dollar General Corp., 207–11
Domhoff, G. William, 8
Don't Ask, Don't Tell, policy on gays in military, 169–170
Dozoretz, Elizabeth (Beth), 71–73
DREAM Act, 170
Drexel, Burnam, Lambert, Inc., 175
Drone warfare, 121–22, 123–125
Drug cartels, 184–185
Drug Enforcement Agency (DEA), 132–133, 136–137, 180, 185–186
Drug Policy Alliance, 136
Drug policy, 56–57, 130–135
Drug testing, of welfare recipients, 55–56
Dubai, 201
Duke Energy Corp., 42
Dunaway, Faye, 159

215

DuPont Corp., 42
Earthquakes, 88-93
East Liverpool, OH, 74-76
Eastman Kodak Co., 42
Echo Bay Mines, Ltd., 45
Economic Policy Institute (EPI), 40
Ecuador, 116
Edelman, Marian W., 19
Edelman, Peter, 19-20, 50-51, 54
Education, 190-193
Edwards, John, 141
Ellington, Duke, 130
Ellsberg, Daniel, 115
Enron, Corp., 10
Environmental Defense Fund (EDF), 15
Environmental policy, 15-16, 19, 33-4, 40-42, 74-76, 77-80, 88-93
Environmental Protection Agency (EPA), 74-76, 77-80
Epstein, Edward J., 116
Espionage Act, 112-113
Estes, Ken, 136-137
Eureka, CA, 204-206
European Union (EU), 105
Everglades, 19
Everybody Loves a Good Drought (Sainath), 162
Ewing, Hickman, Jr., 23-24
Exelon Corp., 91-92
Exner, Judith, 17
EZ Club, 197
Fairchild, Brian, 121
Fallin, Mary, 148-150
Fanjul, Albert, 19
Farm Credit Bank, 44
Farmworkers, 158-159
Fast Track trade authority, 33
Fate of the Forest (Hecht/Cockburn), 2
Faux, Jeff, 40
Fayetteville, AR, 20-21
Federal Bureau of Investigation (FBI), 67, 151-53, 154-56, 157-158, 180, 183-184, 189

Federal National Mortgage Association (Fannie Mae), 73
Federal Reserve, 7-8, 32, 36
Feingold, Russell, 145-147
Feinstein, Mark, 110-111
Field Poll, on death penalty, 145-146
Fifth Amendment, 151-153
Finance industry, 161-163, 173-179, 180-189, 195-196
Fink, Robert, 64, 70-71
Finland, 65
Fire Project (RAND), 198-199
Fires, 84-85, 198-199
First Man, The (Camus), 123
Fisheries policy, 41-42, 45-46
Fisk, Peggy, 21
Florida, 19, 181, 187
Flowers, Gennifer, 27-28
Floyd, Craig, 142
Focus on the Family, 60-61
Foley, Thomas (Tom), 47
Folklore of Capitalism, The (Arnold) 205-206
Forbes, 8
Ford, Gerald R., 18
Foreign Intelligence Surveillance Act (FISA), 164
Forest policy, 2, 25, 41-42, 43-46, 79, 84-85, 138
Forest Service, US, 43-44
Fortune, 8, 159
Foster, Vince, 28-29
Foundations, 194-195
Fox, James A., 126
Foxman, Abraham (Abe), 70-71, 147
France, 1, 70-71, 123
Frankie the Cat, 5-6
Freedom Tower, 200-201
Friedman, Thomas, 204
Friends of the Earth, 42
Fuentes, Amado Carrillo, 186-187
Fukushima nuclear disaster, 88-93, 94-96
Fuller, Kathryn, 41-42

Gaia Hypothesis, 96
Gallup Org., 171
Gantt, Harvey, 47
Gardner, Timothy (Tim), 182
Garment, Leonard, 65-66
Gates, Melinda, 194-195
Gates, Robert M., 119
Gates, William (Bill), 159, 194-195
Gay marriage, 49-50
Gay rights, 49-50, 146-147, 169-170
Gehry, Frank, 194, 196
Geithner, Timothy, 173-174, 205-206
Gellhorn Prize, 4
General Accounting Office (GAO), 75
General Agreement on Trade and Tariffs (GATT), 46
General Electric Co. (GE), 42, 90-91
General Growth Co., 204
Genetic engineering, 77-80
Geneva Conventions, 103
Geography of Nowhere, The (Kunstler) 205-206
Georgia, 82
Gephardt, Richard (Dick), 52
Germany, 1, 65, 92, 106
Gerth, Jeff, 17-18, 23-27, 28-29
Giancana, Sam, 17
Gibbon, Edward, 4
Giger, H.R., 61
Gilbert, Cass, 202
Gillespie, Dizzy, 130
Gingrich, Newton L. (Newt), 47-48
Giuliani, Rudolph W. (Rudy), 66-67, 201-202
GLAAD, 147
Glacier National Park, 159-160
Glass-Steagall Act, 10-12, 63, 174-175, 177
Glasser, Ira, 57
GM crops, 77-80

INDEX

Goldberg, Jonah, 112
Goldman Sachs Group, Inc., 9, 38–39, 62–63, 174, 178
Goldman, Benjamin, 15
Goldstein, Matthew, 189
Goldwater, Barry, 17–18
GOP Convention, of 1968, 18–19
GOP, 1, 11
Gordon, Charles George (Chinese), 122
Gore, Albert (Al), 19–20, 30, 48, 60–61, 69–71, 74–76, 146
Gore, Mary E. (Tipper), 60–61
Gortikon, Stanley, 60
Grabowski, Eugene (Gene), 79
Graham, Lindsey, 152
Leach, James (Jim), 10
Bliley, Thomas, 10
Grameen Bank, 161–162
Gramm-Leach-Bliley Act, 10
Gramm, Phil, 9–10
Gramm, Wendy, 10
Grant Park, 18
Grant, Becky, 4
Grateful Dead, The, 60
Graves, Morris, 1
Grazing fees, 43–44
Great Depression, 10–11, 130, 205–206
Great Lakes, 41–42
Green, Pincus (Pinky), 64–65
Greenberg, Maurice R. (Hank), 176–177
Greenberg, Stanley, 110–111
Greenspan, Alan, 7–8, 32, 36, 202
Grenell, Richard, 118–119
Grocery Manufacturers of America, 79
Grossman, David, 128–129
Groundwater, 83
Guantanamo, prison camp, 171–172

Guardian International Bank, 182–184
Guardian, The, 90
Guatemala, 86
Guevara, Ernesto (Che), 122
Gulf of Mexico, 86–87
Gulf War, 98–100
Haas, Robert, 34–35
Haldeman, H.R., 133–134
Halliday, Denis, 98–99
Hallinan, Terrance, 147
Hallock, John, 154–156
Hamilton, Alexander, 63
Hamilton, David Wright, 82
Hamlet, NC, 197
Hansen, James, 91–92, 94–95
Harlem, NY, 54–55
Hartford Distributors, Inc., 159
Harvard Law Review, 14–15
Harvard University, 8, 14–15, 176
Hatch, Orrin, 14, 16
Health and Human Services Department (HHS), 19–20, 50–51, 54
Health care, 29–30, 140–141
Hedge funds, 176–178, 195–196
Helms, Jesse, 25, 47
Her Way (Gerth/Van Natta), 17–18, 22, 28–29
Hewlett-Packard Corp, 42
High and Low (Kurosawa), 202
High Value Detainee Interrogation Group, 152–53
Hindu, The, 195
Hinton, WV, 208
Hiroshima, nuclear bombing, 92, 107
Hitchcock, Madeleine, 197
Hitler, Adolf, 61, 64
Holden, Bob, 145
Holder, Eric, 68–69, 112–113, 136, 151–153
Hollywood, CA, 9
Holmes, Col. Eugene, 28

Homeland Security Department (DHS), 152–53
Homelessness, 157–160, 198–199
Homosexuality, bias against, 49–50
Hooker, John Lee, 1
Hosgri Fault, 88–89
Housing and Urban Development Dept. (HUD), 51
Housing industry, 38–39, 157–160, 174–175
Houston, TX, 183
Hubbell, Webb, 24–25, 75–76
Hudson, Michael, 169–170
Huffington Post, 118–119
Human Rights Campaign, 147
Human Rights Watch, 109–111
Humanitarian intervention, 30–31, 101–103, 104–108
Humphrey, Hubert H., 132
Hungary, 123
Hurricane Hugo, 183
Hurricane Katrina, 86–87
Hurricane Mitch, 86–87
Hurricanes, 86–87, 183
Hussein, Saddam, 31
Hyde, Henry, 58
Identity politics, 170
Ifshin, David, 23, 27
Ignatieff, Michael, 105
Ikettes, The, 1
Illinois, 9, 17–19, 54, 197–198
Immigration and Naturalization Service (INS), 50, 57
Immigration policy, 50, 57, 157–160, 166–167, 171
In These Times, 82
Independent Grocers Alliance, Inc. (IGA), 208
India, 161–163, 195
Indiana, 17, 55, 207–211
Indianapolis, IN, 207

Inequality, economic, 7–13, 48–49, 167–168, 190–191, 207–211
Insurance industry, 173–179
Internal Revenue Service (IRS), 23–24, 50–51, 56, 66–67, 138, 185–186
International Boundary Waters Commission, 41
International Monetary Fund (IMF), 163,
Interpol, 112–113
Inuit, 95
Iowa, 17
Iran, 31, 64, 100
Iraq, 31, 98–100, 120–121, 198
Israel, 67–71, 165
It Takes a Village (HRC), 108
J.G. Boswell Co., 194
Jackson Stephens Investments, 20–21, 75
Jackson, Jesse Jr., 197–198
Jackson, Rev. Jesse, 197–198
Jamaica, 65–67
James River Co., 46
Japan, 88–93
Jay-Z, 167
Jellyfish, 89
Jenkins, Simon, 104
Jesuits, 206
Jim Crow laws, 168
Johnson, Lyndon B., 166–167
Johnson, Philip, 202
Johnstone, Diana, 121–22
Jones, Don, 17–18
Jones, Paula, 30
Jordan, Vernon, 24–25
Joyce, James, 4
Joyce, William (Lord Haw-Haw), 115
JR Simplot Co., 42
Junior's Hamburgers, 182
Justice Department, 56, 58, 112–113, 151–153, 186
Kahn, Alfred, 14
Kai-Shek, Chiang, 130–131
Kantor, Mickey, 28–29, 40–41

Kassim, Gen. Abd al-Karim, 100
Kaufman, Hugh, 75–76
Kelley Enterprises, 194
Kennedy, Edward (Ted), 7, 14
Kennedy, John F., 131
Kennedy, Robert F., 18, 146
Kent State, shootings, 19
Kent, Steven, 190
Kerry, John, 110–111, 146
Kerst, Gershon, 68–69
Khomeini, Ayatollah Sayyid, 100
King, Martin Luther, Jr, 17–18, 166
King, Peter, 152
Kingdome (Seattle), 201
Kinks, The, 207
Kissinger, Henry, 161
Knesset, 72
Knowledge economy, 190–193
Kolko, Gabriel, 196
Komisar, Lucy, 187
Koppel, Ted, 28
Koran, 97–98
Kosovo Liberation Army (KLA), 101–103, 105–108
Kosovo, 30–31, 101–103, 105–108
Kroft, Steve, 27–28
Kroger Co., 207
Kroll Security Group, Inc., 186
Kucinich, Dennis, 78, 119
Kunstler, James H., 205–206
Kurosawa, Akira, 202
Kyles, Duane, 197
Labor Advisory Committee, 32–33
Labor Department, 50–51
Labor rights, 8–9 34–36, 50–51, 111, 158–159
Labor unions, 8–9, 37–38
Lake District (UK), 20
Lake Lemon, 211
Lake Waban, 19
Las Vegas, NV, 194–196
Lawrence Livermore Labs, 92, 95

LBJ Presidential Library, 166
Legalization, of marijuana, 136–139
Lehman Brothers Holdings, Inc., 62
Lenin, Vladimir I., 5
Lethal injection, 148–150
Levi Strauss Co., 34–35
Levine, Harry, 139
Levy, Bernard-Henri, 119–120
Lewinsky, Monica, 24–25, 30–31, 104
Lewis, Anthony, 104
Lewis, Michael, 175
Libby, Lewis (Scooter), 65–66, 69–70, 176–177
Libeskind, Daniel, 200–201
Libya, 100–101, 118–122
Lieberman, Joseph, 31
Lindsey, Bruce, 69–70
Lingar, Stanley, 145, 147
Lisbon Plan, 104
Little Rock, AR, 20–25, 28–29
Livestock industry, 43–45, 81–85
Living History (HRC), 17–18
Livingstone, Kenneth (Ken), 105
Lockett, Clayton, 148–150
Lockheed Martin Corp., 92
London, UK, 105, 174, 176–177
Loral Corp., 72–73
Los Alamos Labs, 92
Los Angeles riots, of 1992, 35
Los Angeles Times, 110, 136
Los Angeles, CA, 28–29, 35, 39, 110, 134
Losey, John, 77–78
Lost Coast, of California, 2
Lott, Chester T. (Trent), 47
Louisiana, 86–87, 205
Louisville, KY, 207
Lovelock, James, 96
MacCrate, Robert, 25
MacMillan Bloedel, Ltd., 46
Mad Cow disease, 81–82

INDEX

Madison Guaranty S&L, 24–27
Madoff, Bernard (Bernie), 181, 188–189
Magna Carta, 152
Males, Mike, 128–129
Mali, 194
Malthus, Thomas, 87
Managed care, 29–30
Manley, Michael, 67
Manufacturing industry, 12–13
Marbella, Spain, 65
Marc Rich Foundation, 67–68
Marc Rich Group, Inc., 64–65
Marijuana laws, 130–135, 136–139
Marrone, Frank, 201
Marsh, Richard, 82
Marshall Islands, nuclear tests, 92
Marshall, Thurgood, 153
Martin, Robert, 75
Marx, Karl, 8–9, 13
Maryland, 61, 132–133
Mason-Dixon Line, 28
Massachusetts Institute of Technology (MIT), 176
Massachusetts, 18, 35
Massey, Robert, 147
Matisse, Henri, 1
Mattole River, 2
McCaffery, Gen. Barry, 133–134
McCain, John, 101, 175
McCluskey, John, 159–160
McCollum, William (Bill), 126
McConnell, Addison M. (Mitch), 175
McCoy, Jennifer, 110
McDonald's Corp., 54–55, 208
McDougall, James, 22–3, 26–27
McGinty, Kathleen (Katie), 75–76
McGovern, George, 20
Meese, Edwin (Ed), 61

Mein Kampf (Hitler), 61
Meir, Golda, 30
Mendocino National Forest, 138
Mendocino County, CA, 138, 157–158
Merrill Lynch & Co., 12, 174, 178
Mervyn's LLC, 204–205
Metropolitan Life Co., 44
Metzenbaum, Howard, 47–48
Metzgar, Jack, 191–193
Mexico, 32–39, 40–42, 43–46, 79–80, 84–85
Miami Herald, 187
Miami, FL, 187
Michigan, 37, 54, 55–56, 166
Microloans, 161–163
Military Academy, US (West Point), 120–121, 128–129
Miller, Henry, 4
Mills, C. Wright, 8
Milosevic, Slobodan, 101–103, 106–108
Minimum wage, 8–9, 193
Mining industry, 44–45
Mining Law, of 1872, 44–45
Minnesota, 55
Miranda warning, 151–152
Missile defense programs, 141
Mississippi River, 86
Mississippi, 47, 55, 86
Missouri Rock Project, 61
Missouri, 51, 145–146
Mohamud, Mohammed, 154–156
Monarch butterfly, 77–80
Monbiot, George, 90–92, 94–95
Mondale, Walter (Fritz), 19
Money laundering, 184–186
Money: College, 191
Monk, Thelonious, 130
Monks, Robert, 8–9
Monsanto Co., 42, 78–80
Monserrat, 182–189
Montana, 44–45

Montgomery Bus Boycott, 86
Montgomery, AL, 86
Morris, Dick, 25–26, 29–30, 47–50
Mossad, 67–68
Mossadegh, Mohammad, 100
Moynihan, Daniel P., 51–53
Mozambique, 194
Mr. & Mrs. Health, Inc., 182
Mrozek, Thomas, 136
MTV, 61
Mujahideen, 100–101
Mulruney, Brian, 40
Murray, Charles, 7–8
Nadelman, Ethan, 136
Nagasaki, nuclear bombing, 92
Nation, The, 2
National Action Network (NAN), 167
National Economic Council, 63
National Endowment for Democracy (NED), 110–111
National Enquirer, 27–28
National Football League (NFL), 211
National Guard, 39
National Intelligence Estimate, on Iraq, 31
National Law Enforcement Officers Memorial Fund, 142
National Law Journal, 21–2
National Review, 112
National Security Agency (NSA), 57
National Security Council (NSC), 118
National Urban League, 53–54
National Wildlife Federation, 40–42, 45
Native Americans, 168
Natural Resources Defense Council (NRDC), 41–42, 45, 78
Nature, 77–78

Nazis, 115
Nebraska, 83
Nelson, Sheffield, 26
Nevada, 44–45, 194–196
New Deal, 47, 50, 53
New Frontier program, 131
New Hampshire, 35
New Labor Forum, 111
New Mexico, 91–92
New Orleans, LA, 86–87, 205
New Statesman, 104–105
New Urbanism, 205–206
New York Police Dept. (NYPD), 57–58, 138–139
New York Post, 146
New York Times Book Review, 3–4
New York Times, 3–4, 23, 79, 104, 114, 121, 136
New York, 30–31, 47, 54, 57–58, 59, 138–139, 146, 154, 200–203
Nicaragua, 3–4
Nightline (ABC), 28
Nike, Corp., 155
Nixon, Rev. Vic, 20
Nixon, Richard M., 17, 20, 65, 131–132, 133–134
No Knock raids, 58
Nobel Peace Prize, 161–163
Noebel, David, 61
Nolan, Elizabeth (Beth), 69–70
Noranda, Inc., 45
North American Commission on the Environment, 41–42
North American Free Trade Agreement (NAFTA), 29–30, 32–39, 40–42, 43–46, 63
North Atlantic Treaty Organization (NATO), 30–31, 101–103, 104–108
North Carolina, 47, 58–59, 197–198
North Richmond, CA, 3–4
Northeastern University, 126
Novartis AG, 78

Novi Sad, Serbia, 100–101
Nuclear bomb testing, 95–96
Nuclear energy, 88–93, 94–96
Nuremberg Tribunals, 107
O'Neill, Edward (Tip), 132–133
Oakland, CA, 8
Obama, Barack, xiii, 1, 9, 91–92, 112–113, 150, 151–153, 154–156, 190–193, and drones 123–125, and drug war 136–139, and gay rights 169–170, and immigration 166–168, and Libya, 119–122, 164–165, and Wall Street bailouts 173–179, 205–206
Ogallala aquifer, 83
Ohio River, 75–76
Ohio, 74–76, 129
Oil & gas industry, 44, 64–65, 95
Oklahoma State Prison, 148–150
Oklahoma, 148–150
Olmert, Ehud, 67, 69
Omaha, NE, 194–195
Operation Chariot, 95
Operation Redi-Rock, 59
Opium, 133
Oppenheimer, Robert, 95
Oregon City, OR, 3, 157–158
Oregon, xiii, 3, 55–56, 96, 154–56, 157–158
Organization of American States (OAS), 110
Ortega, Carlos, 111
Oster, Patrick, 21
Oyamel Fir Forest, 79
Pacific Gas & Electric Co. (PG&E), 89
Packard, David, 43
Packard, Vance, 8
Pahlevi, Shah Reza, 100
Pakistan, 101, 123
Palestine, 165
Palladino, Jack, 27–28
Palmer, Samuel, 1

Panetta, Leon, 30, 48–49
Panorama (BBC), 186
Pardons, presidential, 64–71
Parents Music Resource Center (PMRC), 60–61
Paris Climate Accords, 94
Paris, France, 1, 70–71, 92, 99, 119–120, 206
Passion & Betrayal (Flowers), 27
PATCO strike, 38
Patriot Act, 164
Patton the Bulldog, 143
Patton, Robert, 149–150
Peacock, Doug, 1
Peltier, Leonard, 73
Penniman, Little Richard, 3
Pennzoil, 42
People for the West, 45
Percy the Cockatiel, 2–3
Peres, Shimon, 67, 69
Peripheral Canal, 95
Perot, Ross, 32–33, 37
Peru, 206
Pesticides, 195
Petrolia, CA, xiii
Phelps Dodge Corp., 44
Philanthropy, corporate, 194–195
Philip Morris Intl., 42
Phillip Brothers, Inc., 64
Picasso, Pablo, 65
Plague on Your Houses, A (Wallace) 198–199
Playboy, 25
Police abuse, 57–59, 142–144
Police shootings, 57–59, 142–144
Politico, 170
Pollard, Jonathan, 70
Pollin, Robert, 11, 162–163
Pollock, Kenneth, 31
Pollution credits, 15–16
Polychlorinated biphenyls, (PCBs), 45–46
Pompidou Center, 1
Popper, Deborah, 84
Popper, Frank, 84
Pornography, 61–62
Porter, Gareth, 114–115

INDEX

Portis, Larry, 119–120
Portland protests, xiii
Portland, OR, xiii, 3, 154–56, 157–158
Posse Comitatus Act, 58
Potossi Prison, 145
Poverty, 7–13, 48–49, 190–191
Powell's Books, 3
Power & Accountability (Monks), 8–9
Power, Samantha, 118–119
Price, Hugh, 53–54
Primus, Walter, 54
Princeton University, 126
Prior, Mark, 188
Prisons, 126–129, 132–135, 145–147
Privacy Rights Education Project, 146–147
Problem From Hell, A (Power), 118
Procter & Gamble Co., 42
Project Gasbag, 95–96
Project Oilsands, 95
Putin, Vladimir, 140
Qaddafi, Muammar, 100–101, 118–122
Quarles Exemption, 151–152
Quayle, James D. (Dan), 60
Queen of Chaos (Johnstone), 121–22
Queens College, 139
QueerWatch, 147
Quigley, William (Bill), 171–172
Quinn, John M. (Jack), 69–71
Rabin, Yitzhak, 67–68, 70
Racism, 166–168
Radiation, 94–96
Raines, Howell, 104–105
Rainforest, 84–85
Ralph Lauren Co., 204
Ranching industry, 43–46, 82–84
RAND Corp., 198–199
Rand, Ayn, 9, 32, 202
Rap music, censorship of, 60–61

Ravenswood Aluminum Co., 67
Raymond, Mark, 187
Reagan, Nancy, 134
Reagan, Paddy, 94–95
Reagan, Ronald, 38, 40, 60, 86, 122, 131–132, 134, 141, 166, 174
Red Bull, 192
Reed College, 3
Reeves-Stanford, Beki, 188
Refco, 22–23
Reich, Robert, 50–51
Reilly, William, 75
Religious fundamentalism, 60–61
Reno, Janet, 56
Retail industry, 204–206, 207–211
Reynolds, Burt, 28
Rhode Island, 198
Rhythm, Riots and Revolution (Noebel), 61
Rice, Susan, 118–119
Rich, Denise, 64–71
Rich, Gabriella, 68
Rich, Marc, 64–71, 147
Ridgeway, James, 3
Riesman, David, 8
Rockefeller, John D., 44
Rocky Mountains, 79–80
Rolling Stones, The, 60
Roman Empire, 97
Romney, W. Mitt, 1
Roosevelt University, 191
Roosevelt, Eleanor, 146
Roosevelt, Franklin D. (FDR), 38, 47, 205
Rose Law Firm, 20–25, 28–29, 76
Rosen, David, 159
Rossi, Giseala, 68–69
Rostenkowski, Daniel (Dan), 47
Rothko, Mark, 19
Rubin, Robert, 9–10, 38–39, 51–52, 62–63
Russell, Bertrand, 116
Russia, 63, 113–114, 140
Rutgers University, 83
Rwanda, 118

Ryan, George, 145–147
Ryan, Paul, 170
Sacramento River Valley, 95
Sage, Louise, 1888
Sainath, P., 162–163, 195
Salinas, Carlos, 41–42
Salomon Brothers, Inc., 64
San Andreas Fault, 89
San Antonio, Texas, 34–35
San Francisco Chronicle, 111
San Francisco, CA, 3, 89, 95
San Onofre nuclear plant, 89
Sanctions, economic, 98–100, 106–107
Sanders, Bernard (Bernie), 105–106
Sandia Labs, 92
Santa Fe, NM, 92
Santorum, Richard (Rick), 191
Sarkozy, Nicolas, 119–120
Sartre, Jean-Paul, 5
Saudi Arabia, 113
Savage, Thomas (Tom), 175–177
Scapegoat Generation (Males), 128–129
Scaramella, Mark, 138
Schafly, Phyllis, 61
Schumer, Charles (Chuck), 58, 72, 146
Schwartz, Bernard, 72–73
Seattle, WA, 201
Securities Exchange Commission (SEC), 180–181, 185, 189
Securities fraud, 180–189
Seese, Dorothy, 143–144
Segregation, racial, 167–168
Sentencing Commission, US, 56–57, 134
Sentencing disparities, for cocaine, 56–57, 134–135
Sentencing Project, 134
September 11, 2001, attacks of, 97–98, 199, 200–203
Serbia, 30–31, 101–103, 104–108
Sese Seko, Mobuto, 118
Shadid, Anthony, 121

221

Shahzad, Faisul, 154
Shakespeare, William, 118
Shalala, Donna, 50–51
Shamir, Israel, 115
Sharpton, Rev. Al, 167
Shearon Harris nuclear plant, 90–91
Shelter Cove, CA, 2
Shopping malls, 204–206
Shrybman, Steven, 41
Sierra Club, 42
Sierra Times, 143–144
Sierra-Pacific Industries, 44
Silverstein, Lawrence (Larry), 200–201
Sinatra, Frank, 18
Single Purpose Trust Agreements, 187–188
Sinjar Records, 120–121
Sirte, Libya, 121–22
Slavery, 19
Smoak, Brandon, 143
Smoak, James, 143
Smoak, Pamela, 143
Smoke and Mirrors (Baum), 132–133
Social Security, 55, 170–171
Socialism, 9
Solidarity Center, 111
Somalia, 155
South Africa, 64, 84, 122
Spain, 65, 72–73
Spectator, The, 104
Spitzer, Eliot, 177
Squier, Robert D. (Bob), 48
St. Ignatius, 97
Stahl, Leslie, 98–91, 107
Standard Oil Co., 44
Stanford Financial Bank, 184
Stanford International, 180–189
Stanford, Leland, 181
Stanford, R. Allen, 180–189
Star Wars, missile defense, 141
Starr Report, 104
Starr, Kenneth, 23–25, 104
State Department, 98–103, 106–107, 113–115, 119–122

Stephens, Jackson, 20–21, 26, 75
Stewardship Working Group, 78–79
Stewart, James, 23
Stiglitz, Joseph, 38
Sting operations, in terror plots, 154–156
Stoekler, Andrea, 188
Stop-and-Frisk policy, 138–139
Stranger, The (Camus), 123
Student loans, 190–193
Subprime loans, 174–175
Sudan, 122
Sugar industry, 19
Suicide rate, 140–41, 209–210
Summers, Lawrence (Larry), 10–11, 173–174, 205–206
Super-predators, theory of, 126–127
Supreme Court, 14–16, 135, 151
SWAT teams, 58–59
Swearingen, Terri, 75–76
Sweet Briar College, 78–79
Switzerland, 65–66
Tar sands, 95
Taraki, Noor M., 100–101
Taxation, policy, 50–51
Teamsters Union, 8
Teller, Edward, 95–96
Tennessee Valley Authority (TVA), 15–16
Tennessee, 15–16, 142–143
Texas, 9–10, 34–35, 44, 158–159, 182–183
Textile industry, 34–35
Thatcher, Margaret, 30, 104–105
The Hague, 112–113
Thinking Reed, The (West), 114
Thornton, Omar, 159
Three Strikes law, 126–127
Times Square bombing plot, 154
Tirado, Gonzalo, 185
Tohoku earthquake, 88–90

Tokyo Electric Power Co. (TEPCO), 91–92
Tolstoy, Leo, 197
Total Fitness Center, Inc., 182–183
Toxic waste, 45–46, 74–76
Tramell, Anita, 148–150
Travelgate scandal, 29
Treasury Department (US), 10–11, 62–63
Triangulation, politics, 29–30
Tron Legacy (Kosinski), 4
Trucking industry, 14–15
Trump, Donald J., 211
Truth About Where You Live (Goldman), 15
Tsarnaev, Dzhokar, 151–153
Tuition, college, 190–193
Tulley, Shawn, 66
Tuna, 45–46, 96
Turner, Ike, 1
Tyson Foods, 20–3, 25
Tyson, Don, 22–23
UBS, Corp., 10
Ukraine, 90–92
Unemployment, 157–160
Unida, Fuerza, 35
United Fruit Co., 86
United Kingdom (UK), 30, 104–105, 123, 174, 176–177
United Nations (UN), 91, 98–100, 101–103, 107, 118–22, 161
University of California at Irvine, 128
University of California, 92
University of Chicago, 54
University of Georgia, 82
University of Maine, 40
University of Maryland, 132–133
University of Michigan, 54
University of Paris, 206
University of Surrey, 94
University of Wisconsin, 82
Urban Institute, 51–52
URS, Corp., 92
US Route 99, 3
USSR, 90–92, 123
V-Chip, 49–50, 61–62

INDEX

Valdez, AK, 19
Van Gogh, Vincent, 68
Van Natta, Dale, 17–18, 24–25, 28–29
Vance-Owen Plan, 104
Vanity Fair, 175, 182
Vanocur, Sander, 32
Veblen, Thorstein, 8
Veneconomia, 188–189
Venezuela, 109–111, 185
Vermont, 108
Vietnam War, 28, 30–31, 211
Village Voice, 2
Violent Crime Control and Law Enforcement Act of 1994 (Clinton Crime Bill), 29–30, 50–51, 56–50,
Vivanco, Jose Miguel, 109–111
Vogel, Wilhelm, 65–66
Voltaire, 5
Voting Rights Act, of 1964, 167
Vuillard, Edouard, 1
Waco, Texas, 182
Wages, 8–9, 33–34, 190–193
Walgreens, Inc., 143–144
Wall Street Journal, 23
Wallace, Deborah, 198–199
Wallace, Roderick, 198–199
Walmart, Inc., 20–21, 25, 193, 208
War on drugs, 56–57, 130–135, 136–139
War on terror, 30–31
Warner, Charles, 148
Warning labels, on music, 60–61
Warren, Vincent, 171–172
Washington Post, 114
Washington, 201
Waste Management Corp. (WMX), 42
Water policy, 19, 41–42, 43–46, 83
Watergate scandal, 20
Watsonville, CA, 158
Wayne, John, 18
Weirton, WV, 74–76
Welch, Casslyn, 159–160

Welfare reform, 29–30, 48–50, 51–60
Wellesley College, 18–19
West Virginia, 74–76, 208
West, Rebecca, 114
Weyerhaeuser Corp., 25
Wharton School of Business, 8
Whistleblowers, 112–117
White River, 2
Whiteout: the CIA, Drugs and the Press (Cockburn/St. Clair), 3–4
Whitewater scandal, 22–25, 75–76
Whitmore, Kay, 42
Wiesel, Elie 69–70
Wikileaks, 112–117
Wild Forest Review, 2–3
Wilde, Olivia, 4
Wildlife, 77–80
Willamette National Forest, 154
Willamette River, 157–158
Williams, Edward B., 65–66
Wilson, James Q., 7
Wilton, CT, 174
Wisconsin Power & Light, 15
Wisconsin, 15, 17, 82
Woolworth Building (NYC), 202
Wordsworth, William, 4, 20
Working Class Perspectives, 191
World Bank, 84–85, 163, 195
World Health Organization (WHO), 98–99, 106–107
World Trade Center, 100, 199, 200–203
World Trade Organization (WTO), 194
World War II, 83, 92, 105, 115–116
World Wildlife Fund, 40–42
Worthen Bank, 20–21, 26
Wright, Betsey, 22–23, 26, 27–28
Wright, Frank Lloyd, 202
WTI incinerator, 74–76
Wynette, Tammy, 28, 30

Wynn, Stephen A. (Steve) 196
Wyoming, 44–45, 205
Xenophobia, 50
Yablokov, Alexy, 91
Yale University, 19
Yaley, Barbara, 3
Yamasaki, Minuro, 202
Yemen, 123
Yepes, Jose A.G., 110
Yolly Bolly Wilderness, 204
Yoon, Carol, 70
Youth crime, 49–50, 56–57, 126–129
Yugoslavia, 101–103, 171
Yukon Territory, 46
Yunus, Mohammad, 161–163
Zaire, 118
Zapatistas, 46
Zarzamora factory, 34–35

When You Choose To Donate $25 Or More

Get **COUNTERPUNCH+** For A Year

- ✓ Exclusive articles
- ✓ Weekly newsletter
- ✓ Full-archive access
- ✓ Special discounts & more!